MINNESOTA/W
TRAVEL ✦ S

D1490687

HENNEPIN AVENUE BRIDGE IN MINNEAPOLIS

Alice Vollmar

MINNESOTA
WISCONSIN
TRAVEL ✦ SMART®

Second Edition

Alice M. Vollmar

John Muir Publications
Santa Fe, New Mexico

John Muir Publications, P.O. Box 613, Santa Fe, New Mexico 87504

Printed in the United States of America.
Second edition. First printing May 1999.

ISSN: 1523-0694
ISBN: 1-56261-438-X

Editors: Peg Goldstein, Chris Hayhurst
Graphics Editor: Heather Pool
Production: Marie J. T. Vigil
Design: Marie J. T. Vigil
Cover design: Janine Lehmann, Marie J. T. Vigil
Typesetting: Melissa Tandysh
Map style development: American Custom Maps—Jemez Springs, NM
Map illustration: Kathleen Sparkes, White Hart Design
Printing: Publishers Press
Front cover photos: *small*—© John Elk III (Old Federal Courts Building, St. Paul)
　　　　　　　　large—Department of City Development, Milwaukee (St. Josaphat's Basilica in
　　　　　　　　　　　　Milwaukee)
Back cover photo: Wisconsin Department of Tourism/Tim Sweet (Windsurfing on Lake Mendota)

Distributed to the book trade by
Publishers Group West
Berkeley, California

MINNESOTA/WISCONSIN TRAVEL•SMART: A GUIDE THAT GUIDES

Most guidebooks are basically directories, providing information but very little help in making choices—you have to guess how to make the most of your time and money. *Minnesota/Wisconsin Travel•Smart* is different: By highlighting the very best of the region and offering various planning features, it acts like a personal tour guide rather than a directory.

TAKE THE STRESS OUT OF TRAVEL

Sometimes traveling causes more stress than it relieves. Sorting through information, figuring out the best routes, determining what to see and where to eat and stay—all of this can make a vacation feel daunting rather than fun. Relax. We've done a lot of the legwork for you. This book will help you plan a trip that suits *you*—whatever your time frame, budget, and interests.

SEE THE BEST OF THE REGION

Author Alice Vollmar has lived in Minnesota for 28 years. She has hand-picked every listing in this book, and she gives you an insider's perspective on what makes each one worthwhile. So while you will find many of the big tourist attractions listed here, you'll also find lots of smaller, lesser known treasures, such as Frank Lloyd Wright's Taliesin in southwestern Wisconsin and the Runestone Museum in Alexandria, Minnesota. And each sight is described so you'll know what's most—and sometimes least—interesting about it.

In selecting the restaurants and accommodations for this book, the author sought out unusual spots with local flavor. While in some areas of the region chains are unavoidable, wherever possible the author directs you to one-of-a-kind places. We also know that you want a range of options: One day you may crave steak or seafood, while the next day you would be just as happy (as would your wallet) with a brat and beer. Most of the restaurants and accommodations listed here are moderately priced, but the author also includes budget and splurge options, depending on the destination.

CREATE THE TRIP YOU WANT

We all have different travel styles. Some people like spontaneous weekend jaunts, while others plan longer, more leisurely trips. You may want to cover as much ground as possible, no matter how much time you have. Or maybe you prefer to focus your trip on one part of the state or on some special interest, such as history, nature, or art. We've taken these differences into account.

Though the individual chapters stand on their own, they are organized in a geographically logical sequence, so that you could conceivably fly into Minneapolis and drive chapter by chapter to each destination in the book. Of course, you don't have to follow that sequence, but it's there if you want a complete picture of the region.

Each destination chapter offers ways of prioritizing when time is limited: In the Perfect Day section, the author suggests what to do if you have only one day to spend in the area. Also, every Sightseeing Highlight is rated, from one to four stars: ★★★★—or "must see"—sights first, followed by ★★★ sights, then ★★ sights, and finally ★—or "see if you have spare time"—sights. At the end of each sight listing is a time recommendation in parentheses. User-friendly maps help you locate the sights, restaurants, and lodging of your choice.

And if you're in it for the ride, so to speak, you'll want to check out the Scenic Routes described at the end of several chapters. They take you through some of the most scenic parts of region.

In addition to these special features, the appendix has other useful travel tools:

- The Planning Map and Mileage Chart help you determine your own route and calculate travel time.
- The Special Interest Tours show you how to design your trip around any of six favorite interests.
- The Calendar of Events provides an at-a-glance view of when and where major events occur throughout the state.
- The Resource guide tells you where to go for more information about national and state parks, individual cities and counties, bed-and-breakfasts, and more.

HAPPY TRAVELS

With this book in hand, you have many reliable recommendations and travel tools at your fingertips. Use it to make the most of your trip. And have a great time!

WHY VISIT MINNESOTA AND WISCONSIN?

Sailboats and fishing vessels ride the waves of two Great Lakes; riverboat paddle wheels churn on the Mississippi River. Bright blue and orange dalahast horses decorate doors and mailboxes in a Swedish town, while not far away onion domes and steeples punctuate a city skyline. Native American culture and music in one region give way to foaming beer steins and apple orchards in another. In the North Woods, black bears look for blueberries and red-eyed loons dive in pristine lakes.

This is the Midwest's Northern Heartland: Minnesota and Wisconsin. Although similar in settlement and geological history, the states are distinct in what they offer visitors and residents. Each resists stereotype with unexpectedly diverse terrain and ethnicity. I encourage travelers to come and be surprised.

This guide highlights several dozen state parks, a handful of national parks and monuments, two state capitals, a wealth of historic sites, art museums both venerable and avant-garde, and a renowned repertory theater. It will take you to popular attractions and those little known. You can hike a solitary North Shore wilderness trail, sip champagne with the Twin Cities' glitterati before an Ordway Theatre musical, and eat blueberry or wild-rice pancakes in a cozy small-town café. Travelers can use this guide to immerse themselves in several destinations or to spend a few days here, a few days there.

Whichever approach you take, prepare to be welcomed by friendly and warm-hearted people, clean air, and an inspiring landscape that will keep you coming back.

HISTORY AND CULTURES

With the melting of glaciers that covered most of this region some 10,000 years ago came the first travelers. These nomadic bands of Asiatic hunters and gatherers crossed the Bering Strait on a land bridge, following herds of tusked mammoths and other big game. Subsequently, a series of cultures arose and declined in what are now Minnesota and Wisconsin. Among them were a copper culture and a culture of mound-builders who built various burial and ceremonial mounds into this landscape—from round, conical, and linear mounds to effigy mounds shaped like birds, bears, snakes, and other animals. Some of these mounds remain today. Grand Mound, on Rainy Lake in northern Minnesota, is the Upper Mississippi region's largest; other mounds can be seen at Saint Paul's Indian Mounds Park and Lizard Mound State Park in Wisconsin.

By the 1600s, Wisconsin's Native American tribes included the Winnebago, eastern Dakota (Sioux), Ojibwa (Chippewa), Fox, Sauk, and Menominee. The Dakota tribe occupied all of Minnesota, with a cultural center near Mille Lacs Lake, until they were forced out of the North Woods and onto the plains by the Ojibwa. French explorers, among them Jean Nicolet, and French fur traders established trade relations with the Native American tribes and set up trading posts. After lively competition, the French eventually capitulated to rival British fur traders, whose posts dominated the region until the War of 1812.

Growing United States government interest in the region's resources—particularly the lumber—changed Native American life forever. Treaties in the region relinquished vast tracts of land to the government. Lieutenant Zebulon Pike came upriver from St. Louis in 1805 and made a down payment to the Dakota tribe—$200 and 60 gallons of whiskey—to buy the land that is now Minneapolis and Saint Paul, with the promise of a "fair amount" of payment in the future. (The fair amount was $2,000, paid 14 years later.) Here, on the bluffs overlooking the Minnesota and Mississippi Rivers' confluence, Fort Snelling was established in 1819. This outpost of civilization in the wilderness remained active until 1849, nine years before Minnesota became a state. Wisconsin's statehood came earlier, in 1848. Native American peoples were relegated to reservations, and the Dakota were exiled from Minnesota for a number of years following the U.S.-Dakota Conflict of 1862, a futile attempt by the desperate and ill-treated Dakota to reclaim their land.

Logging boomed in the region, creating wealthy lumber barons. Discovery of iron in Minnesota and lead in Wisconsin spawned mining operations and even more wealth. By 1830, 5,000 Wisconsin miners had dug out close to 14 million tons of lead, which was used primarily to make ammunition and lead-based paint. In the 1890s, immigrant laborers by the thousands worked in Minnesota's Mesabi, Cayuna, and Vermilion iron ranges.

The first settlers in the region were New England businessmen and entre-preneurs, followed by European immigrants, predominantly Germans, Swedes, and Norwegians. Soon plows turned prairies and logged-out lands into farms, while land unsuited for growing crops gave way to Wisconsin's dairy industry.

These first settlers arrived by water and overland routes. When railroads reached the region, settlement exploded. Adding diversity to the dominant German-Scandinavian culture were immigrants of varying nationalities—Irish, French Canadians, Czechs, Dutch, Flemish, Polish, Danish, Welsh, Swiss, and Luxembourgers. Between 1890 and 1920, Finns, Ukrainians, Yugoslavs, Italians, Bulgarians, Poles, Hungarians, and others settled here. Beginning in 1979, a new wave of immigration brought Southeast Asians to Minnesota and Wisconsin, this time by air, and both states presently record a growing Hispanic population. Even with all this diversity, the Scandinavian/German ethnic personalities of these neighboring states remain predominant. In Minnesota, the more reserved Swedish/Norwegian demeanor tempers the peppery-sausage-making, beer-brewing Germanic heritage; in Wisconsin, it's the other way around.

In recent times, the region's technology and service industries seem far removed from the era of free-roaming Native Americans, explorers, missionar-ies, voyageurs, and the showy Victorian excesses of wealthy lumber, mining, and railroad barons. But yesterday is not gone. The French and Native American influences of the past have a contemporary presence in the names of cities, lakes, and streets—Menomonie, Fond du Lac, Grand Marais, Minneapolis, Milwaukee, Nicollet and Hennepin Avenues, Mille Lacs Lake, and Lake Winnebago.

THE ARTS

The arts flourish in these two states. Architecture from the 1800s is well pre-served and displayed in the cities of Milwaukee and Saint Paul. There are also important art deco buildings, many examples of the Prairie School's design influ-ence, and numerous structures created by Wisconsin-born Frank Lloyd Wright.

Artist Georgia O'Keeffe was born in Wisconsin, and Minnesota-born sculp-tor James Earle Fraser created the buffalo nickel's Indian head. Today you'll find art museums and galleries in nearly every community, a strong regional arts rep-resentation, and active arts colonies.

Ethnic dance groups and musicians perform regularly in Minnesota and

Wisconsin, and exceptional live theater thrives. Wisconsin's American Players Theatre draws sell-out crowds for Shakespearean plays in a rural amphitheater; Minnesota's Guthrie Theater and Children's Theatre Company enjoy nationwide recognition. The larger cities have fine symphonies and chamber orchestras, along with respected ballet and modern dance companies. The Twin Cities support an active jazz scene. Literary notables with regional ties include F. Scott Fitzgerald, Thornton Wilder, Laura Ingalls Wilder, and contemporary poet Robert Bly.

CUISINE

Not long ago, dining out yielded no surprises in Minnesota and Wisconsin. Tastes ran to potatoes and meat, with vegetables more or less an apologetic afterthought.

But things are changing. Chefs have begun to create inventive dishes, often using the region's own produce and meats. Wild rice, for example, a Native American staple harvested here, is enjoying increasing popularity on restaurant menus. You'll find the dark, glossy grain in soups, crusty breads, and pancakes, and as a delightfully seasoned side dish for meats.

Ethnic restaurants—from the fine German restaurants of Milwaukee to the burgeoning Southeast Asian and East Indian eateries of the Twin Cities—are prevalent, especially in the cities. French cuisine also has a presence. And, of course, the region's German and Scandinavian heritage means German bratwurst and beer, Norwegian *lefse*, Danish *kringle*, and Swedish *pepparkakor*.

With thousands of lakes close at hand, freshly caught walleye and lake trout appear on many northern resort menus. In dairy-rich Wisconsin, there's cheese—and more cheese. Stop to nibble samples at the plentiful cheese houses, and you'll walk out with a tangy wedge of cheddar or a mellow Brie. The state's fine meat markets are noted for specialty sausages and cured meats. Breweries and a few wineries offer tours and tasting sessions.

FLORA AND FAUNA

Trees covered all but the southern third or so of the Minnesota/Wisconsin region until the lumber industry moved in. Within decades, almost all of the region's virgin timber had been cut. On the heels of the lumbermen came the farmers, but when much of the deforested land proved less than ideal for farming, reforestation was initiated in both Wisconsin and Minnesota, creating vast second-growth forests. Northernmost Minnesota's remote Boundary Waters Canoe Area (BWCA) contains one of the last large tracts of virgin forest in the area. Here, a boreal forest of jack pine, spruce, aspen, and paper birch overlaps a Laurentian forest of white and red pine and hardwoods, including maple.

Pine forest makes up most of the region's legendary North Woods, giving way to hardwood forest further south—the Big Woods of Laura Ingalls Wilder fame. Here, oak, black walnut, butternut, maple, and elm trees offer summer shade and fall color similar to that of New England.

Most of the lush, tall-grass prairie lands in the southern region of both states was once coveted by farmers. Eventually, more than 90 percent of the prairie was plowed, the genesis of the southern half of the region's panorama of farm buildings flanked by rolling fields of grain, beans, and alfalfa. The few patches of remaining virgin prairie are protected; some land is being returned to prairie, and a portion of the forest lands are preserved in state and national parks and forests. Minnesota has close to 70 state parks, one national park, and two national monuments; Wisconsin counts 45 state parks, five official recreation areas, and 10 state forests.

In parks and preserves, restored prairies, and along roadsides, you'll encounter wildflowers from white trillium to fall goldenrod. Morel mushroom hunters flock to the woods in spring, and wildflower lovers enjoy bright pink phlox and lavender wild asters, sunny marsh marigolds, and pink-and-white showy lady's slippers, bee balm, columbine, and wood violets.

You may come face to face with a moose lunching on tender willow shoots in a wetland, a white-tailed deer grazing in a meadow at dusk, or a muskrat swimming near a lake shore. Other resident critters include fox, beaver, chipmunk, porcupine, bear, elk, and timber wolves. Both city and country birds keep up constant chatter—cardinals, goldfinches, scarlet tanagers, warblers, nuthatches, bluebirds, woodpeckers, swallows, and more. I've seen large red-crested pileated woodpeckers, noisy as pneumatic drills and spewing sawdust, in remote woods and twice on residential streets in Minneapolis. Wisconsin alone claims more than 330 native bird species.

Abundant water attracts a hefty population of Canadian geese, ducks, herons, and other waterfowl, as it does hunters and fishers. The region has long been the place to come for unequaled walleye, muskie, trout, bass, and crappie fishing. In the Great Lakes, anglers catch herring, lake trout, whitefish, salmon, and perch. It's estimated that half of Minnesota's population goes fishing.

LAY OF THE LAND

Ice Age glaciation has much to do with the region's topography: sparkling blue lakes, powerful rivers including the Mississippi, and an extraordinary landscape that includes incredibly fertile farmland based on glacial debris.

Around 75,000 years ago the last southward reach of glacial ice—called the Wisconsin glaciation—extended lobes of ice over all but Minnesota's southeastern corner and Wisconsin's southwestern corner. Devoid of deposits of glacial till and glacial scouring, this region is a world apart—a scenic domain of limestone bluffs and coulees with caves and rushing streams where winding country roads now lead to quaint villages such as Harmony, Choice, Arcadia, and Hillsboro.

As the glacier moved southward over most of the Northern Heartland, it gouged out rocky lake beds, leveled mountains, and occasionally deposited huge boulders called erratics. You'll come across one now and then—a huge mass of rock sitting atop a hill. The glacier also pushed sedimentary, sandstone, dolomite, and limestone layers ahead of it, forming terminal moraines that now mark the glacier's southernmost edge. Moraines snake through Minnesota and Wisconsin as an irregular belt of hillocks and basins with numerous lakes—scenic and also resistant to farming. Upon the glacier's retreat, huge deposits of sand and gravel formed drumlins (long sculpted hills) and eskers (deposits of sand delineating the course of rivers that ran beneath the glacial ice). You can learn about many glaciation phenomena in Wisconsin's Kettle Moraine State Park Northern Unit, one of nine Wisconsin units on the Ice Age Trail, a National Scenic Trail system that follows the glacier's terminal moraine edge.

With the gradual warming of the climate some 13,000 years ago, glacial meltwater filled lake beds and huge chunks of ice were left in depressions or buried in debris to form lakes. Minnesota actually has some 22,000 lakes, though the official count (11,842) is rounded off to 10,000 for Minnesota's oft-repeated moniker, "The Land of 10,000 Lakes." Wisconsin claims 15,000. The region's largest lakes are Lake Michigan on Wisconsin's eastern shore, and Lake Superior, the largest freshwater lake in the world at 288,800 acres and 123 miles of shoreline.

The region's topography in Minnesota ranges from 602 feet above sea level at the Lake Superior shoreline to 2,031 feet above sea level at Eagle Mountain near the North Shore. In Wisconsin the elevation ranges from 580 feet on the Lake Michigan shore to 1,952 feet at Timms Hill.

OUTDOOR ACTIVITIES

Runners and bikers in Minnesota and Wisconsin enjoy numerous trails in spring, summer, and fall, while snowmobiling, cross-country skiing, and dogsledding take over in the winter. Bikers come from all over to pedal trails such as the 33-mile Elroy-Sparta Trail, routed through tunnels on an abandoned railroad bed in southwestern Wisconsin's unglaciated "driftless" region. Minnesota's railbed trails include the 45-mile Cannon Valley Trail, which winds through southeastern Minnesota's hardwood-forested bluff country.

For the hardy hiker, sections of the nearly 300-mile Superior Hiking Trail's route are open along Minnesota's North Shore. The 52-mile segment between Castle Danger and Grand Marais and a 91-mile segment from Crosby Manitou State Park to Kodonce River are rugged and challenging. Hundreds of other trails in the region vary in difficulty, and there's abundant hiking for every age and experience level.

Water draws vacationers from all over the world to this region—for fishing, waterskiing, canoeing, sailing, tubing, and kayaking. In fact, the only way you can explore Minnesota's popular roadless Boundary Waters Canoe Area in the Superior National Forest or Voyageurs National Park is by water. A number of companies lead outdoor adventures ranging from white-water rafting and dogsledding to outdoor experiences for women. You can learn to mush a dog team or just cozy into a blanket-laden sled for the ride.

More daring adventurers raft the Flambeau River's rapids in northern Wisconsin and the turbulent white water on the St. Louis River in northeastern Minnesota. Backpacking and camping are popular. You can also golf on courses designed by Dye and Robert Trent Jones, or saddle up a horse to explore state parks via riding trails. And if you prefer a leisurely outdoors experience, try one of many city parks or lakeshore trails. Enjoying the outdoors here can be as simple as taking a spontaneous afternoon stroll.

PLANNING YOUR TRIP

Before you set out on your trip, you'll need to do some planning. Use this chapter in conjunction with the tools in the appendix to answer some basic questions. First of all, when are you going? You may already have specific dates in mind; if not, various factors will probably influence your timing. Either way, you'll want to know about local events, the weather, and other seasonal considerations. This chapter discusses all of that, while the Calendar of Events in the appendix provides a month-by-month view of major area events.

How much should you expect to spend on your trip? This chapter addresses various regional factors you'll want to consider in estimating your travel expenses. How will you get around? Check out the section on local transportation. If you decide to travel by car, the Planning Map and Mileage Chart in the appendix can help you figure out exact routes and driving times, while the Special Interest Tours provide several focused itineraries. The chapter concludes with some reading recommendations, both fiction and nonfiction, to give you various perspectives on the region. If you want specific information about individual cities or counties, use the Resource guide in the appendix.

HOW MUCH WILL IT COST?

Northern Heartlanders tend to be practical souls who resist overspending which, luckily for the traveler, translates into moderate prices for food, lodging, and attractions. In general, prices tend to be higher in the large metropolitan areas, such as the Twin Cities and Milwaukee. Even so, visitors from the East and West Coasts and other upscale regions will find even the city prices a bargain. It's possible for a budget-conscious family of four to eat three meals in good, medium-priced restaurants, visit two museums, and take in a play or concert for well under $250. Of course, that requires a discriminating eye when choosing dining spots and amusements.

You'll find a variety of dining choices, from fast food, ethnic, and traditional Midwestern fare to gourmet. Many restaurants charge $18 and under for dinner. Most common are restaurants with a $10 to $20 price range. Fewer charge $20 to $35; a select few charge over $35. The Minnesota Restaurant Association's restaurant directory is available from Minnesota Tourism, 800/657-3700. Wisconsin's restaurant association does not publish a directory. Restaurants are also listed in guidebooks to each locality/destination, available from community chambers of commerce or convention and visitors bureaus.

Many museums in this region are free or operate on a donation basis; fees for others are usually under $10. Children and senior-citizen rates are often discounted, and families sometimes receive special rates. Tour fees can range from $2 to $25. Admission to each of the Minnesota Historical Society's 23 sites ranges from free to $5 ($12 family rate, 888/PAST-FUN). Admission to four of the State Historical Society of Wisconsin's seven sites (Pendarvis, Stonefield, Villa Louis, and the Wade House and Wesley Jung Carriage Museum) costs from $2.70 to $7.25. (Exceptions are Old World Wisconsin, $4.50-$9.50; Madeline Island Historical Museum, $2-$4.50; and the First Capitol, free.) A passport ticket allowing unlimited visits to all sites for the season costs $50 for a family and $30 for an individual (call 608/264-6400). Rates vary from $10 to $35 for popular attractions such as Valleyfair Family Amusement Park near the Twin Cities and Wisconsin's House on the Rock.

State Parks in Minnesota charge a daily permit fee of $4 per vehicle; a yearly pass costs $20. In Wisconsin, state park daily stickers cost $7 for nonresidents and $3 to $5 for residents; annual stickers are $25 for nonresidents and $9 to $18 for residents; a one-hour sticker costs $3 for residents and nonresidents. Bikers, equestrians, and cross-country skiers age 16 and older using certain Wisconsin state trails, parks, forests, and recreation areas must have a trail pass. A daily pass costs $3; the annual pass is $10. Passes are sold at park and trail offices, the Bureau of Parks, or Department of Natural Resources (DNR) area and district offices. Some trailheads have self-registration. To order an annual pass using VISA or MasterCard, call 608/266-2181. To order by mail, write to the Bureau of Parks, P.O. Box 7921, Madison, WI 53707. Minnesota has no trail-use fees.

Each chapter in this book includes camping, lodging, and dining options in a variety of price ranges, from economical to luxurious, for the featured city or area. High-quality, reasonably priced lodging is plentiful in this region. Of course, you can spend $200 for a very pampered one-night stay if that's what you have in mind, but double rooms in the $60 to $120 range are the norm. Sources for additional lodging guidance include Wisconsin's bed-and-breakfast directory and lodging directory (www.lodging-wi.com), and the Wisconsin Association of Campground Owners' directory of the state's private campgrounds. All are available at no charge from Wisconsin Tourism: 800/432-8747 or 800/372-2737, www.tourism.state.wi.us. Minnesota's bed-and-breakfast, motel, hotel, and resort lodging directories as well as the Minnesota Alliance of Campground Operators' directory of private campgrounds and RV parks are all free from the Minnesota Office of Tourism: 800/657-3700 or 651/296-5029, www.exploreminnesota.com.

State parks in both Minnesota and Wisconsin contain excellent campgrounds. Reservations are recommended from late June through Labor Day. In Minnesota, state park camping fees are $8 to $12 nightly, based on the individual park's facilities, plus $2.50 for electricity. Reservations can be made up to 90 days in advance by calling "The Connection" at 612/922-9000 or 800/246-CAMP. There is a $6.50 reservation fee. For maps and information, contact the Department of Natural Resources (DNR) at www.dnr.state.mn.us or call 888/646-6367. Campers must also purchase the park's entrance permit, $4 daily or $20 annually.

Wisconsin state parks charge a camping fee of $8 to $12 nightly for nonresidents, and $7 to $10 for residents; rates are based on when you visit and on park facilities. Campsites may be reserved via VISA or Mastercard in most parks by telephoning 888/947-2757 year-round. For more information contact the state parks at www.dnr.state.wi.us/org/land/parks or 608/266-2181. There is a reservation fee (about $10) plus a $7 daily or $25 annual nonresident pass.

CLIMATE

Minnesota and Wisconsin experience four full-blown seasons with wide temperature variations. Temperatures from 70 to 85 degrees Fahrenheit are typical in summer months, but the thermometer can shoot up to 100 degrees and above.

In general, June and August are a bit cooler than July. Pack light clothing for summer, but include a lightweight jacket or sweater—just in case the weather does something unpredictable. An umbrella, or rain gear, is advised for spring, summer, and fall.

Winter, on the other hand, is more predictable; it will be long and cold. Dress for snow and temperatures below freezing—a heavy coat, wool hat, scarf, boots, mittens, and long underwear are de rigueur. On the northern Minnesota border, the January high for International Falls averages 14 degrees and the low averages negative 8; average annual snowfall is 59 inches. The Twin Cities average a 25-degree high and a 6-degree low. In Milwaukee, the January average high is 30 degrees, with an average low of 11 degrees and an average snowfall of 48 inches.

WHEN TO GO

Late spring to early fall is the prime vacation season, and many attractions are seasonal, open from Memorial Day to Labor Day. Summer weekends and holidays can bring crowds to Minnesota's North Shore as well as to bluff and coulee country in southeastern Minnesota and southwestern Wisconsin. Lodging reservations are needed. Make reservations early for Wisconsin's Door Peninsula—a year in advance is not too early.

Radiant fall color brings weekend camera-toting "leaf peekers" to the North Woods, the bluff and coulee country, the Great River Road on both sides of the Mississippi River, and other parts of the region. Accommodations fill quickly. The color peaks around mid- to late September in the north and from late September to early October as you travel south.

Winter has plenty of enthusiasts. Off to the North Woods and lake regions they go, hauling cross-country skis, snowmobiles, or ice-fishing houses. Some lodges and resorts have winter reservation waiting lists, especially along the North Shore and the Gunflint Trail, so plan a winter vacation early. Many communities have Christmas-season events with music, concerts, programs, shopping specials, tours of decorated Victorian houses, parades, and lodging packages.

Mid- to late May, when trees and hillsides turn pastel shades of green, is one of my favorite times to travel the region. Visitors are scarce, and so are mosquitoes (summer visits require insect and tick repellant). Since many attractions have yet to open, it's the perfect time to explore town streets and spend time in cafés talking to the local folks.

ORIENTATION AND TRANSPORTATION

The greater Twin Cities metro area's almost 3 million people and Milwaukee's 1 million make them the region's most populated locations. You'll find the fewest humans (and the most wildlife) in the northern quarter of the two states. Two interstates—I-90 and I-94—serve as major east-west arteries through Minnesota and Wisconsin; I-35 runs north from the Iowa/Minnesota border through Minneapolis/St. Paul to Duluth on the Lake Superior shore. It intersects I-90 in southern Minnesota and I-94 in the Twin Cities. Major north-south Wisconsin highways are U.S. 51 midstate and I-43 from the Illinois border at Beloit to Milwaukee, then along the Lake Michigan shore and up to Green Bay. The changing countryside—from blue lakes and lush farmland to craggy cliffs, rock formations, and fragrant forests of spruce and pine—enlivens the sometimes long drives in this region encompassing 140,222 square miles.

Minneapolis/St. Paul International is the region's major airport. Located off I-494, about 12 miles southeast of downtown Minneapolis and 10 miles southwest of downtown St. Paul, the airport is served by 16 major airlines and regional carriers. It is the main hub for Northwest Airlines.

An information center is located on the lower level of the main terminal. You'll also find free reservation phones for major hotels; limousine, city bus, and taxi services; and car rentals. Major hotels and motels offer complimentary or inexpensive shuttles.

It's wise to reserve a rental vehicle in advance. You'll find all of the nationally known car rental agencies in the Twin Cities, including Avis, 800/831-2847, and National Car Rental, 800/CAR-RENT. Rental recreational vehicles are in high demand during summer months, especially on weekends. A dozen or so Twin Cities metro-area companies specialize in recreational vehicle rentals, including Cruise America Motorhome Rental and Sales, 612/933-6100, and Brambillas', Inc., 612/445-2611.

Milwaukee's General Mitchell International Airport is served by major airlines including Northwest, TWA, and United, as well as by regional carriers. Limousine, taxi service, and car rentals are also available. Call 888/835-9653 for flight and airport information.

Greyhound Bus Line, 800/231-2222, has terminals in Minneapolis and St. Paul, with intercity bus service daily. Twin Cities bus service is provided by Metropolitan Council Transit Operations (MCTO), 612/373-3333. Amtrak, 800/872-7245, serves the region via a major east-west line from Chicago and other eastern cities to Seattle and Portland, with stops in a number of Wisconsin and Minnesota cities. A Twin Cities depot is based in St. Paul's Midway area, 10 minutes from downtown St. Paul and 15 minutes from downtown Minneapolis.

If you are traveling by auto, you'll find a dependable network of roads in the Northern Heartland. Road conditions are good in spring, summer, and fall, although you'll encounter road repair delays. Winter travelers should carry winter survival kits and blankets and be aware of weather forecasts. Although both states operate excellent snow-removal programs, storms often result in icy, snow-packed roads with low visibility. Travel to remote areas can be difficult or impossible in winter. In Wisconsin, the road condition hotline is 800/762-3947; in Minnesota, 800/542-0220. For car travelers, both states operate visitor information centers near the border, off I-94, and elsewhere.

RECOMMENDED READING

Your best sources of free travel information are the state tourism offices, city/area convention and visitors bureaus or chambers of commerce, and each state's department of natural resources. Phone numbers for these and other travel resources appear in the Resources section of this guide.

Be sure to request *The Minnesota Explorer* from Minnesota tourism—a quarterly newspaper jammed with seasonal events all over the state and travel features. The Minnesota DNR also publishes a small magazine, *The Minnesota Volunteer*, with some of the best nature writing around; subscriptions are free to residents (donations welcomed). For nonresidents, a subscription costs $15, available by writing the Minnesota DNR (address listed in Resources).

Regional magazines and alternative newspapers can be a great way to take the pulse of a city or community. *Wisconsin Trails* is a helpful, fun-to-read bimonthly magazine with articles on Wisconsin places, people, and restaurants; for subscriptions, call 800/877-5280. The magazine also publishes books: *Best Wisconsin Bike Trips: 30 One-Day Tours*, by Phil VanValkenberg; *Best Canoe Trails of Southern Wisconsin*, by Michael E. Duncanson; and *Great Golf in Wisconsin*, by John Hughes and Jeff Mayers are highly recommended. *Minnesota Monthly* magazine runs articles about Minnesota with frequent features on bed-and-breakfasts, food, and travel. In the Twin Cities, a tabloid-size newspaper called *City Pages* offers complete calendars of current activities, theater, art exhibits, music, movies, and more. It's free and can be picked up from racks in many public places such as libraries, restaurants, and small food stores. *Mpls St Paul* magazine is another good resource.

Numerous books have been written about the region. In *Landscape of Ghosts* (Voyageur Press, 1993; 800/888-9653), a delightful book with photos by Bob Firth, Minnesota writer Bill Holm takes a wry look at rural Minnesota's past and present people, values, and places. Maxwell MacKenzie's *Abandonings: Photographs of Otter Tail County, Minnesota* (Elliott and Clark, 1995), features color photos of abandoned structures built by Scandinavian immigrants and stories told by settlers.

Conservationist and environmentalist Aldo Leopold recounts his experiences on his farm near Baraboo, Wisconsin, in *Sand County Almanac* (Oxford Press, 1949). Not everybody knows that the naturalist responsible for founding the Sierra Club, John Muir, grew up in Wisconsin and attended the state university. You can read about Muir's life in *The Wilderness World of John Muir* by Edwin Way Teale (Houghton Mifflin Company, 1954).

John Hassler's novels capture the flavor of Minnesota life. Try *Staggerford* (Atheneum Books, 1977). Ole Rolvaag's classic, *Giants in the Earth* (Harper & Brothers, 1928), poignantly details the struggles of pioneer Norwegian farm families on the prairie. For a look at a four-generation Minnesota farm family, read *Mapping the Farm: The Chronicle of a Family* by John Hildebrand (Alfred A. Knopf, 1995).

The most famous books about Minnesota were written by two literary greats, Sinclair Lewis and F. Scott Fitzgerald. *Main Street* by Lewis, first published in 1920, is a thinly disguised portrait of Sauk Centre, the author's hometown. Fitzgerald's classic, *The Great Gatsby*, describes the flamboyant 1920s lifestyle of the wealthy in St. Paul.

Laura Ingalls Wilder's stories of pioneer life in Wisconsin and Minnesota, recounted in her books *Little House in the Big Woods* and *On the Banks of Plum Creek*, first published in the 1930s by Harper & Brothers, are great family travel reading. Then there's Wisconsin's renowned architect Frank Lloyd Wright. One of many books about Wright is *The Prairie School: Frank Lloyd Wright and his Midwest Contemporaries* by Allen H. Brooks (W.W. Norton, 1972).

1
TWIN CITIES

The Twin Cities, St. Paul and Minneapolis, actually have quite distinct personalities. The pulse of Minneapolis races in the city's compact, 12-block-radius downtown, despite the romantic meander of Nicollet Avenue, an outdoor pedestrian mall with fountains and statues, flowers, trees, and summertime musicians. Minneapolis is home to Fortune 500 companies including General Mills and Honeywell and is a noted center for the arts, with two major art museums and a wealth of performing arts companies. East of Minneapolis, in genteel state capital St. Paul, baroque domes and venerable sandstone buildings sit atop hills and steep river bluffs; here, modern skyscrapers flank historic steeples and towers. Streets angle and curve through downtown's three distinct sections: historic Lowertown, St. Paul's birthplace, with a village green and resident arts community; the central business district; and a cultural district on the west side.

A PERFECT DAY IN THE TWIN CITIES
Start with a walk around Lake Harriet, one of Minneapolis's 22 lakes. Breakfast at Nicollet Island Inn above St. Anthony Falls, explore the quaint island village, and take a self-guided tour of Mississippi Mile's old milling district. Next visit the Minneapolis Institute of Arts, then head for St. Paul's historic Summit Avenue. Lunch at W. A. Frost, tour the James J. Hill House, and

explore the Minnesota History Center. Stroll the Mississippi River walkways, dine at the classy Saint Paul Grill, and end the day with a concert or musical at the Ordway Music Theatre.

ORIENTATION

Rimmed by some 200 metro area communities, the Twin Cities sit elbow to elbow on the Mississippi River banks, Minneapolis to the west and Minnesota capital St. Paul to the east. In Minneapolis, streets usually run east-west and avenues, north-south. Although city planners gave St. Paul no such clear design, signs direct you to downtown's major districts. St. Paul attractions are easy to find via a city map, and the river's a good reference point for visitors. Traffic moves east-west through both cities on I-94; I-35 (I-35W in Minneapolis and I-35E in St. Paul) runs north-south. Driving is manageable here, but avoid the rush between seven and eight-thirty in the morning and four to six evenings. To drive from downtown St. Paul to downtown Minneapolis takes about 20 to 30 minutes. Metro transit buses serve the region, and visitors can ride the Minneapolis RiverCity Trolley and St. Paul Capital City Trolley to shop or visit cultural and historic sites. For visitor information, contact Greater Minneapolis Convention and Visitor Association, 4000 Multifoods Tower, 33 South Sixth Street, Minneapolis, MN 55402; 800/445-7412 or 612/348-7000, www.mineapolis.org; and St. Paul Convention and Visitors Bureau, 175 West Kellogg Boulevard, Suite 502, Saint Paul, MN 55102; 800/627-6101 or 651/265-4900, www.stpaulcvb.org.

MINNEAPOLIS SIGHTSEEING HIGHLIGHTS

★★★★ AMERICAN SWEDISH INSTITUTE
2600 Park Ave., 612/871-4907
www.americanswedishinst.org

"There are more Swedish artifacts here than in museums in Sweden," a Swedish visitor once commented. The cherished possessions of Swedish immigrants and their descendants are carefully preserved and displayed in a French chateau–style 33-room mansion with turrets, towers, and exquisitely carved woodwork. Of special note are 11 rare Swedish porcelain tile stoves.

Details: *Open Tue and Thu–Sat noon–4, Wed until 8, Sun 1–5. $2–$3, under 6 free. (1–2 hours)*

★★★★ FREDERICK R. WEISMAN ART MUSEUM
333 E. River Rd., University of Minnesota Campus
612/625-9494

The museum's Frank Gehry–designed steel and brick building has been called a "tin can" and generated controversy when it opened in 1993

MINNEAPOLIS

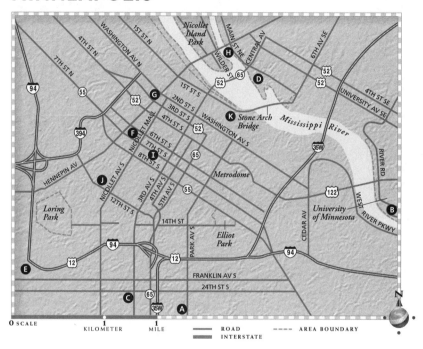

SIGHTS

Ⓐ American Swedish Institute
Ⓑ Frederick R. Weisman Art Museum
Ⓒ Minneapolis Institute of Arts
Ⓓ St. Anthony Falls Historic District, Minnesota Historical Society Visitor Center
Ⓔ Walker Art Center and Minneapolis Sculpture Garden

FOOD

Ⓕ Goodfellows
Ⓖ New French Café & Bar
Ⓗ Nicollet Island Inn
Ⓘ Peter's Grill

LODGING

Ⓙ Doubletree Guest Suites
Ⓚ Hyatt Whitney Hotel
Ⓗ Nicollet Island Inn

Note: Items with the same letter are located in the same place.

FREDERICK R. WEISMAN ART MUSEUM

Alice Vollmar

on the banks of the Mississippi River. Inside, you'll find a beautiful interior display space with skylights. The museum features a large collection of Marsden Hartley works, pop-art murals created by Roy Lichtenstein for the 1965 World's Fair, and works by Robert Motherwell and James Rosenquist.

Details: Open Tue–Fri 10–5, Thu until 8, Sat–Sun 11–5. Free, but a charge for special events. (1 hour)

★★★★ **MINNEAPOLIS INSTITUTE OF ARTS**
2400 Third Ave. S., 612/870-3131
The internationally known institute displays 80,000 objects of fine and decorative arts spanning 4,000 years. An extensive expansion project includes the 1998 addition of Asian Galleries featuring a 1784 jade mountain and two historic Chinese rooms and a literati–style garden transported from their original sites in China.

Details: Open Tue–Sat 10–5, Thu until 9, Sun noon–5. Free; fee for special exhibits except Thu 5–9 (with some exceptions). Free tours Tue–Sun 2, Thu 7, Sat–Sun 1. (1–2 hours)

★★★★ WALKER ART CENTER AND MINNEAPOLIS SCULPTURE GARDEN
725 Vineland Pl., 612/375-7622 or 612/375-7600
This cutting-edge contemporary art center is the third most visited museum in the United States. "Galleries" are defined by trees in the adjacent 11-acre garden, which houses more than 40 sculptures and is noted for the Spoonbridge and Cherry sculpture by Claes Oldenburg and Coosje Van Bruggen.

Details: Sculpture Garden open daily, 6–midnight, free. Art Center open Tue–Sat 10–5, Thu until 8, Sun 11–5. Closed Mon. $3–$4, 11 and under free; Thu and first Sat each month free. Walking tours Thu at 2 and 6, weekends at 2, free with admission. (2 hours)

★★★ ST. ANTHONY FALLS HISTORIC DISTRICT, HISTORICAL SOCIETY VISITOR CENTER
125 S.E. Main St., 612/627-5433
Take a guided tour from the Minnesota Historical Society Visitor Center or follow the St. Anthony Falls Heritage Trail markers to see the only falls on the Mississippi and the old milling district's remaining buildings and ruins. The Upper Lock and Dam Visitor Center (open April through November, at Portland and West River Parkway) has views of the falls and river activity, and stations on the Stone Arch Bridge provide historical background.

Details: Historical Society Visitor Center open May–Oct Wed–Sun 9–5. Historical Society tours $3–$5, under 6 free. (1–2 hours)

ST. PAUL SIGHTSEEING HIGHLIGHTS

★★★★ JAMES J. HILL HOUSE
240 Summit Ave., 651/297-2555
Great Northern Railroad magnate James J. Hill's massive Richardsonian Romanesque home stands like a fortress on St. Paul's Summit Avenue, a four-and-a-half-mile boulevard lined with showy late nineteenth- and early twentieth-century mansions. Nearby stands the ornate 1915 **St. Paul Cathedral** at 239 Selby (651/228-1766), modeled after St. Peter's in Rome, with free tours Monday, Wednesday, and Friday at one.

Details: Open Wed–Sat 10–3:30; guided tours, reservations preferred. $3–$5, 5 and under free. (1–1½ hours)

★★★★ MINNESOTA HISTORY CENTER
345 Kellogg Blvd., 800/657-3773, 888/PAST FUN, or
651/296-6126
In a handsome building made of Minnesota limestone and granite are

ST. PAUL

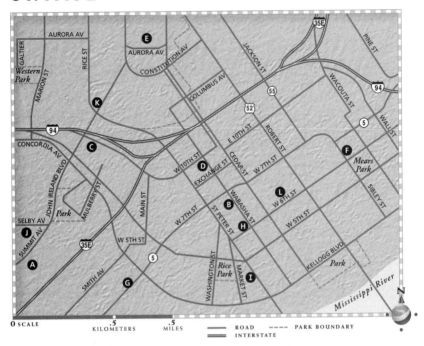

SIGHTS

- **A** James J. Hill House
- **B** Minnesota Children's Museum
- **C** Minnesota History Center
- **D** Science Museum of Minnesota and William L. McKnight 3-M Omnitheater
- **E** State Capitol

FOOD

- **F** Café da Vinci
- **G** Cossetta's Italian Market & Pizzeria
- **H** Sakura
- **I** Saint Paul Grill
- **J** W.A. Frost & Co.

LODGING

- **K** Best Western Kelly Inn
- **L** Radisson Inn Saint Paul
- **I** The Saint Paul Hotel

Note: Items with the same letter are located in the same place.

clever interactive displays that tell the story of Minnesota. The center's Café Minnesota offers exceptional food (lunch and brunch only).
Details: Open Mon–Sat 10–5, Tue until 8, Sun noon–5. Free. (1–2 hours)

★★★★ STATE CAPITOL
Cedar and Aurora Sts. 651/296-3962
An imposing edifice built by Cass Gilbert in 1905, the capitol claims the world's largest unsupported marble dome. Free tours leave daily on the hour and are packed with Minnesota history.
Details: Open Mon–Fri 9–4, Sat 10–3, Sun 1–3. Free. For tours, call 651/296-2881. (1 hour)

★★★ MINNESOTA CHILDREN'S MUSEUM
10 W. Seventh St., 651/225-6050 weekends, 651/225-6001 weekdays
This inviting, inventive museum features hands-on exhibits including a play grocery and restaurant and a simulated storm complete with thunder and lightning.
Details: Open Tue–Sun 9–5, Thu until 8; open Mon Memorial Day–Labor Day only. $3.95–$5.95, infants free. (1 hour)

★★★ SCIENCE MUSEUM OF MINNESOTA AND WILLIAM L. MCKNIGHT 3M OMNITHEATER
30 E. 10th St., 651/221-9444 or 651/221-9412
Popular with all ages, the museum holds interactive science exhibits and the Dinosaur and Fossils Hall. The domed Omnitheater shows science- and nature-based films on its 76-foot domed screen.
Details: Open Mon–Sat 9:30–9, Sunday 10–7; closed Mon Labor Day–mid-December. $4–$7 museum, $5–$7 Omnitheater, $6–$9 combination. (2½ hours)

GREATER TWIN CITIES SIGHTSEEING HIGHLIGHTS

★★★★ HISTORIC FORT SNELLING
MN 5 and 55, St. Paul, 612/726-1171
At Fort Snelling, costumed interpreters reenact fort life in stone

GREATER TWIN CITIES

To A

N

Lake St. Croix

St. Croix River

ST. CROIX TRAIL

95

12
94 12 R Washington

Lake Elmo Regional Park

69E

494

61
10

Mississippi River

N St. Paul

LARPENTEUR AV

S St. Paul

52

35E

Chain of Lakes

S

Rice Creek Regional Park

35E St. Paul

M 52

W St. Paul

55

Ramsey

A

L

LEXINGTON PKWY

F

PILOT KNOB RD

35E H 38

Anoka

35W

68

94 12

C

HENNEPIN AV

HIAWATHA AV

MINNEHAHA PKWY

E 77

CENTRAL AV K

65

47

10

UNIVERSITY AV

I

J 35W

N

62

Minneapolis

94

D

5 35W

100

P 494

13

Hyland Lake Park Reserve

Minnesota River

O B

394

169

12

Hennepin

7

101

Elm Creek Park Reserve

CANTERBURY RD

MARSCHALL RD

94 R

55

Morris T. Baker Park Reserve

Q

Lake Minnetonka

5

G

41

O SCALE
8
8
KILOMETERS MILES

ROAD ——— PARK BOUNDARY

INTERSTATE

buildings and a stockade restored to the fort's 1827 appearance. Visitors can converse with cooks and soldiers and watch military drills and other events on bluffs high above the juncture of the Mississippi and Minnesota Rivers. **Details:** *Open May–Oct Mon–Sat 10–5, Sun noon–5. History center same schedule plus October–May weekdays 9–4. $3–$5. (2–3 hours)*

★★★★ LYNDALE PARK GARDENS
Roseway Rd.
612/661-4800
On rolling lawns with venerable shade trees, park visitors stroll paths through a rose garden, a rock garden, and a bird sanctuary near Lake Harriet and glimpse a slice of the South Minneapolis lifestyle. You can watch sailboats on Lake Harriet and swim at the nearby beach. Follow the lakeside walking path to hear late-afternoon concerts in the Lake Harriet bandshell and buy ice-cream cones and other treats in summer months. **Details:** *Roseway Rd. between E. Lake Harriet Pkwy. and Kings Hwy.; call 612/661-4875 for events information. Open sunrise–10 p.m. Free. (45 minutes to 1½ hours)*

SIGHTS
- Ⓐ Como Park Zoo and Conservatory
- Ⓑ Eloise Butler Wildflower Garden
- Ⓒ Historic Fort Snelling
- Ⓓ Lyndale Park Gardens
- Ⓔ Mall of America
- Ⓕ Minnehaha Falls
- Ⓖ Minnesota Landscape Arboretum
- Ⓗ Minnesota Zoo and Imation IMAX Theater

FOOD
- Ⓘ Bobino Cafe & Wine Bar
- Ⓙ Egg & I
- Ⓚ Emily's Lebanese Delicatessen

LODGING
- Ⓛ Chatsworth Bed and Breakfast
- Ⓜ Covington Inn
- Ⓝ Elmwood House
- Ⓞ Holiday Inn Express Minneapolis (Golden Valley)
- Ⓚ LeBlanc House

LODGING (continued)
- Ⓞ Super 8 Minneapolis West
- Ⓟ Wyndham Garden Hotel

CAMPING
- Ⓠ Baker Park Reserve
- Ⓡ KOA Campgrounds
- Ⓢ Rice Creek Campground
- Ⓣ William O'Brien State Park

Note: Items with the same letter are located in the same place.

★★★ COMO PARK ZOO AND CONSERVATORY
Between Hamline and Lexington Aves. on **Midway**
651/487-8200 or 651/266-6400
This expansive 150,000-acre park contains a Victorian floral conservatory, a free zoo, Japanese gardens, an 18-hole golf course, ski trails, bike and canoe rentals at Lakeside Pavilion, a one-and-a-half-mile walking trail that winds around the lake, and an amusement park.
Details: *Zoo open daily 8–5; buildings open 10–4. Conservatory open Apr–Sept daily 10–6; in winter, until 4. Park and zoo free; conservatory $.25–$.50, age 10 and under free. Fee for rides in amusement park. (1–3 hours)*

★★★ ELOISE BUTLER WILDFLOWER GARDEN
Theodore Wirth Park, Minneapolis, 612/370-4903
You'll visit woodland, wetland, and upland prairie in this delightful wildflower garden with free educational programs nestled in the park's wooded, rolling hills. A plant checklist indicates when the bright red cardinal flower, yellow oxeye daisies, and more than 300 other plants and flowers are in bloom.
Details: *One-half block north of I-394 on Theodore Wirth Parkway in Minneapolis. Open Apr–Oct 7:30 a.m.–dusk. Free. (1 hour)*

★★★ MINNEHAHA FALLS
4825 Minnehaha Ave., Minneapolis, 612/661-4817 or 612/661-4800
The spectacular falls of Minnehaha Creek tumble into a canyon in wooded Minnehaha Park. Walking trails lead from the park to the Mississippi River; hiking and bike paths run along Minnehaha Creek. Other attractions include a picnic area, a historic depot, and historic houses. Be sure to drive a portion of Minnehaha Parkway, which runs west following the creek and is bordered by grassy spaces and picnic spots.
Details: *Open daily 6–11. Free. (1 hour minimum)*

★★★ MINNESOTA LANDSCAPE ARBORETUM
3675 Arboretum Dr., Chanhassen, 612/443-2460
Walk trails and/or drive to see more than 925 acres of plants, landscaped gardens, woodlands, and restored prairie. The flowering crabapple and cherry trees are magnificent in the spring. The central building houses a library, gift shop, and tearoom.

Details: *Nine miles west of I-494 on MN 5. Open 8–sunset daily; building until 4:30; tearoom daily 11–2:30. $5, age 18 and under free. (1–3 hours)*

★★★ MINNESOTA ZOO AND IMATION IMAX THEATRE
13000 and 12000 Zoo Blvd., Apple Valley, 55124, 612/ 432-9000 (zoo); 612/431-4629 or 888/433-4629 (theater)
This natural habitat zoo offers special programs, dolphin shows in Discovery Bay, and holiday events. The 600-seat 3D/2D Theater offers daily shows.
Details: *Open Mon–Sat 9–6, Sun 9–8; Labor Day–April 9–4. Zoo admission $4–$8, 2 and under free; theater admission $5–$8; combination tickets $9–$12.50. (half–full day)*

★★ MALL OF AMERICA
Bloomington, 612/883-8800
Minnesota is home to the largest mall in the United States. Along with about 150 specialty shops are anchor stores Bloomingdale's, Macy's, Nordstrom, and Sears. Kids will head for the enclosed amusement park, Knott's Camp Snoopy (612/883-5600), and the LEGO showcase/hands-on building area.
Details: *Off I-494 and Cedar Ave/MN 77. Mall open 7 a.m.–2 a.m.; stores open Mon–Sat 10–9:30, Sun 11–7. Prices for amusement park rides vary. (1–4 hours)*

FITNESS AND RECREATION
The Twin Cities boast miles of interconnecting paths and parks that are used by hikers, bikers, and skiers alike. Minneapolis Parks and Recreation Board maintains nearly 40 miles of walking paths and almost 40 miles of biking paths, which are described in the board's summer activities guide (for information, call 612/661-4875 or 612/661-4800). Additionally, Hennepin Parks, 612/559-9000, publishes a free parks guide. Parks with hiking and biking include **Hyland Lake Park Reserve** (five and a half miles of hiking/biking trails and four and a half miles of bike-only trails) in Bloomington, 612/941-4362. **St. Paul Parks and Recreation**, 651/266-6400, maintains more than 40 miles of parks, parkways, and trails; call for the *Bike, Hike and Jog User Guide*. In Saint Paul, go to **Crosby Farm-Hidden Falls Regional Park**, 651/645-5713, Shepard Rd. and Mississippi River Blvd., to hike through woods and along the river banks on

nearly eight miles of trails. The region has more than 100 public and private golf courses.

Lakes with popular public swimming beaches include **Lake Harriet** and **Lake Calhoun** in south Minneapolis; Lake Calhoun, 612/370-4964, has canoe rentals, as well. Downhill ski areas include **Hyland Hills**, 612/835-4250, in Bloomington and **Afton Alps**, 612/436-5245, in Hastings.

Fans can watch **Minnesota Twins** professional baseball, 612/375-1116, and **Minnesota Vikings** NFL football, 612/333-8828, in the Hubert H. Humphrey Metrodome, 612/332-0386, 900 S. 5th St., Minneapolis.

FOOD

In downtown Minneapolis, executive chef Kevin Cullen creates award-winning regional cuisine, including Minnesota venison, at **Goodfellows,** 40 S. Seventh St., 612/332-4800, with meals from $20 to $32. At the **New French Café & Bar**, 128 N. Fourth St., Minneapolis, 612/338-3790, excellent nouvelle French cuisine costs $16 to $24. A good breakfast spot in South Minneapolis, with meals from $2 to $6, is the **Egg & I**, 2828 Lyndale Ave., 612/872-7282. When President Clinton came to visit, he ate old-fashioned home cooking downtown at **Peter's Grill**, Baker Center, 114 S. Eighth St., 612/333-1981, where meals cost from $6.65 to $14.95.

You can count on professional service and innovative cuisine, such as salmon with apple dill couscous, at **Nicollet Island Inn,** 612/331-1800. It's near St. Anthony Falls and includes river views and dinner from $13 to $32. **Emily's Lebanese Delicatessen,** 641 University Ave. N.E., Minneapolis, 612/379-4069, is a casual place to dine on fantastic tabbouleh salad, spinach pie, and lamb kebabs for under $11. At popular **Bobino Cafe & Wine Bar**, 222 Hennepin Ave. E., Minneapolis, 612/623-3301, the changing menu features five or six entrées for $10 to $20.

In St. Paul, **W. A. Frost & Co.**, 374 Selby Ave., 651/224-5715, has a great summer garden patio; prices range from $8 to $25. St. Paul's spacious **Café da Vinci**, 400 Sibley St., 651/222-4050, is loaded with artsy atmosphere and specializes in Italian pasta dishes ($8.95–$16.95); while **Cossetta's Italian Market & Pizzeria**, 211 W. Seventh St., 651/222-3476, has award-winning pizza and great deli fare for under $10. The handsome **Saint Paul Grill**, The Saint Paul Hotel, 350 Market St., 651/224-7455, offers excellent food only a short Rice Park stroll away from the Ordway Music Theatre; prices run $12.95 to $35 a la carte. Also convenient to the Ordway is **Sakura**, 350 St. Peter St., 651/224-0185, with Japanese cuisine and a sushi bar from $8 to $15.

LODGING

For sophisticated luxury lodging, stay at **The Saint Paul Hotel**, 350 Market St., 800/292-9292, with rooms from $150 to $165 and suites from $230 to $675; or the **Hyatt Whitney Hotel**, 150 Portland Ave., Minneapolis, 612/375-1234, with rooms for $155 to $185 and suites from $185 to $350.

For a funkier experience, try St. Paul's **Covington Inn**, 651/292-1411, a bed-and-breakfast on a historic line boat docked at Pier One on Harriet Island. Rooms range from $105 to $195. Enjoy a book in the sunny window seat at the **Nicollet Island Inn**, 95 Merriam St., 612/331-1800, a charming country inn on an island in the heart of Minneapolis. Rooms range from $125 to $160. The **Chatsworth Bed-and-Breakfast**, 984 Ashland Ave., St. Paul, 651/227-4288, occupies a handsomely furnished 1902 Victorian house, and includes terry robes or kimonos, a diverse selection of books for serious readers, and rates from $70 to $130.

St. Paul's **Best Western Kelly Inn-State Capitol**, 161 St. Anthony Blvd., 800/528-1234, has rooms from $84 to $89. The **Super 8 Minneapolis West**, 6300 Wayzata Blvd., Golden Valley, 612/546-6277, offers an exceptionally handsome lobby/lounge and rooms; the double rates are $49.88 to $69.88. Nearby, at the well-maintained **Holiday Inn Express Minneapolis (Golden Valley)**, 6020 Wayzatta Blvd., 612/545-8300 or 800/HOLIDAY, there's an indoor pool and rates range from $74.99 to $99.99. The **Wyndham Garden Hotel**, 4460 W. 78th Circle, Bloomington, 800/822-4200, has an indoor pool and restaurant, and doubles run $74 to $94. At downtown Minneapolis' **Doubletree Guest Suites**, 1101 LaSalle Ave., 612/332-6800, rooms are $129 to $189. The **Radisson Inn Saint Paul** in downtown St. Paul, 411 Minnesota, 651/291-8800, offers rooms for $102 to $150 with a full breakfast and cocktails. Feather beds and antiques grace the 1896 Victorian **LeBlanc House**, 302 University Ave. N.E., Minneapolis, 612/379-2570, with rates from

$85 to $105. In south Minneapolis you can cozy into a comfy chair in a spacious living room with original woodwork and a beamed ceiling and read the history of the lovingly restored 1887 **Elmwood House**, 1 E. Elmwood Pl., 888/822-4558 or 612/822-4558, www.iaxs.net/~elmwood/. Its rooms range from $75 to $95.

CAMPING

The greater metro area has close to two dozen campgrounds, private and public. **Baker Park Reserve** on Lake Independence in Maple Plain, 612/559-6700, has 210 sites, 27 with electricity, for $12 to $17. **William O'Brien State Park**, 16 miles north of Stillwater via State 95, 651/433-0500, has 125 campsites—61 with electricity, wheelchair-accessible showers, and flush toilets. **Rice Creek Chain-of-Lakes Regional Park Reserve's Rice Creek Campground** in north metro Lino Lakes, three miles west on County 14 off I-35E, 612/757-3920 or 612/767-2868, has 79 sites, 39 with hookups, rest rooms, and showers for $10 to $14. You'll find private **KOA campgrounds** in Rogers, 15 miles northwest on I-94W, exit 213; two miles west on County 30 and one mile north on Highway 101, 612/420-2255; and east of St. Paul in Woodbury, on County 19 off I-94E, 800/562-0261 or 651/436-6436.

NIGHTLIFE AND SPECIAL EVENTS

Order the *Dining and Entertainment Guide* from Minnesota Tourism, 800/657-3700 or 651/296-5029, as well as the latest *Twin Cities* visitor's guide. Then pick up the *City Pages*, along with the "Friday Variety" section of the *Twin Cities Star Tribune* for current happenings. Musical offerings include **Minnesota Orchestra**, 1111 Nicollet Mall, Minneapolis, 612/371-5656; **Saint Paul Chamber Orchestra**, usually at the Ordway in St. Paul, 651/291-1144; and **Minnesota Opera**, 612/333-2700. Touring Broadway shows are staged at the restored **Historic Orpheum Theatre**, 910 Hennepin Ave. S., Minneapolis, 612/339-7007; and at the **Ordway Music Theatre**, 345 Washington St., St. Paul, 651/224-4222. In St. Paul, jazz music accompanies original and wonderful "Minnesota cuisine" at the **Dakota Bar and Grill,** 1021 Bandana Blvd. E., east of Snelling Ave., 651/642-1442; and at the hot Greenwich Village–style **Artists' Quarter**, 366 Jackson St., 651/292-1359, which has hosted Mose Allison and Benny Golson. **Fine Line Music Café**, 318 First Ave. N., Minneapolis, 612/335-8181 or 612/338-8100, swings with jazz and rock bands of local and national repute. Dance companies perform at

Minneapolis's historic **Hennepin Center for the Arts**, 528 Hennepin, 612/332-4478, and elsewhere.

In Minneapolis, go to the **Guthrie Theater**, 725 Vineland Pl., 612/377-2224, a noted repertory theater for the classics; or to **Mixed Blood**, 1501 S. Fourth St., 612/338-6131, for fun, startling, and bold plays that are always good. Also try the renowned **Children's Theatre Company** at 2400 Third Ave. S. in Minneapolis, 612/874-0400, for plays applauded by children and adults. There are also theaters and nightclubs at the **Mall of America**, off I-494 and Hwy. 77 in Bloomington, 612/883-8800. Casinos close to the Twin Cities include **Mystic Lake**, 2400 Mystic Lake Blvd., Prior Lake, 800/262-7799; and **Treasure Island**, off Hwy. 61 between Hastings and Red Wing, 800/222-7077.

St. Croix River Valley Drive

Take I-35W or I-35E (they meld into I-35) north of the Twin Cities to MN 97, just south of Forest Lake. Follow 97 east to the Swedish town of Scandia and visit the Swedish-heritage **Gammel Gården Museum**, 651/433-5053 (open weekends May–October).

Continue east to the St. Croix River, a national scenic riverway, and head north on State Highway 95, which winds along the bluffs of the St. Croix. In Taylors Falls, follow signs to the **Historic Angel Hill District**, a New England–style village. Tour the restored 1855 Greek Revival/Federal–style **Folsom House**, 612/465-3125 (open daily 1–4:30 p.m. Memorial Day weekend–mid-October). At **Interstate Park** (across from downtown), hike trails past glacial potholes, up rocky bluffs for river views, and through the woods. Take a river cruise to view the scenic rock cliffs of the Dalles of the St. Croix.

To return to the Twin Cities, follow U.S. 8 west. Between Taylors Falls and Shafer, see giant-scale art at the 14-acre **Franconia Sculpture Park**. In Lindstrom, dine on the Dinnerbel's deck, continue west to I-35, then take the interstate south to return to the Twin Cities.

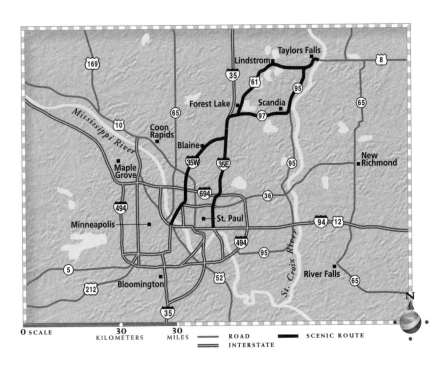

2
DULUTH AND
THE NORTH SHORE

Duluth and the Lake Superior North Shore lie in the northeastern Minnesota Arrowhead region, home of the magnificent, nearly 3 million-acre Superior National Forest. This land of rocky outcroppings contains exposed Precambrian rocks more than 2.5 billion years old.

Fur trade once flourished in this area. A major fur trading post was established at Grand Portage by 1776 and is now honored as a national monument.

About 150 miles south of Grand Portage, perched on rocky cliffs overlooking Lake Superior, world port Duluth has a large natural harbor and is a railway and shipping hub. Ships arrive via the St. Lawrence Seaway from more than 30 countries to take on cargoes of coal, grain, crude oil, and iron ore. The harbor was critical to Minnesota's once-booming iron ore mining industry. Most of the high-grade iron ore is gone now, but taconite mining continues on the Iron Range. Iron ore wealth helped build the architectural treasures that line the streets of Duluth today. The rugged terrain in this region provides some of the best and most challenging hiking and skiing in the state, as well as unparalleled scenic beauty.

A PERFECT DAY IN DULUTH

Start your visit to Duluth amid the flocks of seagulls at Canal Park and watch a seagoing ship pass under the famed Aerial Lift Bridge. Stroll on the Lakewalk,

31

DULUTH

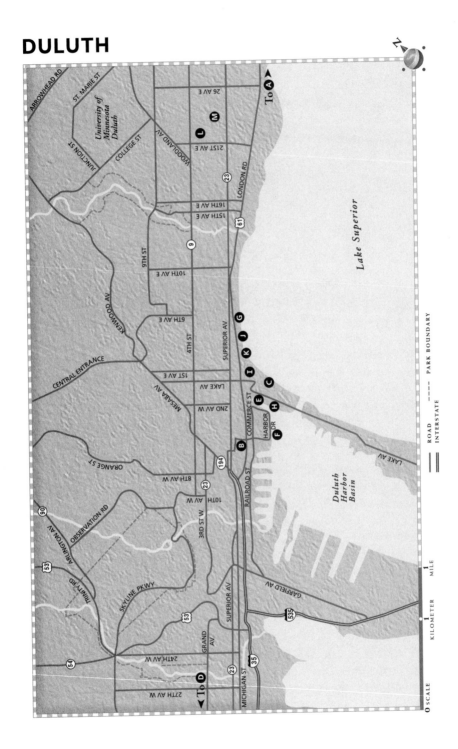

explore Canal Park area shops, visit the Lake Superior Maritime Visitor Center, and treat yourself to lunch at the Lake Avenue Cafe. Drive to the Railroad Museum and climb aboard one of the world's largest steam-powered locomotives. Next, head for Jay Cooke State Park, cross the St. Louis River on a swinging bridge, and hike a trail or two. Then, catch Skyline Drive's harbor views, take time to smell the roses at Leif Erikson Park, take a dinner harbor cruise, and end the day with a romantic lakeside amble.

DULUTH SIGHTSEEING HIGHLIGHTS

★★★★ LAKE SUPERIOR MARITIME VISITOR CENTER AND CANAL PARK
600 Lake Ave. S., 218/727-2497

The Maritime Center offers a recap of maritime history via pictures, a film show, and artifacts. You can watch gigantic vessels pass through the canal and under the Aerial Lift Bridge, which rises 138 feet to allow ships to enter and leave the harbor.

Details: Late May–early Sept daily 10–9; other seasons until 4:30 daily, except mid-Dec–Apr when open only Fri–Sun. Boat-watcher's hotline: 218/722-6489. Free. (1 hour)

★★★★ LAKE SUPERIOR RAILROAD MUSEUM
The Depot, 506 W. Michigan St., 888/733-5833 or 218/727-8025

SIGHTS

- Ⓐ Glensheen Mansion
- Ⓑ Lake Superior Railroad Museum
- Ⓒ Lake Superior Maritime Visitor Center and Canal Park
- Ⓓ Lake Superior & Mississippi Railroad
- Ⓐ North Shore Scenic Drive
- Ⓔ William A. Irvin
- Ⓕ Vista Fleet

FOOD

- Ⓖ Bennett's on the Lake
- Ⓗ Grandma's
- Ⓘ Lake Avenue Cafe
- Ⓙ Pickwick Restaurant

LODGING

- Ⓚ Duluth Hampton Inn on Lake Superior
- Ⓖ Fitger's Inn
- Ⓛ Manor on the Creek
- Ⓜ Olcott House

Note: Items with the same letter are located in the same area.

Displays feature the first locomotive to operate in Minnesota, plus other vintage trains, railroad equipment, and a collection of dining car china and silver. Hands-on/climb-aboard opportunities abound. The museum also operates the North Shore Scenic Railroad, with North Shore two- and six-hour excursions from May through October. Call the museum for the schedule and fares.

Details: Memorial Day–Labor Day daily 9:30–6, Fri until 8; other seasons Mon–Sat 10–5, Sun 1–5. $5–$8, under 6 free, family rate $22.50. One fee admits you to the Depot's children's museum, railroad museum, historical society exhibits, and the Duluth Art Institute. (1–3 hours)

★★★★ NORTH SHORE SCENIC DRIVE, DULUTH TO TWO HARBORS

North Shore Scenic Drive Association: www.northshore scenicdrive.com

For scenic views of Lake Superior, from thundering waves crashing at the foot of rocky cliffs to serene bays backdropped by towering pine and spruce, take the 22-mile Scenic Highway 61 drive from Brighton Beach up to Two Harbors. (half–full day)

★★★★ VISTA FLEET, HARBOR DR.

Entertainment Convention Center dock, 218/722-6218

Get a close-up view of loading docks and ships in the harbor. Cruises pass underneath the Aerial Lift Bridge and enter Lake Superior.

Details: Cruises mid-May–mid-October daily 9:30–7:30; tours hourly 11:30–3:30, then every two hours. $4–$9, under 3 free. (2 hours)

★★★ GLENSHEEN MANSION

3300 London Rd., 218/724-8864 or 724-8863, www.d.umn .edu/glen/

Tour the 39-room Jacobean Revival mansion built by millionaire Chester Congdon, on landscaped grounds with formal gardens.

Details: May–Oct daily 9:30–4; Nov–Apr Sat–Sun 11–2. $4–$8.75, under 6 free. Reservations recommended. (2 hours)

★★★ LAKE SUPERIOR & MISSISSIPPI RAILROAD

506 W. Michigan St., 218/624-7549 or 218/727-0687

Clatter along the St. Louis River on a vintage train with coaches from the early nineteenth century.

Details: *Departs from the Western Waterfront Trail parking lot at Grand Ave. and 71st Ave. W. across from Duluth Zoo. Operates mid-June–late Aug Sat–Sun 11 and 2. $5–$7. (1½ hours)*

★★★ WILLIAM A. IRVIN
Harbor Dr., 218/722-5573 or 218/722-7876
The permanently docked flagship of the USS Great Lakes Fleet offers tours. You can also tour the historic tugboat *Lake Superior.*

> **Details:** *Docked at the Duluth Entertainment Center. Open May–Oct; call for tour times. $4–$6.50, under 3 free. (1 hour)*

NORTH SHORE SIGHTSEEING HIGHLIGHTS

★★★★ GRAND MARAIS
MN 61 888/922-5000 or 218/387-2524
www.grandmaraismn.com
This picturesque North Shore fishing village shelters an arts colony and has a natural harbor with a lighthouse. Visit the **Johnson Heritage Post Art Gallery**, on Wisconsin Street downtown, 218/387-2314, to see the work of North Shore artists. Go to **Cook County Museum**, also on Wisconsin Street downtown, 218/387-2838, for artifacts and logging and commercial fishing history.

> **Details:** *Grand Marais Visitor Center is 1½ blocks south at the signal light. Open year round. (half day minimum)*

★★★★ GRAND PORTAGE NATIONAL MONUMENT
Grand Portage, 218/387-2788 or 218/475-2202
The site contains the reconstructed North West Fur Company Trading Post, complete with stockade, great hall, and furnishings. There are daily demonstrations of fort activities. You can also hike the portage used by Native Americans and voyageurs, but it's a demanding, often muddy, not especially scenic trek of nearly nine miles and five hours one way.

> **Details:** *Off MN 61, 36 miles north of Grand Marais; watch for the sign after you pass the casino. May–mid-Oct daily 9–5. $2, under 16 free; $5 family rate. (1–2 hours)*

★★★★ GRAND PORTAGE STATE PARK
MN 61 W., Grand Portage, 218/475-2360

NORTH SHORE AREA

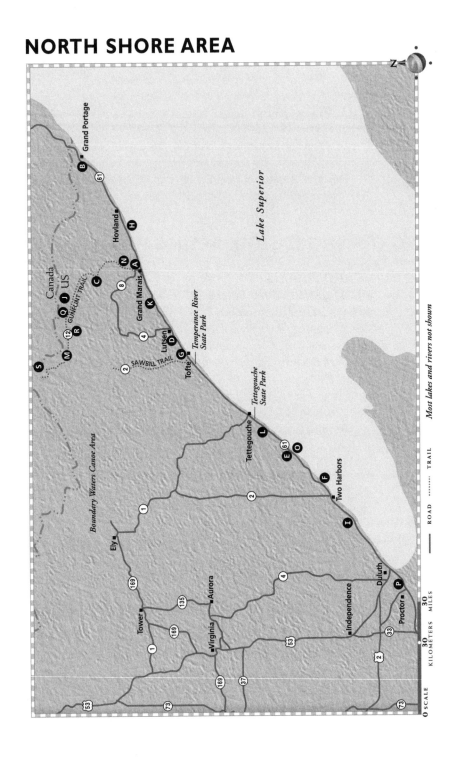

Most lakes and rivers not shown

ROAD .... TRAIL

SCALE

0   30 KILOMETERS
0   30 MILES

Hike boardwalk trails to view the 120-foot High Falls of the Pigeon River, the state's highest waterfall. This state park opened in 1994 as a day-use facility with interpretive programs jointly operated by the DNR and the Grand Portage Band of Ojibwa.

Details: *150 miles northeast of Duluth, just inside the Canadian border, on the upper side of MN 61, just past the town of Grand Portage. Open in daytime. $4 daily park permit. (1 hour)*

★★★★ **SPLIT ROCK LIGHTHOUSE STATE PARK**
2010A MN 61 E., Two Harbors, 218/226-6372 or 218/226-6377

Learn North Shore history and tour the lighthouse and keeper's quarters in summer months on the edge of a craggy cliff.

Details: *On MN 61, 20 miles northeast of Two Harbors. Open mid-May–mid-Oct 9–5. $3–$5, household $12, under 6 free, in lieu of park permit. Other months only visitors center open Fri–Sun noon–4 (closed Dec), $4 daily park permit but no admission fee. (1 hour)*

SIGHTS

- Ⓐ Cook County Museum
- Ⓐ Grand Marais
- Ⓑ Grand Portage National Monument
- Ⓑ Grand Portage State Park
- Ⓒ Gunflint Trail
- Ⓐ Johnson Heritage Post Art Gallery
- Ⓓ Lutsen Ski Area
- Ⓔ Split Rock Lighthouse State Park

FOOD

- Ⓐ Angry Trout
- Ⓕ Betty's Pies
- Ⓖ Bluefin Restaurant
- Ⓐ Blue Water Café
- Ⓑ Lakeside Dining Room

FOOD *(continued)*

- Ⓓ Lutsen Resort
- Ⓗ Naniboujou Lodge
- Ⓘ Scenic Cafe
- Ⓐ Sven and Ole's

LODGING

- Ⓙ Bearskin Lodge
- Ⓚ Cascade Lodge
- Ⓛ Cove Point Lodge
- Ⓐ East Bay Hotel
- Ⓐ Econolodge
- Ⓑ Grand Portage Lodge
- Ⓜ Gunflint Lodge
- Ⓓ Lutsen Resort and Sea Villas
- Ⓝ Pincushion Mountain Bed and Breakfast
- Ⓖ Superior Shores

CAMPING

- Ⓙ Flour Lake Campground
- Ⓞ Gooseberry Falls State Park
- Ⓐ Grand Marais Recreation Area RV Park-Campground
- Ⓑ Grand Portage Campground and Marina
- Ⓜ Gunflint Pines Resort
- Ⓟ Indian Point Campground
- Ⓠ Iron Lake Campground
- Ⓟ Jay Cooke State Park
- Ⓣ Judge C. R. Magney State Park
- Ⓡ Nor'wester Lodge
- Ⓢ Trail's End Campground

Note: Items with the same letter are located in the same place.

NORTH SHORE FISHING HISTORY
To learn about the once-thriving commercial herring and lake trout fishing industry spawned by Norwegian immigrants, visit the North Shore Commercial Fishing Museum/Information Center in Tofte.

★★★ **GUNFLINT TRAIL**
800/338-6932, www.gunflint-trail.com
This 63-mile road leads north and west from Grand Marais into the BWCA wilderness and Superior National Forest's close to 3 million acres of public land. You'll find highly rated wilderness lodges, fishing, wildlife (including moose and eagles), lots of hiking, and winter skiing. Bring your hiking boots and lots of mosquito repellent if you're visiting this area during the summer months.

Details: Contact the Gunflint Trail Association for guides, 800/338-6932. Free. (half day minimum)

★★ **LUTSEN SKI AREA**
218/663-7281
In addition to skiing, the facility offers Gondola Sky Rides, alpine slides, and mountain biking. Gondola rides climb to the Moose Mountain summit and offer excellent ridgeline views, especially scenic in autumn. There are hiking trails here, as well.

Details: 90 minutes northeast of Duluth, off MN 61. Memorial Day–mid-Oct 10–5, closes later mid-summer; late May–mid-Oct weekends 10–5. Gondola ride: $5–$8.25, under 7 free; alpine slide $4.50–$29; mountain biking trail pass $12–$18. Bike rental $7–$23. All-day pass: $21. (1 hour minimum)

FITNESS AND RECREATION
Hiking and skiing (cross-country and downhill) dominate the recreation scene. Duluth's visitor's guide, 800/438-5884, lists eight hiking and five ski trails with their locations, along with bike, canoe, and snowmobile rental sources. **Lutsen Mountains** ski area, 218/663-7281, has the best downhill skiing in the Midwest and offers various ski packages. There's also downhill skiing at **Spirit**

Mountain in Duluth, 800/642-6377. You can hike segments of the **Superior Hiking Trail** which, when completed, will stretch from Duluth to the Canadian border. Seasoned hikers can try the 75-mile BWCA **Border Route Trail**, which leads from Kekekabic Trail on the Gunflint Trail to the Pigeon River below South Fowl Lake, or stretch their legs on state park and other area trails, or loop combinations. The U.S. Forest Service, 218/387-1750, offers an information packet listing 33 hikes. Included are the six-mile **Temperance River Trail** with pools and rocky ledges; the two-mile **Devils Kettle Trail** at Judge C. R. Magney State Park with waterfalls, rapids, and a disappearing 50-foot waterfall; and the short but steep **Honeymoon Bluff Trail**, off County Road 66 at the Flour Lake Campground entrance, with an overlook on Hungry Jack Lake. For more detailed information, get the *Guide to the Superior Hiking Trail* sold in local shops or available from the Superior Hiking Trail Association, 218/834-2700.

Head to **Village Inn & Resort's Homestead Stables** at Lutsen Mountains for guided horseback rides, 800/642-6036 or 218/663-7241. Golf courses include **Superior National Golf Course** in Lutsen, 218/663-7195, with 18 holes of championship golf. You'll find numerous charter fishing companies in Duluth, including **Captain Gary's Charters**, 800/457-9402, and **Lake Superior Sport Fishing Charters**, 218/724-4214 or 218/724-9104. The area also offers kayaking, rock-climbing, and canoeing. Winter sports include cross-country and downhill skiing and dogsledding. For yurt-to-yurt or lodge-to-lodge skiing and hiking contact Gunflint Trail Association, 800/338-6932; Lutsen-Tofte Association on MN 61 in Tofte at the Twin Fish Houses, 888/616-6784 or 218/663-7804, www.mn-northshore.com; or Lodge to Lodge Trekking, 800/322-8327, www.boreal.org/adventures/hiking.html.

FOOD

You'll find excellent food here. In Duluth, go to **Lake Avenue Cafe**, DeWitt-Seitz Marketplace, 218/722-2355, for tasty artichoke-spinach pizza and international specialties from $5 to $17. Duluth's **Pickwick Restaurant**, 508 E. Superior St., 218/727-8901, is a classic establishment that has been family-operated since 1914. It offers good steaks and traditional fare from $8 to $45. **Grandma's**, 522 Lake Ave. S., Duluth, 218/727-4192, serves sandwiches, soups, steaks, and pasta in a casual, fun atmosphere for $8 to $25. At **Bennett's on the Lake**, 218/722-2829, Fitger's Complex at 600 E. Superior St., the menu features duck, sea bass, and a variety of creative American dishes in a tastefully appointed dining room for $13.95 to $22.95. Feast on pan-seared sea scallops in orange sauce with candied walnuts at the **Scenic Cafe**, 13 miles east of Duluth, 546 North Shore Scenic Dr., 218/525-6274, with meals from $7 to $16. **Bluefin Restaurant**, on the North Shore near Tofte, 218/663-7860, ext. 333, features locally caught fish and exceptional cuisine for $13 to $23. Pie lovers make a beeline for **Betty's Pies**, 215 MN 61 E. in Two Harbors, 218/834-3367.

A longtime North Shore resident with a fondness for pie directs visitors to the Rustic Inn Cafe, 13 miles east of Two Harbors, 218/834-2488.

North Shore–area lodges serve fantastic meals. Try the wild rice soup and raisin rye bread in **Lutsen Resort's** Scandinavian dining room, off MN 61 at Lutsen, 218/663-7212; dinner costs from $10 to $23. Afternoon tea, served from three to five daily, with scones and short-bread cookies for $8.50, is a delight at **Naniboujou Lodge**, 15 miles east of Grand Marais via MN 61, 218/387-2688. The lodge is a former private club with a great hall decorated in Cree Indian motif. The **Angry Trout** in Grand Marais, 218/387-1265, serves pasta, fish, and salads with attention to healthy preparation. The town's **Blue Water Café**, 218/387-1597, is where local folks gather. **Sven and Ole's**, 218/387-1713, may be the only place you'll find Scandinavian pizza; meals cost from $5–$13. There's also Grand Portage Casino's **Lakeside Dining Room**, 218/475-2401, with dinners from $5.95 to $14.95.

LODGING

At **Fitger's Inn**, 600 E. Superior St., Duluth, 888/FITGERS, 218/726-2982, you'll lodge in a renovated 1857 brewery for $90 to $250. The **Duluth Hampton Inn on Lake Superior**, 310 Canal Park Dr., 800/426-7866 or 218/720-3000, features a comfortable reading room and offers rates from $89 to $169. The romantically handsome restored 1904 Georgian-style mansion, the **Olcott House**, 2316 E. First St., Duluth, 800/715-1339, is endowed with mahogany wood and antiques. Breakfast is served on china and crystal and rooms are $80 to $180. Oregon Creek meanders through the yard at **Manor on the Creek**, 2215 E. 2nd St., Duluth, 800/428-3189, with rooms from $98 to $199.

Natural pine Norwegian decor and a fieldstone fireplace in the Great Hall welcome guests to **Cove Point Lodge**, 50 miles north of Duluth on Lake Superior at Beaver Bay, 800/598-3221, with rooms for $65 to $179 and suites from $139 to $259. Those under the age of six stay free. **Lutsen Resort and Sea Villas**, 800/258-8736, on the Lake Superior North Shore, has lodge guestrooms, new log cabins, and townhouses for $55 to $249.

Cascade Lodge, on the North Shore in Cascade River State Park, 800/322-9543, www.cascadelodgemn.com, has a family-style restaurant, lodge rooms from $66 to $85, cabins with fireplaces for $105 to $175, and off-season discounts. **Gunflint Lodge**, 45 miles up the Gunflint Trail, 143 S. Gunflint Trail, 800/328-3325, has been run by the Kerfoot family since 1927 and has cabins with modern conveniences for $159 to $331. **Bearskin Lodge**, 124 E. Bearskin Rd. on the Gunflint Trail, 800/338-4170, is a highly regarded upscale resort with lakefront log cabins, townhouses, and a lodge. Rooms at this wintertime cross-country ski resort are often booked a year in advance and cost $541 to $1,836 weekly. **Pincushion Mountain Bed and Breakfast**, 968 Gunflint Trail, 800/542-1226, has rooms for $90 to $99. Discounts are offered in May and June.

Grand Portage Lodge in Grand Portage, 800/543-1384, has double rooms for $57 to $67, and allows those under 18 to stay free. The **EconoLodge**, E. MN 61, Grand Marais, 800/247-6020 or 218/387-2500, has a lakeview lobby and rooms from $69 to $140. Or stay in the new wing of the **East Bay Hotel** on the beach at Wisconsin St., Grand Marais, 800/414-2807 or 218/387-2800, with lakeside dining and rooms for $79 to $155.

CAMPING

Private campgrounds include **Grand Portage Campground and Marina**, 800/543-1384, with full hookups on Lake Superior at Grand Portage. Rates are $10 to $17 daily or $250 per month. **Gunflint Pines Resort**, 45 miles up the Gunflint Trail, 800/533-5814, offers campsites with RV hookups. The resort includes 19 sites, boat rentals, a lodge, playground, and swimming, and charges $17 to $23 for two people. **Nor'wester Lodge**, 7778 Gunflint Trail, 800/992-4FUN, offers five lakeside sites, showers, full hookups, a playground, and a sand beach. It charges $25 for two people, $4 per additional person.

Private campgrounds near Duluth with showers, electricity, and full hookups include **Indian Point Campground**, 75th Ave. W. and Grand Ave. (Hwy. 23), on the St. Louis River Bay near the zoo, 218/624-5637, with 50 sites and wheelchair-accessible facilities.

Public camping options are nearly overwhelming. **Jay Cooke State Park**, 218/384-4610, south of Duluth off I-35 near Carlton, has beautiful stands of birch, St. Louis River views, 80 sites (20 with electricity), and handicapped-accessible showers.

Many of the eight state parks lining the North Shore have campsites: **Judge C. R. Magney**, 218/387-3039, has 31 drive-in sites with showers but no electricity. **Gooseberry Falls**, 218/834-3855, has 70 sites with showers but no electricity. It is imperative to have weekend campsite reservations on the North Shore in summer and fall. (See Planning Your Trip for camping reservation information and phone numbers.) Forest Service campgrounds, 218/387-2609, have water but no electricity or showers for $9 per night at state forest campsites, $8 to $12 and $5 for each extra vehicle at national forest campgrounds. The only forest service campgrounds taking reservations are along the Gunflint Trail at **Trail's End**, **Iron Lake**, and **Flour Lake**. Call 218/387-2609 to reserve. The **Grand Marais Recreation Area RV Park-Campground**, West MN 61, on the west end of the harbor in Grand Marais, 218/387-1712, has 300 campsites ranging from primitive tenting to full RV hookups for $16.58 to $21. The area also offers bathhouses and an indoor pool. Call 800/998-0959 for reservations.

NIGHTLIFE AND SPECIAL EVENTS

Sleep is the top-rated evening activity after hiking on the North Shore or Gunflint Trail. Some lodges and state parks do have evening nature walks, campfire talks, and naturalist-led programs. Casinos have become very popular in this region. You'll find **Fond-du-Luth Casino** in Duluth at 129 E. Superior St., 800/873-0280, and **Grand Portage Casino** at Grand Portage, 800/543-1384. Duluth's **Bayfront Festival**, **Chester Bowl**, and **Lake Place** parks host musical events all summer long, including the **Bayfront Blues Festival** in August, 800/438-5884. In June, the annual **Grandma's Marathon**, 218/727-0947, fills Duluth with runners and their families and fans. **Grand Slam Restaurant and Entertainment Center**, 395 Lake Ave., Duluth, 218/722-5667, with indoor baseball, softball, and amusement rides, is popular with kids. There are also dinner cruises of the harbor, 218/722-6218, or North Shore cruises on *Grampa Woo III* at Beaver Bay, 218/226-4100, www.grampawoo.com.

Check out performing-arts events at **The Depot**, 506 W. Michigan St., 218/727-8025, in Duluth, and the **Grand Marais Playhouse/Art Colony** in Grand Marais, 218/387-1284. Or sip an espresso drink or tea at the **Brew Ha Ha** coffee shop, 111 W. Wisconsin St., Grand Marais, 218/387-9850.

Lake Superior North Shore Drive

From Duluth, follow MN 61 up the north shore for spectacular views. The spectacle of storms on the North Shore can be almost magnetic. They quickly transform clouds, sky, and lake from benign to threatening and make for a grand show, back-dropped by tall pines and spruce. Stop to hike in the numerous state parks—don't miss **Gooseberry Falls State Park**, where the Gooseberry River tumbles over a series of waterfalls. In **Temperance River State Park**, the river courses through a black-walled gorge, and you can see potholes created long ago. **Tettegouche State Park** contains the Baptism River's falls and cascades, as well as lush inland forests of maple, basswood, and spruce.

Spend some time in **Grand Marais** with its picturesque lighthouse, good restaurants, and arts community. Then continue on MN 61 to **Grand Portage**, visit the monument and state park, then backtrack to Grand Marais and drive the wilderness terrain of the **Gunflint Trail**. Stay overnight in one of the fine lodges and decide where to go next. Options include taking MN 61 back to Duluth to catch the state parks you missed on the way up or taking the highway to Scenic MN 1 at Tettegouche State Park and following it to Ely.

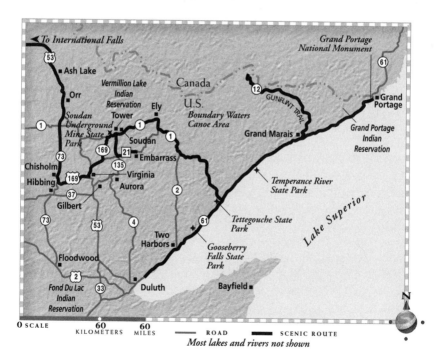

From Ely, take MN 1 southwest to Soudan and Tower. Take the underground mine tour at **Soudan Underground Mine State Park**, then follow MN 135 south about 13 miles to County Road 21, west of Embarrass. Stop at the visitors center at the intersection and sign up for a tour of Finnish pioneer homesteads and saunas (10 a.m. and 2 p.m. daily Memorial Day–Labor Day; $2–$5, under 5 free). The guide will ride with you in your car on the 15-mile, two- to three-hour trip. Then head back to 135. Go southwest to U.S. 53. Go northwest and take U.S. 169 west to Chisolm. Stop at **Iron World** for a colorful introduction to mining history and Iron Range culture via exhibits, demonstrations, ethnic costumes, and food. Finally, from Chisholm, take MN 73 and U.S. 53 north to **International Falls** and **Voyageurs National Park.**

3
THE NORTHERN WILDERNESS

In Superior National Forest, the roadless Boundary Waters Canoe Area contains some 2,000 lakes. The 1.3 million-acre BWCA stretches along the U.S.–Canadian border for 150 miles, adjoining Voyageurs National Park. The 218,000-acre national park is a similar roadless wilderness. It contains four major lakes—Rainy, Kabetogama, Sand Point, and Namakan—and 26 smaller ones with countless rocky islands. Motorized craft are allowed in Voyageurs—not the case in the BWCA. BWCA explorers travel by canoe, just as the French Canadian voyageurs did when the water served as their highway between Lake Superior and Lake of the Woods.

Lake of the Woods claims 65,000 miles of shoreline and 14,000 islands. People come here for walleye, muskie, and northern pike fishing. They also come to get away—really away. Lake of the Woods is as far north as you can go in the contiguous United States. On Lake of the Woods, a fluke of cartography awarded Minnesota a separate chunk of land known as the Northwest Angle. To drive there, you pass through a portion of Manitoba. Or you can go by boat from Warroad.

A PERFECT DAY IN THE WILDERNESS

Breakfast in Ely, visit the Wolf Center, and drive to Voyageurs National Park. Take the narrated boat tour on the *Pride of Rainy Lake*, see the exhibits at the visitors center, check into a lodge, go for a hike, go fishing, or hire a small plane for an aerial view of the park. Then fill up on good home cooking in the lodge dining room and hear anglers exchange fishing tales. At dusk, go for another walk, keeping an eye out for bears. At night, sit on the dock listening to loons and waves lapping the shore. Go to bed and sleep, sated with the fresh clean air.

ELY AREA SIGHTSEEING HIGHLIGHTS

★★★★ BOUNDARY WATERS CANOE AREA HEADQUARTERS
International Wolf Center, MN 169, Ely
218/365-7681

More than 1 million acres of wilderness and 1,500 miles of water await canoeists. Permits are required for entrance, so contact the permit station/headquarters. Ely is the launching point for the Boundary Waters, so the town is filled with outfitters and guides who can supply everything you need for a canoe trip into the wilderness. May through September, Northwest Airlines flies into Ely, a 45-minute flight from the Twin Cities.

Details: BWCA headquarters open mid-May–Sept daily 6:30–8. The cost of BWCA trips vary. (2¹/₂ days minimum)

★★★★ INTERNATIONAL WOLF CENTER
MN 169, Ely, 800/ELY-WOLF or 218/365-4695

The center features a "Wolves and Humans" exhibit, other displays, and educational programs. Try howling with the center's resident pack of wolves.

Details: May–Oct daily 9–5:30; other months Fri–Sun 10–5. $2.50–$5, under 6 free. (1 hour)

★★★ DOROTHY MOLTER CABIN MUSEUM
MN 169, Ely, 218/365-4451

The original cabins of Dorothy Molter, "The Root Beer Lady," have been reconstructed in Ely. Molter lived alone on Knife Lake in the BWCA for more than 50 years and served homemade root beer to the canoeists that stopped by.

Details: May–Sept daily 10–6. $1.50–$3; $6.50 family rate. (30 minutes–1 hour)

★★★ VERMILION INTERPRETIVE CENTER
1900 E. Camp St., Ely, 218/365-3226
The center covers 12,000 years of local history and tells the story of
the Vermilion Iron Range.

Details: *Memorial Day–Labor Day daily 10–4; winter by appointment. $1–$2, under 5 free. (30 minutes–1 hour)*

ELY AREA

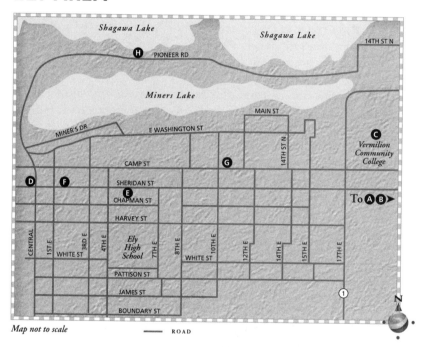

Map not to scale ——— ROAD

SIGHTS

A Boundary Waters Canoe Area
  Headquarters
B Dorothy Molter Cabin Museum
A International Wolf Center
C Vermillion Interpretive Center

FOOD

D Chocolate Moose
E Minglewood Café
F Vertins Café, Pub, and Supper Club

LODGING

G Budget Host Motel
H Holiday Inn SunSpree Resort

Note: Items with the same letter are located in the same place.

LAKE OF THE WOODS SIGHTSEEING HIGHLIGHTS

★★★★ BELTRAMI ISLAND STATE FOREST
Lake of the Woods Area Tourist Information Center
800/382-FISH

To immerse yourself in the countryside, follow the Wilderness Drives in this 669,030-acre state forest. A must-see is the **Homesteader's Drive** on Bankton Forest Road, with aging cemeteries and lilacs abloom near ruined buildings on old homesteads. Also try **Blueberry Picker's Drive** for the best picking—along roadsides or small forest clearings where jack pines grow. This drive also passes historic Norris Civilian Conservation Corps (CCC) Camp, now the Red Lake Wildlife Management Area.

Details: Get a detailed Wilderness Drives map from the Lake of the Woods Area Tourist Information Center, west of Baudette on Hwy. 11, P.O. Box 518, Baudette, MN 56623, 800/382-3474 or 218/634-1174; www.lakeofthewoodsmn.com. Free. (2 hours minimum)

★★★ FORT ST. CHARLES
Magnuson Island

Visit the restored fort on the site of the original log fort/trading post erected in 1732 by French voyageurs and commanded by Pierre La Verendrye.

Details: Reachable by boat—call Lake of the Woods Tourism for directions, 800/382-FISH. Open 24 hours. (30 minutes)

VOYAGEURS NATIONAL PARK SIGHTSEEING HIGHLIGHTS

★★★★ SIGHT-SEA-ER TOUR BOAT
Kabetogama Lake Visitor Center, 218/875-2111

Naturalist-guided tours of the lakes range from a six-hour trip to historic Kettle Falls Hotel to a two-hour sunset cruise. Free interpretive programs and trips are also available. Call for a schedule of *Sight-Sea-Er* tours.

Details: From U.S. 53, take Hwy. 122 north to Kabetogama Lake Center. Center open early May–Sept daily 9–5. Center free; cruises $8–$35. (1 hour minimum)

VOYAGEURS NATIONAL PARK

Alice Vollmar

★★★★ **PRIDE OF RAINY LAKE CRUISES**
218/286-5470 at Rainy Lake Visitor Center, 218/286-5258
The attractive center includes displays about the park and free naturalist-guided canoe trips and programs. Cruises with a naturalist aboard include a 90-minute gold mine tour and a two-hour bald eagle–watch tour. Call the center for schedule.

> **Details:** *From International Falls, take MN 11 east 12 miles. Center open early May–Sept daily 9–5. Center free; cruises $6.25–$35. (2 hours minimum)*

INTERNATIONAL FALLS SIGHTSEEING HIGHLIGHTS

★★★★ **KOOCHICHING COUNTY HISTORICAL MUSEUM/ BRONKO NAGURSKI MUSEUM**
Third St. and Sixth Ave., International Falls, 218/283-4316
Discover the area's colorful past—gold-rush days, logging, and home-steading—and the story of NFL legend and native son Nagurski.

> **Details:** *Located in Smokey Bear Park. Open Memorial Day–Labor*

THE NORTHERN WILDERNESS

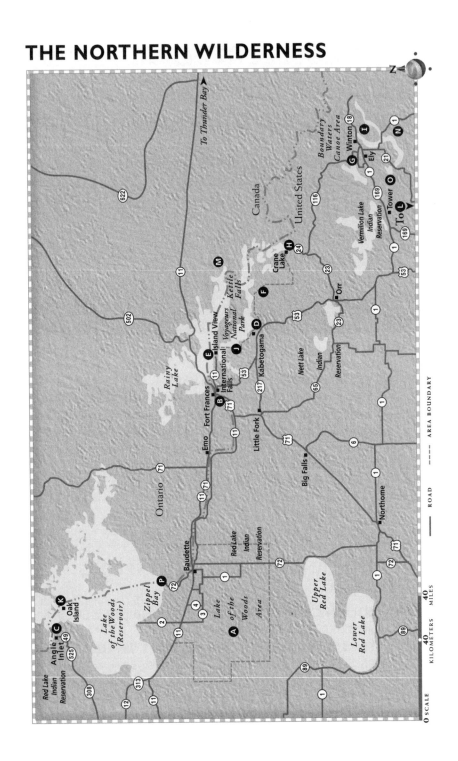

Day daily 9–5, other seasons Mon–Fri 9–5; closed holidays. $1–$3, under 5 free. (1 hour)

★★★ GRAND MOUND HISTORY CENTER
6749 Hwy. 11, International Falls, 218/285-3332

The center interprets the Laurel Indian culture, from 200 B.C. to A.D. 800, and tracks succeeding Indian cultures. It is the site of the largest prehistoric burial mound in Minnesota. Walk through lovely woods to see other mounds.

Details: 17 miles west of International Falls on MN 11. June–Labor Day Thu–Sat 10–5, Sun noon–5. $1.50–$3, under 6 free. (1 hour)

★★ BORDER BOB'S
200 Second Ave., International Falls, 218/283-4414

You can buy everything here, from fresh fish and art to taxidermy services and barbecue.

Details: Near the Canadian border. Open daily. Free. (30 minutes–2 hours)

SIGHTS
Ⓐ Beltrami Island State Forest
Ⓑ Border Bob's
Ⓒ Fort St. Charles
Ⓑ Grand Mound History Center
Ⓓ Sight-Sea-Er Tour Boat
Ⓔ Koochiching County Historical Museum/ Bronko Nagurski Museum
Ⓔ Pride of RL Cruises

FOOD
Ⓕ Ash Trail Lodge
Ⓓ Bait 'n Bite
Ⓖ Burntside Lodge
Ⓑ Grandma's Pantry

FOOD (continued)
Ⓔ Island View Lodge
Ⓗ Nelson's Resort
Ⓘ Silver Rapids Lodge

LODGING
Ⓒ Angle Outpost
Ⓙ Arrowhead Lodge and Resort
Ⓚ Bonnie Brea Resort
Ⓛ Finnish Heritage Homestead
Ⓜ Kettle Falls Hotel
Ⓗ Nelson's Resort
Ⓖ Prothero's Trading Post
Ⓔ Rainy Lake Houseboats
Ⓝ River Point Resort
Ⓘ Silver Rapids Lodge
Ⓑ Super 8 Motel
Ⓗ Voyagaire Houseboats

CAMPING
Ⓞ Bear Head Lake State Park
Ⓟ Morris Point Resort
Ⓘ Silver Rapids Lodge and Campground
Ⓕ Sunset Resort Campground
Ⓙ Woodenfrog Campground
Ⓟ Zippel Bay State Park

Note: Items with the same letter are located in the same place.

FITNESS AND RECREATION

Fishing is the big recreation here. We're talking big fish—8, 10, 20, 30, even 40 pounds. Visitors are sure to see eagles, osprey, pelicans, and cormorants, and possibly moose and bear. Blueberry-picking is a popular pursuit—for bears and for humans. More than 20 outfitters base in Ely to provide supplies and guidance for canoe trips in the BWCA. Among them are 75-year-old **Wilderness Outfitters**, 1 E. Camp St., 800/777-8572; **Canoe Country Outfitters**, operating since 1946, 629 E. Sheridan, 800/752-2306; and **Piragis Northwoods Outfitting**, 105 N. Central Ave., 800/223-6565. You can walk or ski around Miners Lake in Ely on the four-mile **Trezona Trail**, which connects to the International Wolf Center. **Zippel Bay State Park** on Lake of the Woods has 3,000 acres with a three-mile sand beach and six-mile trail system for hiking and horseback riding, three and a half miles of ski trails, five miles of snowmobile trails, and abundant wildlife (see Camping, below, for location). **Bear Head Lake State Park,** near Ely, offers 4,375 acres with hiking, skiing, and snowmobile trails, plus boat and canoe rentals at the park contact station (see Camping, below). If you come in winter, try mushing your own dogsled team. Companies offering dogsled outings include Ely-based **White Wilderness Sled Dog Adventures**, 800/701-6238, with naturalist/guides and heated tents or lodge-to-lodge trips; and **Outdoor Adventure Dog Sled Trips**, 800/777-8574, also in Ely, offering day trips, winter camping, and cabin/lodge accommodations. For helpful information, read *Boundary Waters Journal* magazine (800/548-7319).

FOOD

In Ely, the **Chocolate Moose**, Central and Main, 218/365-6343, serves homemade muffins, wild-rice pancakes, cappuccino, walleye, and buffalo. The eclectic **Minglewood Café**, 528 E. Sheridan St., 218/365-3398, offers a health-food focus; and **Vertins Café, Pub, and Supper Club**, 145 E. Sheridan, 218/365-4041, has three dining rooms and is noted for homemade soups, steaks, and sticky buns. Visit **Burntside Lodge**, 2755 Burntside Lodge Rd., 218/365-3894, for walleye and steak in a historic lodge with lakeside dining. **Silver Rapids Lodge**, 218/365-4877, five miles east of Ely via Highways 169 and 16, offers sunset views with its Sunday brunch.

Grandma's Pantry in tiny Ranier (Voyageurs National Park area), three miles east of International Falls on MN 11, 218/286-5584, serves wonderful homemade soups and meals. You'll also find fun shops and galleries in the area. In the Lake Kabetogama area, the **Bait 'n Bite**, Hwy. 122/9634 Gappa Rd., 218/875-2281, is run by someone with a sense of humor: "Eat Here and Get

Worms," reads the sign. It's actually a family dining place with good homemade soups and dinners from $6.95 to $10.95. You can pick up tackle and bait here, too.

Resorts in this area with public dining rooms include **Ash Trail Lodge**, 25 miles south of International Falls on U.S. 53, then follow Hwy. 129/Ash River Trail, 218/374-3131; and **Nelson's Resort**, 7632 Nelson Rd. on Crane Lake, 218/993-2295, with a full menu, garden-fresh produce, dining rooms with polished wood floors, lake views, and dinners for $8 to $20. Overlooking Rainy Lake, **Island View Lodge**, 12 miles east of International Falls via MN 11, 800/777-7856 or 218/286-3511, offers fine dining and serves three meals a day.

LODGING

Summer is the busy season here; rates vary seasonally. In Ely, the **Holiday Inn SunSpree Resort**, 400 N. Pioneer Rd., 800/365-5070, features a whirlpool, indoor pool, and a marina with boat rentals. An unusual and fun lodging choice west of Ely is the **Finnish Heritage Homestead** bed-and-breakfast, 4776 Waisanen Rd., Embarrass (take Hwy. 21 west from Ely to Embarrass, then go south on Hwy. 362/Waisanen Rd. half mile), 218/984-3318, on an 1891 farm complete with animals and a wood-fired sauna. Guest rooms have handmade quilts, bathrobes, and thoughtful touches for around $69; inquire about packages. Area motels include the **Budget Host Motel**, 1047 E. Sheridan St., 218/365-3237, with double rooms from $60 to $65. Resorts include **Silver Rapids Lodge** on White Iron Lake Chain, 800/950-9425, and **River Point Resort** at Kawishiwi River/Birch Lake, 800/456-5580.

In the Voyageurs National Park area, lodging includes **Nelson's Resort** on Crane Lake, 218/993-2295. In operation since the 1930s, it wins raves with log cabins and lodge dining rooms with fireplaces. Rates range from $108 per person daily with three meals to $93 with dinner only. Fishing guides cost $280 per day for three people, and boat rentals are $65 to $115 per day. To get there, take U.S. 53 to Orr, then drive east on Highway 23 for about 28 miles to Nelson Road.

Arrowhead Lodge and Resort on Kabetogama Lake, 218/875-2141, a traditional Minnesota fishing resort with lodge rooms and cottages, offers complete fishing packages ranging in price from $334 for three days to $852 for seven days. The price includes meals, lodging, boat, gas, dock service, and maid and linen service. Daily rates are also available. Or check into the historic **Kettle Falls Hotel, 888/KF-HOTEL,** which reputedly was once a wilderness brothel. It can only be reached by boat, and its quaint restored rooms with

ORR

The town of Orr sits between Virginia and International Falls on U.S. 53. The **Orr Wetlands/Bog Walk** *leads you through swamp, marsh, and bog via a boardwalk from the Voyageurs National Park and Orr Area Information Center, 800/357-9255, a half mile south of Orr on U.S. 53. Take the tour, during which you'll have the opportunity to sample the naturalist's bog tea and identify water parsnip, pitcher plants, and swamp rue, then grab fixings for a picnic at the Pelican Bay IGA deli in Orr and drive to the* **Vermilion Falls Trail***. There you can eat lunch and hike in to see Vermilion River rush through a narrow chute and cascade over a series of rapids. To get there from U.S. 53 in Orr, drive 23 miles east and north on Highway 23 and Highway 24, then five miles west on Forest Road 491.*

Later, visit the **Vince Shute Wildlife Sanctuary***, a wilderness haven for black bears run by the American Black Bear Association. From an enclosed 10-foot-high observation platform, you can watch bears socialize and eat. Iridescent dragonflies do dine on mosquitoes, but bring insect repellent anyway. To get there, go one mile south of Orr on U.S. 53, then take Highway 23 west for 13.3 miles. Pass the Highway 514 junction, then drive north (right) on the first gravel road 2.1 miles to the sanctuary. Plan to stay in Orr in a northwoods-style room in* **Hundred Acre Woods Bed and Breakfast***, 5048 Old Hwy. 53, 218/757-0070. A fireplace, whirlpool, and sauna welcome guests, and rooms from $99 to $150 include breakfast and innkeeper Veronica Holman's potica, a walnut-filled Slovenian bread.*

shared baths are $65. The hotel dining room serves breakfast, lunch, and dinner; nearby are attractively furnished villas with rates from $100 to $150.

Houseboat rentals are also a popular way to experience the lakes: **Voyagaire Houseboats** on Crane Lake, 800/882-6287, rent from $225 to $850 daily and $995 to $4,490 a week. To get there, follow Highways 23 and 24 east from U.S. 53 at Orr. **Rainy Lake Houseboats** on Rainy Lake, 800/554-9188 or 218/286-5391, rent for $210 to $810 daily and $1,055 to $3,895 weekly. To get there, take MN 11 east for 10 miles from International Falls.

In International Falls, motels include the **Super 8 Motel**, on U.S. 53, 800/800-8000, with rooms from $49 to $51. In the Lake of the Woods area, **Prothero's Trading Post** at Angle Inlet, 800/376-3151, has handcrafted log cabins with window boxes and log furniture. You'll find reading material as well as the history of long-time owners Grace and Dale Prothero in the trading post sitting area. Weekly rates are $390 for two people, $60/$50 for each additional adult/child under 12. Daily rates are $65 per couple, $20 per additional person. Boats rent for $20 a day. There are few stores here so bring food with you. **Angle Outpost**, 800/441-5014, on Lake of the Woods, is owned and run by David and Jessica Fandrich, who make you feel at home and serve excellent food. Cabins rent from $24 to $45 per person a night. Meals can be included in the package for slightly higher rates. Don McClanathan's **Bonnie Brae Resort**, 800/772-8411, on pretty Oak Island, has attractive housekeeping condominium units, log fourplex units, three semi-modern cabin units, a log lodge, hiking trails, and lots of pelicans winging overhead. Rates of $230 to $330 per person for three days and nights include a 25-minute fly-in from Baudette or boat-in from Young's Bay on Northwest Angle, plus a boat, motor, and gas. Bring your groceries with you.

CAMPING

Some resorts in this area also have camping. A good private campground near Ely is the **Silver Rapids Lodge and Campground**, 218/365-4877, on the White Iron Chain. It has 15 lakeside full-hookup sites, 19 of which come with electricity and water. It also offers two tent sites, and a restaurant. Fees range from $15 to $24 per night and $90 to $168 per week. **Bear Head Lake State Park**, between Tower and Ely off MN 169/1, 218/365-7229, has 73 drive-in sites, five sites for backpackers, and one site reserved for those who come in by canoe. In the BWCA, camping is allowed on designated campsites as identified on BWCA maps.

In the Voyageurs National Park area, private campgrounds include **Sunset Resort Campground** on Ash River, 800/232-3161, with six full-hookup and 30 wooded tent sites with electricity, water, and showers for $16 to $20. Public **Woodenfrog Campground** on Kabetogama Lake off of Highway 122, 218/757-3274, has 60 secluded, wooded sites with water and a good beach, but no showers or electricity. Sites cost $9.

Lake of the Woods–area private campgrounds include **Morris Point Resort**, 218/634-2570, on a 300-acre peninsula north of Baudette. It has 20 sites with electricity, 15 full hookups, 20 tent sites, and a shower building for $13 to $20. Public camping is available at 2,906-acre **Zippel Bay State Park**,

218/783-6252, 10 miles northeast of Williams on Lake of the Woods. It has 57 rustic sites, and showers but no electricity.

NIGHTLIFE AND SPECIAL EVENTS

Frankly, folks don't come here for the nightlife. However, hanging out in a bar—which is likely to sport mounted fish, pine paneling, and lighted beer signs—can be a fun way to meet the local people and learn what it's like to live in this remote place. Resorts often have games and pool tables. **Nelson's Resort** on Crane Lake, 218/993-2295, has entertainment in the lounge Thursday through Saturday. In the Ely area you can go to **Fortune Bay Casino** in Tower, 800/992-7529, for evening activity. A fun summer event is Ely's **Blueberry Arts Festival** in July, 800/777-7281. January brings **Icebox Days** to International Falls, 800/325-5766, with the Freeze Yer Gizzard Blizzard 10-kilometer race, a beach party, and turkey bowling.

4
MINNESOTA'S
NORTH WOODS

This is the pine forest known as the home of Paul Bunyan and his blue ox, Babe. It is also what most Minnesotans identify as the lakes region—the lakes and wetlands created millions of years ago by glacial moraine and meltwater. Less rugged and wild than the landscape at the top of the state, the North Woods region has become a vacation playground. Here, in more or less the midsection of Minnesota, resorts range from small and secluded to upscale and posh. Nearby cities and towns contain shopping, amusement parks, casinos, and plenty of other entertainment to occupy vacationers.

Mille Lacs Lake, the second largest Minnesota lake at 20 miles across and with 100 miles of shoreline, is renowned for good walleye fishing. Near Bemidji, the headwaters of the mighty Mississippi River lie in Itasca State Park, which was discovered in 1832 by Henry Schoolcraft and his guide, Chief Ozawindib. Here, as it begins its 2,348-mile trip to the Gulf of Mexico, the Mississippi River is a shallow stream that is easy to cross. East of Bemidji stretches the vast Chippewa National Forest, a habitat for bald eagles and numerous other wild creatures.

A PERFECT DAY IN THE NORTH WOODS

Start with an early morning bog walk in Lake Bemidji State Park to catch the songbirds' serenade. Grab breakfast in Bemidji, stock up on picnic food, and

BEMIDJI AREA

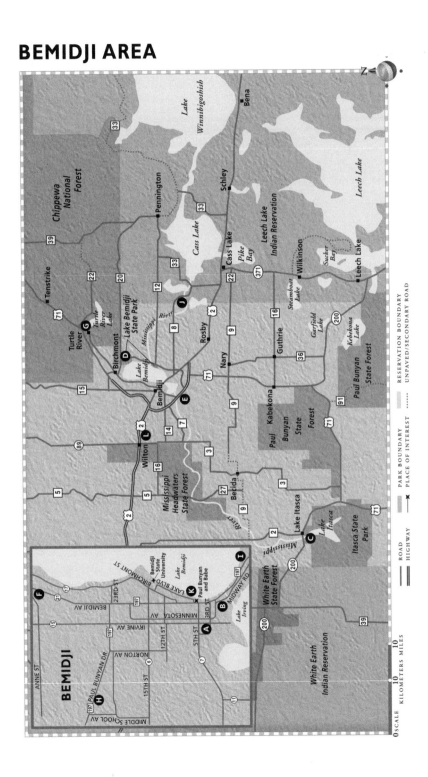

head for Itasca State Park. Visit the Mississippi Headwaters and hike the Schoolcraft Trail. Take the Wilderness Drive, then hike to remote Bohall Lake and eat a picnic lunch. From Douglas Lodge, hike the two-mile Dr. Robert's Trail, or hike to the observation tower. Take the Lake Itasca boat tour, eat dinner at Douglas Lodge, then cozy into your own log cabin for a night in the Itasca State Park woods.

BEMIDJI AREA SIGHTSEEING HIGHLIGHTS

★★★★ ITASCA STATE PARK
U.S. 71 Lake Itasca, 218/266-2114

Established in 1891 to protect remnant stands of virgin pine and the Mississippi River source, this 32,690-acre park has an interpretive program with naturalist-led activities, including hikes and tours. The main attraction is the Mississippi River Headwaters. The park's historic Douglas Lodge has a dining room open daily and cabin rentals May through September. In Preacher's Grove you can see a stand of red pines more than 250 years old. Take the 10-mile Wilderness Drive past a 2,000-acre virgin forest that is home to Minnesota's largest white pine. There are also daily narrated naturalist tours of Lake Itasca on the boat *Chester Charles*.

Details: *20 miles north of Park Rapids on U.S. 71. Open year-round daily 8–10. $4 daily park permit per vehicle, $20 season pass. Chester Charles tours July–mid–Aug daily 11, 1, and 3, except Sun 1 and*

SIGHTS
Ⓐ Bemidji Woolen Mills
Ⓑ Chocolates Plus
Ⓒ Itasca State Park
Ⓓ Lake Bemidji State Park
Ⓔ Old Schoolhouse

FOOD
Ⓒ Douglas Lodge
Ⓕ Slim's Bar & Grill

LODGING
Ⓖ A Place in the Woods
Ⓗ AmericInn
Ⓘ Edgewater Motel on Lake Bemidji
Ⓙ Finn 'n' Feather Resort
Ⓒ Itasca State Park
Ⓚ Lakewatch Bed and Breakfast

CAMPING
Ⓛ Bemidji KOA
Ⓒ Itasca State Park
Ⓓ Lake Bemidji State Park

Note: Items with the same letter are located in the same place.

3; late June and mid-Aug–Sept daily 1 and 3; late May–early June and Sept daily 1; 218/732-5318 or 218/266-2101 for reservations. $8, 3 and under free. (1 day minimum)

★★★★ LAKE BEMIDJI STATE PARK
3401 State Park Rd. N.E., Bemidji, 218/755-3843
A highlight is the 1,200-foot boardwalk through a bog rich in plant life, including lady's slipper orchid and pitcher plant. The park has six other trails that wind through old-growth maple-basswood forest, lowland forest, and pine forest, and offers naturalist-guided tours.
Details: *North end of the lake on Hwy. 20. Open daily 8–10. $4 park permit. (30 minutes–1 hour)*

★★★ BEMIDJI WOOLEN MILLS
301 Irvine Ave., Bemidji, 218/751-5166
This is the place to buy woolen goods—from woodsman pants and shirts to knitting yarns and Hudson Bay Point blankets.
Details: *Mon–Sat 8–5:30, Sun 10–5. Free. (30 minutes–1 hour)*

★★ CHOCOLATES PLUS
102 1st St., Bemidji, 218/759-1175
Here chocolate lovers can buy fresh truffles and other goodies.
Details: *Mon–Sat 10–9, Sun noon–5. (20 minutes)*

★★ OLD SCHOOLHOUSE
**Carr Lake and Old Schoolhouse Rd., Bemidji
218/751-4723**
View the work of 500 area artists in a renovated 1917 school building.
Details: *One mile south of Bemidji via MN 197, then one mile west on Carr Lake and Old Schoolhouse Rd. Mon–Sat 10–5:30. Free. (30 minutes)*

BRAINERD AREA SIGHTSEEING HIGHLIGHTS

★★★★ CROW WING COUNTY HISTORICAL SOCIETY MUSEUM
320 Laurel St., Brainerd, 218/829-3268
Housed in a 1917 sheriff's residence and jail, this museum offers a

BRAINERD AREA

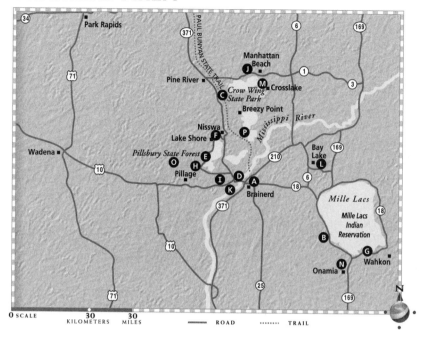

SIGHTS

A Brainerd International Raceway
A Crow Wing County Historical Society Museum
B Mille Lacs Indian Museum and Trading Post
C Minnesota Resort Museum
D Northland Arboretum
E Swedish Timber House

FOOD

B Grand Casino Mille Lacs
F Grand View Lodge

FOOD (continued)

F Italian Gardens
G Izaty's Golf and Yacht Club
H Kavanaugh's Resort and Restaurant
I Madden's on Gull Lake
J Manhattan Beach Lodge
F Sherwood Forest

LODGING

K Brainerd Days Inn
C Driftwood Family Resort
A Econo Lodge Motel
F Grand View Lodge

LODGING (continued)

G Izaty's Golf and Yacht Club
H Kavanaugh's Resort and Restaurant
I Madden's on Gull Lake
L Ruttger's Bay Lake Lodge

CAMPING

M Greer Lake Campground
N Mille Lacs Kathio State Park
O Rock Lake Campground
P Wilderness Point Resort

Note: Items with the same letter are located in the same place.

glimpse of a sheriff's lifestyle and has displays on the history of the region, including Native American and logging artifacts.

Details: Memorial Day–Labor Day Mon–Fri 9–5, Sat until 1; other seasons Mon–Fri 1–5, Sat 9–1. $3, children free. (1 hour)

★★★★ MILLE LACS INDIAN MUSEUM AND TRADING POST
Onamia, 320/532-3632

Detailed exhibits trace the history of the Mille Lacs band of Ojibwe up to the present, including dance traditions and craft demonstrations. The trading post sells American Indian–made wares.

Details: North of Onamia 12 miles on U.S. 169. Mid-April–Labor Day Mon–Sat 10–6, Sun noon–6; other seasons Thu–Sat 10–6, Sun noon–5. $3–$5, under 6 free; $12 family rate. (1–2 hours)

★★★ MINNESOTA RESORT MUSEUM
Driftwood Family Resort, Pine River, 800/950-3540

Learn about early resort life in Minnesota from displays in a 6,500-square-foot building at this family-run resort.

Details: Located on the Whitefish Chain of Lakes, 5 1/2 miles north of Jenkins, off Hwy. 15. Open May–Sept daily 10–5. $1–$2. (30 minutes–1 hour)

★★★ NORTHLAND ARBORETUM
NW Seventh St., Brainerd/Baxter, 218/829-8770

More than three thousand species of plants and a Nature Conservancy jack pine savanna are contained on 600 acres with 12 miles of hiking and skiing trails. The Paul Bunyan Recreational Trail starts here.

Details: MN 210 between Brainerd and Baxter, on NW 7th St.; can enter on Excelsior Road in summer. Gates open 24 hours. Gatehouse hours Mon–Fri 8–4. $1–$3; pay fee in honor-system box on porch if gatehouse is closed. (30 minutes minimum)

★★ BRAINERD INTERNATIONAL RACEWAY
MN 371 N., Brainerd, 612/475-1500 or 218/829-9863

The BIR hosts national competitions in NHRA drag and AMA motorcycle racing. There's also on-track camping.

Details: AMA racing in July and August, NHRA drag racing in August. Events last all day. Call for ticket prices and a complete schedule of events. (1 day)

★★ SWEDISH TIMBER HOUSE

7678 Interlachen Rd., Lakeshore, Nisswa, 218/963-7897
Shop for Scandinavian gifts in a log house that was constructed in Sweden, dismantled, and shipped to the United States.
Details: *May–late Oct daily 10–5, December until Christmas Fri–Sun 10–5. Free. (30 minutes minimum)*

FITNESS AND RECREATION

The **Paul Bunyan Trail**, a 100-mile recreational corridor for biking, hiking, and snowmobiling, begins in Brainerd and connects to the Blue Ox Trail from Bemidji, which leads north to International Falls, 800/450-2838. There is, of course, fishing for prized muskie, northern pike, largemouth bass, brown and rainbow trout, and panfish. Hunting for wild strawberries, raspberries, and blueberries is also popular. Golf courses at Madden's on Gull Lake and Grand View Lodge resorts (see Lodging) are among the finest in the Midwest. Winter sports range from cross-country and downhill skiing to curling and snowshoeing. You'll find 33 miles of hiking trails and a 17-mile bicycle route at **Itasca State Park**, plus boat, canoe, bike, and snowshoe rentals at Itasca Sports Rental, 218/266-2150 or 218/657-2420, across from the park headquarters on the main park drive. You can rent a multispeed mountain bike for $3.50 an hour or $20 a day—there's a family rate for four people or more of $3 per person per hour or $15 per person per day. Canoes and rowboats can also be rented for $3 an hour or $18 a day. **Lake Bemidji State Park**, 218/755-3843, offers 15 miles of hiking trails, 9 miles of ski trails, and 3 miles of snowmobile trails, and has boat and snowshoe rentals. There are also amusement park attractions and waterslides near Brainerd. Near the southwestern end of Mille Lacs Lake, 10,585-acre **Mille Lacs Kathio State Park**, 320/532-3523, has miles of hiking, horse, ski, and snowmobile trails—plus boat, canoe, ski, and snowshoe rentals. The park is five miles northwest of Onamia on Highway 26.

FOOD

The best places to eat here are resort dining rooms open to the general public as well as to guests. **Kavanaugh's Resort and Restaurant**, 2300 Kavanaugh Dr., 800/562-7061 or 218/829-5226, is one of my favorites, with well-prepared food from $15 to $23 in a pleasant dining room with views of Sylvan Lake. Dine in a romantic North Woods resort atmosphere at **Grand View Lodge**, 800/432-3788 or 218/963-2234. The resort is off of MN 371 and Highway 77 north of Brainerd, and offers a five-course dinner for $25. A family-style meal at their **Italian Gardens** is $18; dinner at the **Sherwood Forest** is $11 to $17.

On Big Turtle Lake the restored **Manhattan Beach Lodge**, three miles north of Crosslake via Hwy. 66, 218/692-3381, offers a diverse menu and daily fresh fish specials for $7 to $18. The food is also good at **Madden's on Gull Lake**, 8001 Pine Beach Peninsula, 218/829-2811; and at **Izatys Golf and Yacht Club**, Mille Lacs Lake's south shore, 800/533-1728 or 320/532-3101. You can hardly beat the $11 to $14 price for the ample dinner buffet at **Grand Casino Mille Lacs**, U.S. 169 on Mille Lacs Lake's west shore, 800/626-5825. There are numerous dining spots in Bemidji. For great burgers and chili from $3 to $6 in a North Woods setting, go to **Slim's Bar & Grill**, 142 Anne St., 218/751-8196. Or try ordering the walleye at **Douglas Lodge** in Itasca State Park, 218/266-2114. Dinners at Douglas range from $6 to $16.

LODGING

Resorts are as plentiful as lakes here, and the larger ones have extensive planned activities and recreation programs. In the Brainerd area, **Madden's on Gull Lake**, 8001 Pine Beach Peninsula (take U.S. 371 north and Hwy. 77 west out of Brainerd), 800/642-5363, www.maddens.com, is a large golf resort on expansive landscaped grounds with six tennis courts, pools, and saunas. Guests stay in cottages, lodges, and villas. Rates for a lodge room are $81 to $223 for two people; a two-bedroom cottage costs from $227 to $284 for two people. Each additional child is $15, additional adults are $30.

A stroll down a flower-lined walk brings you to a fine sand beach at **Grand View Lodge**, South 134 Nokomis, Nisswa (14 miles north on MN 371 out of Brainerd, take a left on Hwy. 77 and another left at the Grand View sign), 800/432-3788, www.grandviewlodge.com. The emphasis here is on golf (27 holes of championship golf plus The Preserve with 18 holes) and tennis (11 courts and free children's clinics). This highly rated resort nestled in the woods has a main lodge on the National Historic Registry; rates are $165 to $295.

Kavanaugh's Resort and Restaurant, 2300 Kavanaugh Dr. S.W., Brainerd (on Sylvan Lake in the Pine Beach area), 800/562-7061, www.kavanaughs.com, is a smaller-scale resort than Madden's or Grand View. It offers cottages and townhouses with fireplaces and kitchens, as well as tennis, an indoor pool, and a spa. A one-week stay for two costs $630 to $1,145. There's a three-night to one-week minimum during summer. Ask about packages.

Driftwood Family Resort, 800/950-3540 or 218/568-4221, on the Whitefish Chain of Lakes near Jenkins/Pine River in the Brainerd lakes area, is a family-run resort with activities for all ages, a pool and sand beach, daily pony rides for kids, and no televisions. The owners' Norwegian heritage endows the resort with Scandinavian touches including a Friday night smorgasbord. Rates for three nights with two meals daily are $192 per adult, $116 ages 4 to 11, and $68 ages 1 to 3.

On the south shore of Mille Lacs Lake, **Izaty's Golf and Yacht Club**, 40005 85th Ave., 800/533-1728, has a lodge, beach villas, cottages, lakeside townhouses, a Dye-designed 18-hole golf course, and rentals for water sports and fishing. Summer rates for two range from $85 to $219 per night. Also in the Brainerd Lakes region, **Ruttger's Bay Lake Lodge**, on MN 6 near Deerwood, 800/450-4545, enjoys a picturesque, wooded setting with quality accommodations, an 18-hole championship golf course, a 9-hole executive course, and a nice beach. Doubles range from $122 to $260 per night. Brainerd-area motels include **Brainerd Days Inn**, 1630 Fairview Dr. N.W., Baxter, 800/329-7466, with summer rates from $58 to $69; and **Econo Lodge Motel**, Hwy. 371 S., Andrew St., 800/553-2666, with rooms from $46 to $66.

In the Bemidji area, **A Place in the Woods**, 14 miles north of Bemidji on Hwy. 71, 800/676-4547, occupies a 45-acre wooded peninsula on Turtle River Lake. Its handsome cabins have round-log walls, porches and decks, cathedral ceilings, and lofts. A cabin for two costs $510 for three nights, $920 per week. The lodge has a fieldstone fireplace and a library. At **Finn 'n' Feather Resort**, a highly recommended family resort on Lake Andrusia in the Bemidji area, 800/776-3466, attractive new log homes have screened-in porches and fire-places. Rates start at $145 for two people and $205 for four people. Resort amenities include a lodge, beaches, and water sports equipment. From Bemidji, take U.S. 2 south to Roosevelt Road/Highway 8, then drive east nine miles to the resort.

At **Lakewatch Bed and Breakfast**, 609 Lake Blvd. N.E., Bemidji, 218/751-8413, guests stay in a renovated 1904 home overlooking Lake Bemidji and enjoy down comforters, private baths, and a full breakfast with rates from $50 to $80.

Itasca State Park, 800/466-2267 or 218/266-2114, offers accommodations for a decent price: $45 to $80 for two people. Motels in the Bemidji area include **AmericInn**, 1200 Paul Bunyan Dr. N.W., 800/634-3444, with a sauna, indoor pool, and double rooms from $69 to $74; and **Edgewater Motel on Lake Bemidji**, 1015 Paul Bunyan Dr. N.E., 800/776-3343, with a sand beach and rates from $53 to $78.

CAMPING

You'll find pleasant, wooded campsites in state parks here. See the Practical Tips chapter for reservation and fee information. **Itasca State Park**, 20 miles north of Park Rapids on U.S. 71, 218/266-2114, has showers, flush toilets (wheelchair-accessible), and several campgrounds with a total of 237 sites. **Mille Lacs Kathio State Park**, just south of the southwestern edge of Mille Lacs Lake on Highway 26, 320/532-3523, has 70 sites, wheelchair-accessible showers, and flush toilets. **Lake Bemidji State Park**, on Hwy. 20 about six miles northeast of Bemidji, 218/755-3843, has 98 sites, 43 with electricity, wheelchair-accessible showers, and flush toilets. This is a popular campground, so make your reservations ahead of time.

For private campgrounds, try **Wilderness Point Resort**, 800/231-4050. (Drive two miles north of Nisswa on MN 371, turn right on Highway 107/Wilderness Road, then continue another three miles to the end of the road.) It has six lakefront tent sites; 30 shaded, secluded sites with water and electricity; showers; a swimming beach; and boat rentals. The **Bemidji KOA**, 5707 U.S. 2 W. (two miles east of Wilton), 218/751-1792, has pine-shaded tent sites, a range of hookups, hot showers, flush toilets, and a playground. Fees are $20 per night for tents, $22 to $25 for RVs, and $1 to $2 per additional person.

State forests in the area have primitive campgrounds. Campers pay $9 per night, and most sites have pit toilets and drinking water. Pillsbury State Forest's **Rock Lake Campground**, 218/828-2565, with 43 sites, is west of Pillager. (Take MN 210 a half mile west from Pillager, turn right on Highway 1, go six miles, turn left, and follow the road around the lake.) To get to Crow Wing State Forest's **Greer Lake Campground** from Crosby, take MN 6 north 12 miles to Highway 36, go west three miles to Highway 14, go south one and a half miles, then turn right and follow the signs for two miles. Call the campground at 218/828-2565 for information on its 34 campsites.

NIGHTLIFE AND SPECIAL EVENTS

Paul Bunyan Playhouse, 218/751-7270, has popular summer theater productions in the historic Chief Theatre in downtown Bemidji. If you're in the mood for gaming, go to **Grand Casino Mille Lacs** on Highway 169, west shore of Lake Mille Lacs, 800/626-5825. You'll find blackjack, slots, video games, and a huge all-you-can-eat buffet.

5
OTTER TAIL
COUNTRY

Only in recent years has tourism begun to make its way into Otter Tail Country, a lush green land of hardwood forest and country roads angling and curving past blue lakes—a breathtakingly pretty place. So far, efforts to attract tourists have had a gentle impact, tending more toward a smattering of regional arts and crafts shops in small towns and modest cities, and one-of-a-kind attractions encountered now and then along a country road. For example, a retired farmer indulges his passion for flowers by creating glorious open-to-the-public gardens on a former farm feedlot, and a rural town with an ambitious cultural center hosts a nationally recognized annual Great American Think-Off philosophy competition. There's a picturesque old mill surrounded by trees and verdant sweeps of grass, and a town that draws all manner of media coverage for its annual summer turtle races. Here, amusement parks and waterslides are scarce.

People have been coming to Otter Tail Country resorts for years—usually to fish. These quiet resorts are mostly small operations, comfortable and well-kept, beloved by owners and guests but not fancy.

A PERFECT DAY IN OTTER TAIL COUNTRY
Start off with a walking tour of Fergus Falls, then visit the outstanding Otter Tail County Historical Society Museum. Buy picnic lunch supplies in town, bring

67

along a good book, and spend a couple of peaceful hours at beautiful Phelps Mill County Park. Then go to Floralane via Highway 14 and see Clarence Bjorklund's flowers. Backtrack to Otter Tail Lake for an early dinner at The Pier, then drive to Vergas via MN 78, U.S. 10, and MN 228. Take Highway 4 west to the Log House and Homestead, where a rose and a tray laden with fruit, cheese, and cakes await your arrival.

OTTER TAIL SIGHTSEEING HIGHLIGHTS

★★★★ FLORALANE GARDENS
Perham, 218/346-6724
Clarence Bjorklund's ever-expanding gardens are a creation born of love for blooming plants and shrubs. "I should have been a gardener all along," says Bjorklund, a retired farmer of Swedish descent. Garden paths lead past beds of perennials and annuals, including 400 dahlias, in which Bjorklund has built fountains and placed sculptures, including a pair of geese "flying" overhead and a bizarre arch made of welded wagon wheels. The flowers are in prime form July 10 to August 10. Talking to the spirited, feisty farmer/gardener is part of the fun. There's also a sales room with dried flower arrangements.

Details: Six miles south of Perham on MN 78, then one mile west on Hwy. 14/Richland Rd. Open late May or early June–Oct daylight hours. $2 donation. (30 minutes minimum)

★★★★ PHELPS MILL COUNTY PARK
218/739-2884
This is one of the most beautiful and most photographed spots in Minnesota. The old Phelps Mill, one of the first to use roller-mill technology, stands on the lush banks of the broad, meandering Otter Tail River in an expansive park. Shade trees and picnic grounds flank the mill. It's not been in use since 1939, but you can walk through the mill and read interpretive displays explaining how it once worked. The interior is being restored by the Friends of Phelps Mill/Otter Tail County Historical Society, and you are on your own to explore. You'll find ice cream, candy, and handcrafted items across the street at Phelps Mill Store.

Details: Four miles west of Otter Tail Lake. At the northeast edge of Fergus Falls, take Hwy. 1 north to Hwy. 10, then go east to the mill. Open daylight hours. Free. (1 hour minimum)

SEVEN SISTERS PRAIRIE

This lush countryside abounds in off-the-beaten-path discoveries, such as the Nature Conservancy's Seven Sisters Prairie with seven rounded knobs on a hill overlooking Lake Christina, western plants uncommon to the area, and waterfowl. Drive three miles northeast of Ashby on MN 78. Park by the Nature Conservancy sign on the north side of the road. The 148-acre prairie is open to the public.

★★★ RUNESTONE MUSEUM
206 Broadway, Alexandria, 320/763-3160

A larger-than-life Viking statue towers above the museum that holds the famed and controversial Kensington Runestone—a large stone inscribed with runic inscriptions found by a Swedish farmer near the town of Kensington, Minnesota, in 1898. Was the inscription made by Vikings? If so, that means they visited here in 1362. Or is the inscription a fake—a bit of trickery on the part of the Swedish farmer and his minister, who were up on Viking lore and known to enjoy a good laugh? The controversy has lasted for years. Alexandria has preserved the stone and its story in a museum that also includes community settlement history and pioneer buildings.

Details: Mon–Fri 9–5, Sat 9–4 (11–4 winter), Sun 11–4 (closed in winter). $3–$5, under 6 free; $12 family rate. Wheelchair accessible. (30 minutes–1 hour)

FERGUS FALLS SIGHTSEEING HIGHLIGHTS

★★★★ OTTER TAIL COUNTY HISTORICAL SOCIETY MUSEUM
1110 Lincoln Ave. W., Fergus Falls, 218/736-6038

Visitors can tour a comprehensive agricultural wing complete with a lifelike sow nursing her piglets and a farmer driving a yesteryear tractor, as well as an interesting Native American exhibit. A scarecrow guards the pioneer garden planted in front of the museum. You can sample garden produce at the Fall Garden Fair in September.

OTTER TAIL COUNTRY

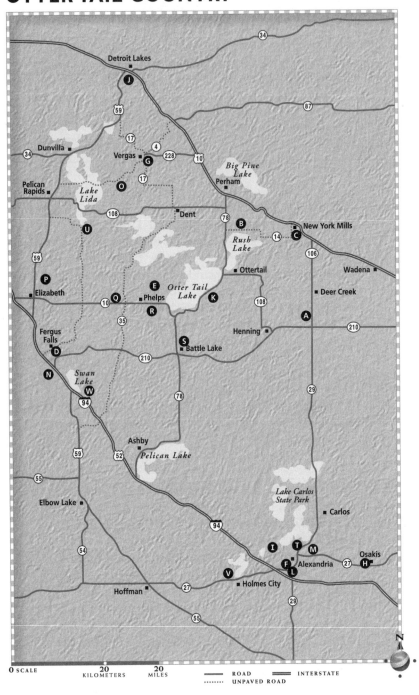

Detroit Lakes
J

34

59

87

17

4

228

10

Dunvilla

34

Vergas
G

O

17

Big Pine Lake

Perham

Pelican Rapids

Lake Lida

108

Dent

78

B

14

New York Mills
C

106

Rush Lake

59

U

Wadena

Deer Creek

P

E

Otter Tail Lake

Ottertail

Elizabeth

10
Q

Phelps

R

K

108

A

210

35

Henning

Fergus Falls
D

210

S
Battle Lake

N

Swan Lake

W

78

29

94

Ashby

59

52

Pelican Lake

55

Lake Carlos State Park

Elbow Lake

Carlos

54

94

I

T
M

Osakis
H

F
L
Alexandria

27

V

Holmes City

Hoffman

27

29

55

N

O SCALE

20
KILOMETERS

20
MILES

ROAD   INTERSTATE

UNPAVED ROAD

Details: Open year-round Mon–Fri 9–5, Sat 1–4, Sun 1–4 June–Sept. 50 cents–$2. (1–1½ hours)

★★★★ **PRAIRIE WETLANDS LEARNING CENTER**
Fergus Falls, 800/726-8959 or 218/739-2291
This 300-acre tract of land includes 23 wetlands, 19 acres of virgin prairie, and approximately 175 acres of restored prairie grasslands. You can drive or walk the rather rough road through the prairie. The center conducts educational programs.

Details: Adjacent to the Otter Tail County Fairgrounds, on the MN 210 bypass at the south edge of Fergus Falls. Open daylight hours. Free. (30 minutes–1 hour)

NEW YORK MILLS SIGHTSEEING HIGHLIGHTS

★★★★ **FINN CREEK OPEN AIR MUSEUM**
New York Mills, 218/385-2233

SIGHTS
- Ⓐ Finn Creek Open Air Museum
- Ⓑ Floralane Gardens
- Ⓒ New York Mills Regional Cultural Center
- Ⓓ Otter Tail County Historical Society Museum
- Ⓔ Phelps Mill County Park
- Ⓓ Prairie Wetlands Learning Center
- Ⓕ Runestone Museum

FOOD
- Ⓖ Billy's Bar
- Ⓗ Just Like Grandma's Tea Room
- Ⓘ Lake Café
- Ⓙ Lakeside 1891
- Ⓓ Mabel Murphy's Eating & Drinking Establishment
- Ⓚ Pier Supper Club
- Ⓓ The Viking

LODGING
- Ⓛ AmericInn
- Ⓜ Cedar Rose Inn Bed and Breakfast
- Ⓝ Day's Inn
- Ⓞ Log House & Homestead on Spirit Lake

LODGING (continued)
- Ⓟ Nim's Bakketopp Hus
- Ⓘ Radisson-Arrowwood
- Ⓞ Super 8 Motel
- Ⓠ Weslake Resort
- Ⓡ Whispering Waters
- Ⓒ Whistle Stop Inn Bed and Breakfast

CAMPING
- Ⓢ Glendalough State Park
- Ⓣ Lake Carlos State Park
- Ⓤ Maplewood State Park
- Ⓥ Sun Valley Resort and Campground
- Ⓦ Swan Lake Resort

Note: Items with the same letter are located in the same place.

Near New York Mills you can visit an early 1900s farmstead complete with an original Finnish home and sauna.

Details: *Three miles east of New York Mills on U.S. 10, then 2¹/₂ miles south on MN 106 toward Deer Creek and a half mile west on a gravel road. Open Memorial Day–Labor Day noon–5. Donation welcome. (30 minutes–1 hour)*

★★★★ **NEW YORK MILLS REGIONAL CULTURAL CENTER**
24 Main Ave., New York Mills, 218/385-3339
In a vintage brick building, the center houses a fine-art gallery, performance space, gourmet coffee nook, and gift shop. There's a regional art show yearly, and the center hosts numerous cultural programs and activities, including the annual Great American Think-Off (to bring philosophy down to the common person's level), culminating in a debate the third weekend in June by the final four contestants.

Details: *Open year-round Tue–Sat 10–5, Sun 11–3 (summer only); open by appointment Mon. Free except for special events and shows. (30 minutes)*

FITNESS AND RECREATION

Fishing is the top recreation in this region. Which lake is best? That depends on who you talk to and what you want to catch. Big Pine Lake, according to contest statistics, has yielded good-sized walleye, northerns, and crappie in recent years.

Other diversions include summer boating, waterskiing, hiking, and horseback riding; as well as winter snowshoeing, snowmobiling, and cross-country skiing. Several state parks in the area have trails. **Maplewood State Park** has 25 miles of hiking trails, plus horse, ski, and snowmobile trails; and **Lake Carlos State Park** has 13 miles of hiking trails along with horse, ski and snowmobile trails (see Camping for directions to these parks). **Glendalough State Park**, four miles north of Battle Lake off MN 78, 218/864-0110, has eight miles of hiking trails.

Golf options include **Perham Lakeside Country Club**, one mile north of Perham on Highway 51 or 8, 218/346-6070, an 18-hole championship course; and Alexandria's 18-hole **Radisson-Arrowwood**, 320/762-1124 (see Lodging for location). The **Pebble Lake Golf Course**, 218/736-7404, also with 18 holes, is two miles south of Fergus Falls via Pebble Lake Road and Highway 82.

Fergus Falls has seven miles of marked bikeways in the city. Northeast of

Fergus Falls, one bike path follows Highway 1 north. The Pebble Lake bike route runs south from Vernon Avenue and Adams Park. The visitors bureau, 800/726-8959, puts out a free area guide with marked bikeways.

FOOD

The **Pier Supper Club** on Highway 78 near Ottertail, 218/367-2260, has a dining room with wide lake views—great for watching the sunset. The club is known for walleye, prime rib, and scrumptious cheesecake. Dinner, the only meal served here (except for a $13 Sunday brunch), costs from $13 to $18. There's a dock if you come by boat, and casual, limited-menu deck dining supplements the main dining room. At **Just Like Grandma's Tea Room**, 115 W. Main, Osakis, 320/859-4504, you can get wild-rice salad and other dishes based on home-style recipes that could have come from a church congregation's cookbook. Soups, salads, sandwiches, good breads, and several hot entrées are available, plus ice cream, great pie, and other desserts. Everything is served in a combination tearoom/bed-and-breakfast in a restored 1902 Victorian home. Gifts and the works of regional artisans are sold in an adjacent vintage schoolhouse, barn, annex, and summer kitchen. The fragrance of potpourri, cinnamon, and spices lingers in the buildings.

At **Mabel Murphy's Eating & Drinking Establishment**, Highway 210 W. and I-94, Fergus Falls, 218/739-4406, prime rib and steak are the specialties in a rambling restaurant. It's busy and popular, and serves large portions of good food for $9 to $22 in an upbeat atmosphere. Go to **The Viking**, 203 Lincoln Ave., Fergus Falls, 218/736-6660, for breakfasts, homemade pastries, and comfort food in an old-fashioned café with wooden booths and counter stools.

The attractive **Lake Café** in the Radisson-Arrowwood, Alexandria, 320/762-1124, serves breakfast, lunch, and dinner. Try the coco shrimp or the filet mignon; dinner costs $6 to $22. The food gets praise at **Lakeside 1891**, off U.S. 59 at 200 W. Lake Dr., 218/847-7887. The restaurant overlooks Little Detroit Lake.

Vergas residents recommend the hamburgers at **Billy's Bar**, downtown across from the hardware store, 218/342-2451. Decorated with neon beer signs and mounted deer heads, it's a busy place where local people convene.

LODGING

The **Log House & Homestead on Spirit Lake** near Vergas, 800/342-2318, is a charming place to go for pampering with all sorts of extra touches, right down to the water-filled crystal vase waiting to receive the rose that's laid on each guest's pillow. You'll receive first-rate service, a morning newspaper at your door, and gourmet food. Former owners Yvonne and Lyle Tweten brought the best of their world-travel experiences to the inn and passed on their high standards of innkeeping to their daughters, Suzanne Tweten and Patrice Allen. Rates for four rooms and a suite run from $85 to $155. They have a wonderful Christmas tea in December. To get there, take County 4 west out of Vergas for about four miles, enter the driveway and take an immediate left to the Homestead.

Radisson-Arrowwood, on Lake Darling, 2100 Arrowwood Ln., Alexandria, 800/333-3333 or 320/762-1124, is a superb resort with something for everyone—formal and casual dining, golf, tennis courts (indoor and outdoor), volleyball courts, 30-horse riding stable, whirlpool, fitness center, walking/jogging paths, bike and snowmobile rentals, and a playground. There are organized activities for all ages. Rates range from $109 to $219. From I-94, take the Alexandria exit, go north on MN 29, west on Highway 82, and north on 22 to Arrowwood Drive. Also in Alexandria, the **Cedar Rose Inn Bed and Breakfast**, 422 7th Ave. W., 888/203-5333, is a 1903 Tudor Revival–style home with original stained glass, a fireplace, private baths, and a full country breakfast for $75 to $130.

In New York Mills you can sleep in a caboose, an elegant mahogany-paneled Pullman Car, or a room in a 1903 Victorian house for $49 to $125 at the **Whistle Stop Inn Bed and Breakfast**, 800/328-6315 or 218/385-2223. It's located one block south and one block east of the four-way stop sign in town. Nearby in Fergus Falls, **Nims' Bakketopp Hus** on Long Lake, 218/739-2915, is a chalet-style home with a fireplace, spa, and suites. You'll eat breakfast on antique china. Rates range from $70 to $105.

Whispering Waters, 218/495-2552, on the northeast shore of East Lost Lake, is the quintessential Minnesota mom-and-pop fishing resort. It's clean, quiet, and run by friendly and helpful Jan and Don Gladson. You'll find basic lodging but nothing fancy here. Rates are $365 to $540 for one week; a minimum stay of two days, for $144 to $216, is required. It's open mid-May through September. From Fergus Falls, go 16 miles east on Highway 1 and Highway 10. Cross Otter Tail River and turn right at the resort sign.

Weslake Resort, located on West Lost Lake, 800/258-9056, www.weslakeresort.com, is run by Gary and Sharon Nelson and their children, Karine and Chris. You'll find cabins and a large family lodge for big groups, and pleasant grounds. The resort has a small store and lots of activities, and more attention is paid to decor than at some of the other fishing resorts in the area, but don't expect upscale and posh. Rates start at $645 per week for one to four people in a two-bedroom cabin on the lake. Prices go down in spring and fall.

Motels in the area include **Day's Inn** at the intersection of MN 210 and I-94, Fergus Falls, 800/329-7466, with rates from $49 to $75; and the **Super 8 Motel**, I-94 and MN 210 junction, exit 54, Fergus Falls, 800/800-8000 or 218/739-3261, with rooms for $39 to $48. In Alexandria, rates at the **AmericInn**, 4520 MN 29, 800/634-3444, are $61 to $70 for doubles.

CAMPING

Public campgrounds are located in several state parks. **Maplewood State Park**, 21 miles north of Fergus Falls via U.S. 59 to Pelican Rapids, then seven miles east on MN 108, 218/863-8383, has 9,250 heavily forested acres with 60 drive-in sites. Half of those sites come with electricity, handicapped-accessible showers, and flush toilets. **Lake Carlos State Park**, north of Alexandria off MN 29, 320/852-7200, has 124 drive-in sites, 81 with electricity, handicapped-accessible showers, and flush toilets. **Glendalough State Park**, two miles northeast of Battle Lake, 218/864-0110, has 26 cart-in sites. These are popular parks, so reserve early.

Private campgrounds include the **Swan Lake Resort** near Fergus Falls, 218/736-4626. The resort offers 30 shaded sites with hookups, 10 tent sites, free showers, a swimming beach, and 20 acres with trails for $14 to $20 per night. On Mill Lake, **Sun Valley Resort and Campground**, 10045 MN 27 W. (seven miles west from Alexandria), 320/886-5417, has 30 shaded sites, hookups, and showers, and charges $19 a night for two people.

NIGHTLIFE

Phelps Mill County Park is the site of the popular **Phelps Mill Festival**, 218/739-2884, with fine arts, live entertainment, crafts, and American and ethnic foods the second weekend in July. Finn Creek Open Air Museum holds a **Summer Folk Festival**, 218/385-2233, the last weekend in August, with dancers, musicians, threshing, and blacksmithing. In Perham, turtle races are held Wednesday mornings all summer on Main Street near the city hall, 800/634-6112. A major music festival takes place in Detroit Lakes: **WE FEST**, held in early August, is billed as "the country music and camping event of the summer." The celebration draws thousands to the festival grounds on Soo Pass Ranch, 218/847-1681 or 218/847-1340.

6
PRAIRIE LANDS

A green and gold checkerboard of fields stretches across the gently rolling land of southwestern Minnesota below the Minnesota River—until you reach the extreme southwest, where Minnesota becomes more western than midwestern. This is the Coteau des Prairies, a glacial drift upland rising from 500 to 800 feet above the plains. Under the Coteau lie tilted ridges of Precambrian sandstone and Sioux quartzite in hues of pink and red—remnants of a previous mountain range. The quartzite, estimated to be 1.5 billion years old, is dramatically exposed in Pipestone National Monument, the Jeffers Petroglyphs, and Blue Mounds State Park. Native Americans have long quarried the quartzite for its softer red stone layer, which they fashion into pipes. Hence the red stone's name: pipestone. Today, Native Americans alone are allowed to quarry the pipestone at Pipestone National Monument. South of Pipestone, in Blue Mounds State Park, virgin prairie grass and prickly-pear cactus grow on land that slopes upward and ends abruptly at a cliff. The cliff-line extends 1 1/2 miles and is 90 feet high at some points. In the same region, the Jeffers Petroglyphs preserve ancient rock carvings dating to 3,000 B.C. and earlier.

A PERFECT DAY IN THE PRAIRIE LANDS
Pack a picnic and head for Blue Mounds State Park. Stop to browse at the visitors center, then hike through the prairie to the cliff-line. Hike the upper

cliff-line trail to Lower Mound Lake, go for a swim, then hike the lower trail back. Afterward, drive to Pipestone, view the quarries, and picnic on the grounds, then leave for Jeffers Petroglyphs via MN 30 east. Contemplate the glyphs, then head for Sanborn via MN 30 east and U.S. 71 north and check into the Sod House on the Prairie bed-and-breakfast. Drive to Springfield for a light meal at Victorian Gardens or to Wanda for heartier fare at Grandma's Granary. Finish the day by lantern light in the remarkably comfy sod house and fall asleep to a chorus of insects, as pioneers once did.

SIGHTSEEING HIGHLIGHTS

★★★★ BLUE MOUNDS STATE PARK
Hwy. 20 E. Luverne, 507/283-1307

This park's 2,028 acres encompass prairie and grassland, a dramatic cliff-line, lush wildflowers and wildlife, and a bison herd. Some say Native Americans drove buffalo over the cliff to effect a kill (piles of buffalo bones were once found at the base of the cliff). Patches of prickly-pear cactus atop quartzite outcrops bloom yellow in late June and early July. Coyotes, meadowlarks, white-tailed deer, and nighthawks live here; on late summer days, swallows dive, crickets create a shrill chorus, and grasshoppers leap everywhere. A scramble up rocky crevices leads to an overhang overlooking the broad valley below. Parklands are thick with goldenrod, lacy pink thistle, prairie cordgrass, milkweed pods bursting with white silk-bearing seeds, flowering white Queen Anne's lace, and monarch butterflies by the hundreds. The 13 miles of hiking trails lead through prairie with big bluestem grass and side oats grama, pass two lakes, and enter oak woods. Stop at the interpretive center for program and guided hikes information. There is a swimming beach, fishing, and camping.

Details: Six miles north of I-90 and Luverne, 16 miles south of Pipestone; enter the park off U.S. 75. Interpretive center, 507/283-4548. Park open daily 8 a.m.–10 p.m. Permit required. (half–full day)

★★★★ PIPESTONE NATIONAL MONUMENT
Pipestone, 507/825-5464

Digging at this quarry began in the 1700s and pipe-carvers prized the red stone. Dakota (Sioux) controlled the quarries and distributed

PRAIRIE LANDS REGION

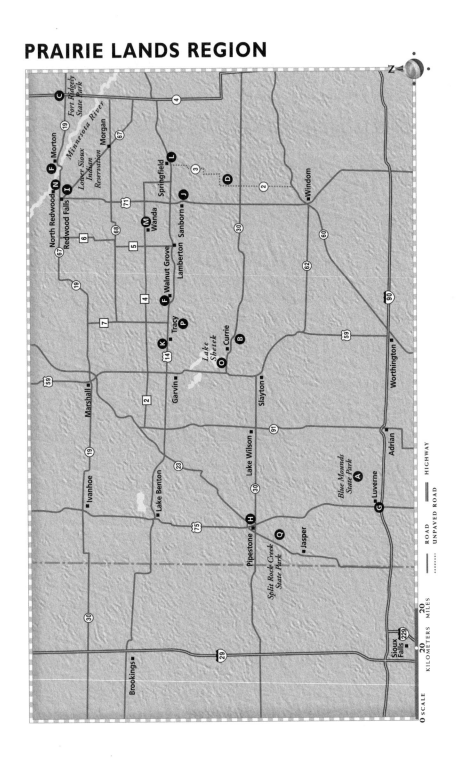

the stone only through trade. The T-shaped calumet pipes became known as peace pipes because they were used by Native Americans at treaty ceremonies. Pipes came into white society via trade, and as contact with whites increased, pipes also became a source of income. Pipestone Monument was created in 1937, open to the public but with quarrying restricted to Native Americans. A circle tour passes active and old quarry sites, Winnewassa Falls, Leaping Rock, craggy outcroppings, a clear stream, and pioneer inscriptions in the stone. Wildflowers and meadow sedge flank the paths, and river bulrush grows near the stream. Native Americans carve pipes in the cultural resource center from Memorial Day to Labor Day.

Details: *Just north of Pipestone; follow signs from U.S. 75, MN 23, or MN 30. Open Memorial Day–Labor Day Mon–Thu 8–6, Fri–Sun 8–8; other seasons daily 8–5. $2–$4; free to Native Americans and children under 16. Visitors center and self-guided trail are wheelchair-accessible. (1–2 hours minimum)*

SIGHTS

- **A** Blue Mounds State Park
- **B** End-o-Line Railroad Park and Museum
- **C** Fort Ridgely State Park
- **D** Jeffers Petroglyphs
- **E** Laura Ingalls Wilder Dugout Site and Museum
- **F** Lower Sioux Agency
- **G** Luverne
- **H** Pipestone
- **H** Pipestone National Monument
- **I** Redwood Falls
- **J** Sod House on the Prairie

FOOD

- **G** Blue Mound Inn
- **G** Coffey Haus
- **G** Cafe Dakota

FOOD (continued)

- **H** Historic Calumet Inn Restaurant
- **H** Gannon's
- **G** Magnolia Steak House
- **K** Mediterranean Club
- **E** Nellie's Cafe
- **L** Ruby's Heritage House
- **M** Southside Bar & Grill/Grandma's Granary
- **L** Victorian Gardens
- **M** Wanda Country Steak & Drink

LODGING

- **G** Comfort Inn
- **D** Dakota Inn
- **H** Historic Calumet Inn
- **G** Hillcrest Motel
- **G** Luverne Super 8 Motel
- **N** Redwood Inn

LODGING (continued)

- **J** Sodhouse on the Prairie
- **G** Sunrise Motel
- **H** Super 8 Motel Pipestone
- **N** Super 8 Motel Redwood Falls

CAMPING

- **I** Alexander Ramsey Park and Zoo
- **A** Blue Mounds State Park
- **O** Lake Shetek State Park
- **H** Pipestone RV Campground
- **P** Plum Creek
- **Q** Split Rock Creek State Park

Note: Items with the same letter are located in the same place.

★★★★ SOD HOUSE ON THE PRAIRIE
Sanborn, 507/723-5138

Visitors can tour two authentic sod houses (built in 1987 and 1988 by Stan McCone) to compare a "rich" man's soddy and a dugout. The site has restored prairie grasses and information about sod-house pioneers and life on the once-treeless prairie. (The rich man's soddy also operates as a bed-and-breakfast, open all year.)
Details: *1 mile east and ¹/₂ mile south of U.S. 71/U.S. 14 junction; 20 miles east of Walnut Grove. Open Apr–Oct. $3, under 7 free. (30 minutes–1 hour)*

★★★ END-O-LINE RAILROAD PARK AND MUSEUM
Currie, 507/763-3113 or 507/763-3409

After the town of Currie bought some railroad property, including the turntable at the north end of town, they added a caboose, motorcar, and locomotive, plus an engine house, a twentieth-century section foreman's house, an 1873 furnished general store, a school, lots of railroad memorabilia, and more. Thus was born a museum that continues to be supported by an involved community. A six-mile bicycle/pedestrian trail connects the museum with Lake Shetek State Park.
Details: *South of Lake Shetek State Park at the MN 30/Hwy. 38 intersection. Memorial Day–Labor Day Mon–Fri 10–noon and 1–5, Sat–Sun 1–5; last tour at 4. $1–$5 donation, under 6 free. (1 hour)*

★★★ JEFFERS PETROGLYPHS
between Jeffers and Comfrey, 507/628-5591 or 507/697-6321, www.minhs.org

In the midst of virgin prairie, these rock carvings span 5,000 years. More than 2,000 figures and designs, including a distinctly drawn thunderbird, are carved on a red quartzite outcrop some 700 feet long. Operated by the state historical society, the site has an interpretive center and trails.
Details: *Three miles east of U.S. 71 on Hwy. 10, then one mile south on Hwy. 2. May–Labor Day Fri, Sat, and Mon holidays 10–5, Sun noon–5; Sept–mid-Oct Sat 10–5, Sun noon–5. Free. (1–2 hours)*

★★★ LAURA INGALLS WILDER DUGOUT SITE AND MUSEUM
330 Eighth St., Walnut Grove, 800/761-1009
507/859-2358, or 507/859-2155

In the town of Walnut Grove, the Wilder Museum interprets Laura's life on the prairie. You can drive one and a half miles north on Highway 5 to the site of the dugout in which Laura and her family lived on the banks of Plum Creek. The popular and crowded Wilder pageant, "Fragments of a Dream," is held in a natural outdoor amphitheater on the first three weekends in July. You can see the land as Laura saw it at the Nature Conservancy's Wahpeton Prairie with tall grass, woods, and an oxbow pond.

Details: Pageant gates open 7 p.m.; $6–$7. Museum open Mar–Dec; $1. Dugout site: $3 per car. (1–2 hours)

★★ LUVERNE
I-90 and U.S. 75, 888/283-4061

A town of more than 4,300 people, Luverne makes a logical base for forays into Blue Mounds State Park. Notable quartzite structures include the imposing **Rock County Courthouse**, on Luverne between Cedar and McKenzie Sts., and the **Hinkly House Museum**, 217 N. Freeman Ave. The latter was built by a family who mined local quartzite for many buildings, and it has underground caverns for storing dynamite. Near the Hinkly House stands the **Carnegie Cultural Center**, 205 N. Freeman Ave., with displays of arts, crafts, and historical items.

Details: Hinkley House: 507/283-2115. Open summer Tue, Thu, Sat 2–4. $2, free for children with adults. Cultural Center: 507/283-8924. Open daily 2–4, Thu until 9. Donation. (2 hours)

★★ PIPESTONE
U.S. 75/MN 30 junction
800/336-6125

This town is renowned for its historic downtown district with 20 quartzite buildings, including one adorned with gargoyles. A walking-tour map is included in the community's free guide. **Pipestone County Museum** is located in the former city hall (built in 1896 out of Sioux quartzite) and has exhibits on the county's history, pioneer artifacts, a Native American gallery, and a library/reading room.

Details: The Chamber of Commerce Information Center near the 75/30 intersection offers information, 507/825-3316. County Museum: 113 S. Hiawatha, 507/825-2563. Open daily 10–5, until 8 during the Hiawatha Pageant. $2, under 12 free. (1 hour)

OTHER REGIONAL SIGHTS

★★★★ LOWER SIOUX AGENCY
Redwood Falls/Morton, 507/697-6321

The agency was the site of the first battle of the U.S.-Dakota Conflict of 1862. Starvation and poor treatment led to retaliation by Dakota confined on this reservation. An excellent interpretive center thoughtfully explores the genesis of the conflict. A stone agency warehouse remains. You can hike three miles of trails with interpretive stations and follow a path to the Redwood Ferry site.

Details: Hwy. 2, nine miles east of Redwood Falls. Open May–Labor Day Mon–Sat 10–5, Sun noon–5; after Labor Day–Oct daily 1–5; Dec–Feb Sat–Sun 1–5. $1.50–$3, under 6 free; $6 per family. (1–2 hours)

★★★ FORT RIDGELY STATE PARK
Fairfax, 507/426-7888 or 507/697-6321

The site has a restored commissary and marked building foundations. Interpretive center displays emphasize military strategy of the U.S.-Dakota Conflict of 1862.

Details: Seven miles south of Fairfax, off MN 4. Open Tue–Sat and Mon holidays 10–5, Sun noon–5. State park permit required. (1 hour)

★★ REDWOOD FALLS
U.S. 71 and MN 67/19, 800/657-7070

Highlights include hiking and camping in the 217-acre Alexander Ramsey Park, and the **Redwood County Historical Society Museum/Minnesota Inventors Hall of Fame**, 507/637-3329, in the former County Poor Farm facility.

Details: Alexander Ramsey Park: MN 19/U.S. 71 becomes Bridge St. in Redwood Falls. From Bridge St., go north on Grove St., turn left on Oak St., then follow it to the park. Open daily sunrise–10 p.m. Free. Redwood County Museum: On MN 19 W. Open May–Sept Thu–Sun 1–4. $2. (1–2 hours)

FITNESS AND RECREATION

Blue Mounds State Park has 13 miles of hiking trails. **Split Rock Creek State Park**, six miles south of Pipestone off MN 23 and Highway 2, and **Lake**

ALEXANDER HARKIN
STORE AND NEW ULM

On a bluff above the Minnesota River, the shelves of the historic **Alexander Harkin Store**, 507/354-2016, hold lots of original 1870s wares left when the store closed. A checkerboard, for instance, still sits atop a barrel near the wood-burning stove. Costumed interpreters—surrounded by vintage dishes, bottles of horse liniment, blocks of lye soap, cigars, "straight" shoes, and camphor—tell the store's history. Visit the store on Highway 21, eight miles northwest of New Ulm.

Take the rest of the day to explore German-heritage **New Ulm**, at the junction of U.S. 14, MN 15, and MN 99. The city's visitors center is at 1 North Minnesota Street (888/4-NEW ULM or 507/354-4217). New Ulm's architectural treasures include the striking brown-and-white 1910 Brown County Historical Museum, Center and Broadway, a great place to learn about early settlement history; and the August Schell Brewery, with original brick buildings, a museum, and landscaped gardens. Don't miss Domeier's German Store, 1020 S. Minnesota St., which is jammed with imported goods; the Glockenspiel's polka band; wooded Flandrau State Park; or the 102-foot-tall monument topped by the statue of heroic Hermann keeping watch over the city. You can browse in fun shops, visit the historic Wanda Gag (226 N. Washington) and John Lind (Center and State) houses, and eat red cabbage and ribs at Veigel's Kaiserhoff (221 N. Minnesota). Spend the night in the Victorian 1893 Deutsche Strasse Bed-and-Breakfast, 404 S. German St., 507/354-2005; or drive 14 miles west on U.S. 14 to Sleepy Eye and check into the 1900s Queen Anne W. W. Smith Inn (stained glass, cozy library), 101 Linden St. S.W., 800/799-5661.

Shetek State Park, north of Currie off Highway 38, also have hiking trails. Luverne has a city park with tennis courts on the banks of the Rock River and an indoor community swimming pool. In Pipestone, **Ewert Recreation Center**, 115 N. Hiawatha, 507/825-5834, has a swimming pool, weight/exercise room, whirlpool, racquetball/handball courts, steam room, golf practice net, gym, and tanning bed. Redwood Falls' exceptional **Alexander Ramsey Park and Zoo** has both easy and challenging trails, plus a waterfall.

FOOD

You'll find good quality food locally, but limited fine dining. Expect roasted chicken, burgers, and steak. Dinner here costs from $6 to $20. Prices are lower in town cafés. In Pipestone, try the **Historic Calumet Inn Restaurant**, 104 W. Main, 507/825-5871; or **Gannon's**, U.S. 75 and MN 23 intersection, 507/825-3114.

In addition to the usual assortment of fast-food options, Luverne's **Coffey Haus**, 111 E. Main, 507/283-8676, offers espresso drinks, muffins, pastries, soups, sandwiches, and desserts. There's also the **Blue Mound Inn**, two miles north of Luverne on U.S. 75, 507/283-2718, with a weekday lunch buffet, weekend evening buffet, and Sunday smorgasbord. It's closed on Monday. Locals recommend **Magnolia Steak House**, I-90 and U.S. 75, 507/283-9161. **Cafe Dakota**, located in the Jackpot Junction Casino (800/WIN CASH), near Morton, is another dining option. Near Sanborn in Springfield, **Victorian Gardens**, 8 W. Central, 507/723-6594, has gourmet coffee drinks, sandwiches, and desserts that make the trip worthwhile. Nearby, **Ruby's Heritage House**, 11 S. Marshall, 507/723-4716, serves full meals. Or go to the **Southside Bar & Grill/Grandma's Granary** (with grain-elevator salt and pepper shakers), in tiny Wanda, 507/342-5682. Folks from the area dine there or across the street at **Wanda Country Steak and Drink**, 507/342-5694. Another good spot is the **Mediterranean Club**, U.S. 14 in Tracy, 507/629-4400. In Walnut Grove, **Nellie's Café**, 550 U.S. 14, 507/859-2384, serves real mashed potatoes and home-style cooking and draws a big crowd on Sunday mornings.

LODGING

In the Pipestone area, **Historic Calumet Inn**, 104 W. Main St., 800/535-7610, is a renovated 1888 Sioux quartzite hotel, with antiques-furnished rooms and rates from $60 to $65. The hotel is adjacent to the Center for Performing Arts, so inquire about theater and romantic getaway packages. **Super 8 Motel**, 605 8th Ave. S.E., junction of U.S. 75, MN 23, and MN 30, 800/800-8000 or 507/825-4217, has rooms for $57 to $60.

Luverne-area lodging includes the **Luverne Super 8 Motel**, I-90 (exit 12) and U.S. 75 S., 800/800-8000, which charges $57 for a double; and a **Comfort Inn**, 800/228-5150, a few blocks to the north off U.S. 75. **Hillcrest Motel**, near Blue Mounds State Park, 800/588-3763, offers rooms for $40. The small, remodeled **Sunrise Motel**, 114 S. Sunshine, 800/868-4748, has rooms for $24 to $36.

In Sanborn, the one-room **Sodhouse on the Prairie**, 800/258-3974, replicates an 1880 structure with two double beds, a rocking chair, oil lamps, a wood stove, a nearby outhouse, and meadowlarks in full song. Pheasants provide a spontaneous wake-up call. It's open year-round and charges $85 per night for two or $126 to $140 per family.

In Redwood Falls the **Dakota Inn**, 410 W. Park Rd., 800/287-5443, is a lodge-style hotel owned by Jackpot Junction Casino, with gaming packages and free casino shuttle. Rooms run $39 to $60. There's also the **Super 8 Motel**, 800/800-8000, 1305 E. Bridge St., with rooms for $55; and the **Redwood Inn**, 507/637-3521, 1303 E. Bridge, with rates of $35 to $65.

CAMPING

Three area state parks have campgrounds; however, they are in high demand in summer, so reserve early. In Luverne, **Blue Mounds State Park**, Hwy. 20 E., 507/283-1307, has 73 semi-modern sites, a swimming beach, 13 miles of hiking trails, lake fishing, canoeing, seven miles of snowmobile trails, wheelchair-accessible showers, and flush toilets. (See Planning Your Trip for fee/reservation details.) **Split Rock Creek State Park**, six miles south of Pipestone via Hwy. 23, 507/348-7908, has 28 sites, four and a half miles of hiking trails, and boat and canoe rentals. **Lake Shetek State Park**, south of U.S. 14 off U.S. 59, 507/763-3256, is set on 1,109 acres, has 98 drive-in sites, 10 walk-in sites, wheelchair-accessible showers, and flush toilets, plus a cabin and miles of hiking trails. **Pipestone RV Campground**, 919 N. Hiawatha Ave., 507/825-2455, has 50 sites with electricity, tent and teepee camping, and a heated outdoor pool. **Plum Creek Park**, 507/859-2358, southwest of Walnut Grove on the site of the original walnut grove that gave the city its name, has a campground with 40 wooded and electrified sites with showers. In Redwood Falls, **Alexander Ramsey Park and Zoo**, 507/637-5755, has 28 sites—some with electricity—for $10 each.

NIGHTLIFE AND SPECIAL EVENTS

Festivals take place all summer long in this part of Minnesota. Luverne hosts the **Tri-State Band Festival** for marching bands the first Saturday in September. The town's **Buffalo Days** celebration includes a parade, an arts and crafts fair, free buffalo burgers, and an open house at Blue Mounds State Park (first weekend in June; 507/283-4061). Luverne's **Palace Theater**, 104 E. Main, a 1915 vaudeville house revived as a movie theater on Main Street, hosts performances by the **Green Earth Players**, a local theatrical performing group, 507/283-8526. Pipestone's biggest event is the popular **Hiawatha Pageant**, held in an outdoor amphitheater north of town. The 200-member cast puts on its colorful show the last two weekends in July and the first weekend in August ($8, under 7 free; 507/825-4126 or 507/825-3316). (If you aren't a Henry Wadsworth Longfellow *Song of Hiawatha* fan or you dislike crowds, avoid these weekends.)

The **Pipestone County Fair** takes place in August, and a full calendar of entertainment is scheduled at the **Pipestone Center for Performing Arts,** a state-of-the-art theater in a historic building on Main Street. Programs include community theater and classics. For tickets and information, call the Historic Calumet Inn, 800/535-7610.

For music and late-night activity, try **Jackpot Junction Casino**, 800/WIN-CASH. Past entertainers have included the Oak Ridge Boys, Crystal Gayle, and Wayne Newton. For a slice of pioneer prairie life, catch the **Laura Ingalls Wilder Pageant, "Fragments of a Dream,"** in Walnut Grove's outdoor amphitheater. It takes place the first three weekends in July (507/859-2174 or www.walnutgrove.org).

7
BLUFF COUNTRY

Southeast of Rochester, in the Richard J. Dorer Memorial Hardwood Forest, lies a magical land of deep valleys and river gorges, limestone cliffs and swift-running trout streams, caves, and sinkholes—Bluff Country. Although this land was spared glacial abrasion, meltwater rushed in, down-cutting and carving the bluffs and valleys in which small farms and villages thrive today. It's a little pocket of New England-in-Minnesota, with white Victorian houses; old stone buildings; narrow churches with tall steeples; hills forested in oak, maple, and black walnut; and undulating, winding country roads.

This far southeastern corner of Minnesota enjoyed obscurity for years. Only morel mushroom hunters, berry-pickers, farmers (including a community of Amish), wood-carvers, and artists called it home. That changed with the advent of the Root River Trail, a 35-mile paved bicycle trail running from the Fountain to the town of Rushford. Swarms of weekend bicyclists now pedal the trail and back roads, and once-quiet streets now bustle with activity. Nearly every village in the area has bed-and-breakfasts or inns and shops selling Amish goods and regional artisans' work. Even so, it's still possible to go there midweek in spring and late fall, or anytime in the winter, and find solitude hiking the state trail; hear a wild turkey gobbler; spot hawks, white-tailed deer, and bald eagles; and see few other "outsiders" on village streets.

A PERFECT DAY IN BLUFF COUNTRY

Hike or bike part of the Root River Trail early in the morning, or go to the Eagle Bluff Environmental Learning Center to watch for raptors and hike down the steep bluff to the river. Take a leisurely walking tour of Lanesboro, then drive to Harmony. Eat lunch amid local folks at the Country Bread Basket and take an Amish country tour. Return to Lanesboro via a scenic route. Dine at the remarkable Victorian House restaurant in Lanesboro. Perhaps go to a Commonweal Theatre play. Then settle into a cozy room in Mrs. B's Historic Lanesboro Inn or any of the town's excellent bed-and-breakfasts.

SIGHTSEEING HIGHLIGHTS

★★★★ EAGLE BLUFF ENVIRONMENTAL LEARNING CENTER
Lanesboro, 507/467-2437, www.eagle-bluff.org

Situated on a bluff high above the Root River, the center is a great spot to see raptors cruising the valley below. Eagle Bluff Center offers information on programs and research conducted at the center, as well as a map of the demonstration areas and seven-mile trail system. One trail leads down to the Root River. There's also a bat condominium, a raptor perch, and an osprey nesting platform. Ongoing programs include a shiitake mushroom–growing project.

Details: *From Lanesboro, take Hwy. 8 west two miles to Hwy. 21. Follow 21 northwest 1.2 miles to the Eagle Bluff ELC sign. Follow the signed gravel road north two miles. Year-round Mon–Fri 8–4:30, Sat–Sun 10–4:30. Hiking trails and center are free. Tours and programs, by reservation only, have varying fees. (1–3 hours)*

★★★★ FORESTVILLE STATE PARK
Hwy. 5, Wykoff/Preston, 507/352-5111

The park offers excellent brown-trout streams, tours of **Mystery Cave** (six miles south of U.S. 16 on Hwy. 5), and the restored 1899 site of **Historic Forestville** (507/765-2785). In summer, costumed interpreters inhabit the town's stocked brick store, Meighen residence, and farm buildings. Park wildlife includes wild turkey, red and gray fox, raccoon, opossum, snapping turtle, and deer. Remnant stands of white pine remain, and black walnut trees send down volleys of green-clad nuts in fall.

Details: *Four miles south of U.S. 16 on Fillmore County Hwy. 5,* and two miles east on Fillmore County Hwy. 12. Daily 8–10. $4 daily permit includes Historic Forestville. Mystery Cave open Memorial Day–Labor Day daily and spring/fall weekends. $1–$7 in addition to park permit. (half–full day)

★★★★ **HARMONY**
U.S. 52/MN 44/MN 139; Tourist Information: 45 Center St. E., 800/247-MINN, www.harmony.mn.us
A town of around 1,000, Harmony serves as an agricultural and business hub, as well as the gateway to the 17.8-mile **Harmony-Preston Valley State Trail**. Harmony is the place to buy handcrafted Amish furniture and other products. Horse-drawn buggies are common on Harmony streets, and several operators offer tours, including Michel's Amish Tours, 45 Main Ave. N., 800/752-6474 or 507/886-5392, and Amish Country Tours, 90 Second Ave. NW, 800/278-8327 or 507/886-2303. On the tours you'll stop at Amish farms, where goods for sale range from jams and honey to quilts and furniture. The guides explain Amish customs and offer historical and anecdotal details. It is courteous to refrain from taking pictures of Amish people. You can also tour Amish farm country independently by driving east of town

AMISH FARM NEAR HARMONY

Alice Vollmar

BLUFF COUNTRY

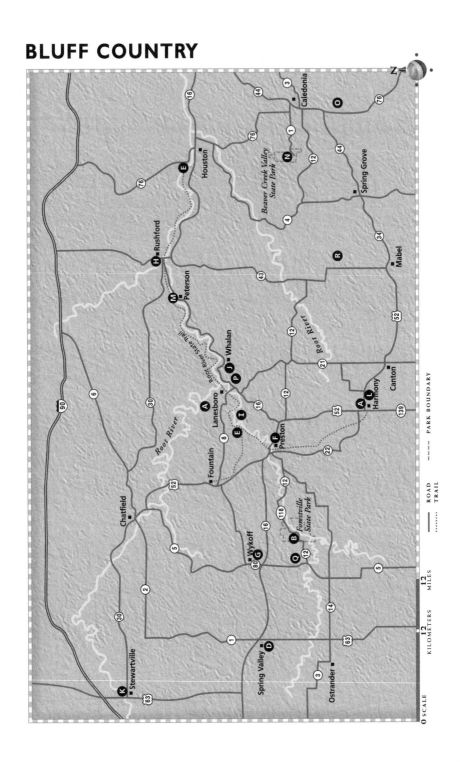

Z

Caledonia

76

16

44

3

76

O

76

Spring Grove

76

12

44

N

Houston

E

Beaver Creek Valley State Park

4

34

Mabel

Rushford

H

R

Peterson

M

43

Root River

52

Whalan

J

12

P

Root River State Trail

A

Lanesboro

21

Canton

Harmony

L

I

16

A

E

Fountain

8

52

F

Preston

139

6

30

22

90

Root River

12

52

118

Forestville State Park

Chatfield

Wykoff

16

B

5

G

80

Q

12

5

2

14

30

Spring Valley

D

1

63

Ostrander

3

Stewartville

K

63

SCALE
0 ████ 12
KILOMETERS

0 ████ 12
MILES

——— ROAD   - - - PARK BOUNDARY
········· TRAIL

on MN 44 and turning north onto the first gravel road. Then drive country roads at random, watching for farms with windmills, horse-drawn field machinery, and huge gardens.

At the Village Green, the **Village Depot & School**, 90 Second Ave. NW, 507/886-2409, sells Amish furniture, quilts, and other goods. Harmony's grocery store has a hitching rail, and buggy rides are offered for a fee in town during summer months. There are also nearly 4,000 toys to see at the **Harmony Toy Museum**, 30 Main Ave. S, 507/867-3380.

Details: *13 miles south of Lanesboro via MN 16 and U.S. 52.* *(Half–full day)*

★★★★ LANESBORO
MN 16 and 250; Visitors Center: 100 Milwaukee Rd.
800/944-2670

Backdropped by sheer bluffs in a deep valley, Lanesboro, a town of about a thousand on MN 16, sits on the banks of the meandering Root River and is on the Root River State Trail. Its downtown streets hold many of the original brick and stone buildings erected by German, Irish, and Scandinavian settlers in the middle to late 1800s. Attractions in the compact downtown historic district on or near Parkway Avenue North and Coffee Street include **Scenic Valley Winery**, 507/

SIGHTS
- **O** Eagle Bluff Environmental Learning Center
- **B** Forestville State Park
- **C** Harmony
- **D** Methodist Church Museum and Washburn-Zittleman House
- **E** Root River Trail

FOOD
- **F** Branding Iron
- **A** Country Bread Basket
- **G** Gateway Inn

FOOD (continued)
- **H** Mill Street Inn Restaurant
- **I** Old Barn Resort
- **J** Overland Inn

LODGING
- **K** AmericInn Motel
- **L** Carrolton Country Inn
- **L** Country Lodge Motel
- **G** Historic Wykoff Jail Haus
- **P** JailHouse Historic Inn
- **C** Selvig House Bed and Breakfast
- **M** Wenneson Hotel

CAMPING
- **N** Beaver Creek Valley State Park
- **O** DunRomin' Park
- **P** Eagle Cliff Campground
- **B** Forestville State Park
- **Q** Maple Springs Campground
- **I** Old Barn Resort, Hostel and Campground
- **R** Supersaw Valley Campground

Note: Items with the same letter are located in the same place.

LANESBORO

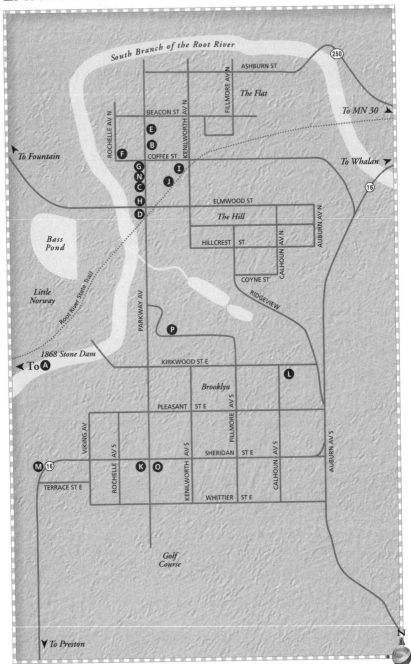

South Branch of the Root River

250

ASHBURN ST

FILLMORE AV N

The Flat

To MN 30

ROCHELLE AV N

BEACON ST

KENILWORTH AV N

To Fountain

E

B

F

COFFEE ST

To Whalan

G

I

N

J

16

C

H

D

ELMWOOD ST

The Hill

AUBURN AV N

Bass
Pond

HILLCREST   ST

CALHOUN AV N

Little
Norway

COYNE ST

RIDGEVIEW

Root River State Trail

PARKWAY AV

P

1868 Stone Dam

To A

KIRKWOOD ST E

L

Brooklyn

PLEASANT   ST E

FILLMORE AV S

VIKING AV

ROCHELLE AV S

KENILWORTH AV S

SHERIDAN   ST E

CALHOUN AV S

AUBURN AV S

M 16

K O

TERRACE ST E

WHITTIER   ST E

Golf
Course

To Preston

N

Map not to scale   —— ROAD   ·········· TRAIL

467-2958, specializing in wines made from locally grown fruit; **Cornucopia Art Center and Gallery**, 507/467-2446, showcasing regional artists' work; specialty shops; the restored art deco–style **St. Mane Theater**, hosting performances of the Commonweal Theatre Company, 800/657-7025, a professional acting company; **River Valley Cheese Factory**, 507/467-7000, with cheese made from Amish farm milk; **Lanesboro Historical Preservation Society Museum**, 507/467-2177; and the **DNR Root River Trail Office**, 507/467-2552, on the lower level of the historical museum. There's also a livestock auction barn at the edge of town off Coffee Street and Highway 8; and **Avian Acres**, 800/967-BIRD, a one-of-a kind native bird supply store/petting zoo southwest of town on Norway Drive.

Details: (half day)

★★★ METHODIST CHURCH MUSEUM AND WASHBURN-ZITTLEMAN HOUSE
221 and 222 W. Courtland St., Spring Valley, 507/346-7659
In this pleasant little town 25 miles west of Lanesboro on MN 16, the Methodist Church Museum occupies an 1876 National Historic Registry church attended by Laura Ingalls Wilder and her husband, Almanzo Wilder, in 1890 and 1891. Two floors of exhibits include religious and pioneer artifacts and memorabilia, such as a wooden coffin with a glass viewing window—used for victims of contagious disease.

SIGHTS
- **A** Avian Acres
- **B** Commonweal Theatre Company
- **C** Cornucopia Art Center and Gallery
- **D** DNR Root River Trail Office
- **D** Lanesboro Historical Preservation Society Museum
- **E** River Valley Cheese Factory
- **B** St. Mane Theater
- **F** Scenic Valley Winery

FOOD
- **G** Das Wurst Haus
- **H** Mrs. B's Historic Lanesboro Inn Restaurant
- **I** Old Village Hall Restaurant and Pub
- **J** Picnic Basket
- **K** Victorian House of Lanesboro

LODGING
- **L** Cady Hayes House Bed and Breakfast
- **M** Green Gables Inn
- **N** Historic Lodge Inn
- **O** Historic Scanlon House
- **H** Mrs. B's Historic Lanesboro Inn

CAMPING
- **P** Sylvan Park
- **P** Riverview Campground

Note: Items with the same letter are located in the same place.

Across the street, the 1866 Washburn-Zittleman House contains 1870s furnishings, quilts, and toys.

Details: Memorial Day–Labor Day daily 10–4, Sept–Oct weekends 10–4. $1–$4 for guided tours of the museum and house. (1–1½ hours)

★★★ ROOT RIVER TRAIL
800/428-2030

Root River State Trail is a 35.3-mile biking and hiking trail in an abandoned railroad bed that leads from Fountain through Lanesboro, Whalen, Peterson, and Rushford. Toward its western end, the trail links up with the 17.8-mile **Harmony-Preston Valley State Trail**. Each trail town is unique, and most offer food and lodging. In Fountain, the **Fillmore County Historical Center**, U.S. 52 and Hwy. 8, 507/268-4449, displays farm tools and exhibits on regional history.

Details: (Full day minimum)

FITNESS AND RECREATION

Biking is *the* sport in this area. Bring your own bike or rent a 10-speed or 12-speed in Lanesboro from **Capron Hardware**, 119 Parkway Ave. N., 800/726-5030 ($4 per hour, $12 per day). They also rent kids' one-speed bikes as well as "Kiddie Karts." At **Little River General Store**, 104/106 Parkway Ave. N., 800/994-2943 or 507/467-2943, bike rentals cost $10 for two hours, $18 for the day, and canoes rent for $25 to $30. The store also rents skis and runs a bike/canoe/ski shuttle on request. You can rent bikes, inner tubes, and canoes from **Root River Outfitters** in Lanesboro, 507/467-3400; and canoes from **Lanesboro Canoe Rental**, 507/467-2948. **Old Barn Resort**, 507/467-2512, rents bikes and inner tubes. If you plan to rent bikes or equipment in the area, call ahead for reservations.

The most popular bike route is the **Root River State Trail,** 507/467-2552, beginning in Fountain and ending east of Rushford or vice versa. Signs direct you to trailheads at each of five towns along its length. You can also bike south 5.5 miles from the Root River Trail at Isinours Junction to Preston, and 12.3 miles from Preston to Harmony on the newer **Harmony-Preston Valley State Trail**. The hard-surfaced country roads in the region also provide good biking. *Biking with the Wind*, a book by David Dixen, Peter Seed, and Nancy Wilson, describes several Lanesboro-area routes. It's available at the Little River General Store, area bookstores, and from DSW, Inc., 906 N. 4th St., Stillwater, MN 55082.

Forestville State Park, near Spring Grove, 507/352-5111, has 17 miles of hiking trails, 15 miles of horse-riding trails, five and a half miles of snowmobile trails, and 11 miles of ski trails. **Beaver Creek Valley State Park,** 507/724-2107, five miles west of Caledonia on Highway 1 off MN 76, has eight miles of hiking trails in virgin hardwood forest. This is a scenic domain with a privately owned operating gristmill and great ridge-top trails 250 feet above pretty Beaver Creek. There are numerous freshwater springs, and watercress grows in the creek. The **Richard Dorer Memorial Hardwood Forest**, 507/724-5264, has trails for hiking, skiing, horseback riding, and snowmobiling. Opportunities for canoeing and fly-fishing abound in the spring-fed streams throughout the area and in both state parks mentioned above.

FOOD

Homemade pies memorable enough to warrant a return trip are common in these small communities. You'll find decent food in most towns, and creative gourmet cuisine in several Lanesboro restaurants.

Jean Claude Venant, the French chef/co-proprietor of the **Victorian House of Lanesboro**, 709 Parkway Ave. S., 507/467-3457, serves exquisitely seasoned lamb and the best tomato bisque I've encountered. If you ask, Venant will relate the funny story about how he came to live and exercise his culinary talents in a small town in Minnesota. The house-turned-restaurant has stained glass, antiques, and lots of charm. A full dinner including dessert costs $21 to $27. Reservations are required.

Das Wurst Haus, in the heart of downtown Lanesboro, 507/467-2902, features owners Arv and Jan Fabian's smoked sausage, homemade root beer, and music by their live polka band. **Old Village Hall Restaurant and Pub**, 111 Coffee St., 507/467-2962, serves creative lunch and dinner dishes, including pan-seared game and four pastas. The restaurant has a deck on the Root River Trail. **Mrs. B's Historic Lanesboro Inn Restaurant**, 101 Parkway N., 507/467-2154, uses local produce and meats. You may dine on sweet potato tart with carmelized onions and roast pork loin with peach sauce. A five-course meal is served evenings at seven for a set price of $25 (by reservation only). A lunch menu featuring sandwiches on homemade bread, soups, and desserts is also offered. The **Picnic Basket**, 100 Parkway Ave. N., 507/467-2977, will fix one for you, filling it with fruit, sandwiches, freshly baked cookies, and such.

The **Old Barn Resort**, 507/467-2512, three miles north of Preston on Highway 17, then east for one mile on the Root River Trail, has a large dining room and traditional Midwestern fare for $2 to $10. At the **Branding Iron**, in Preston, 507/765-3388, the hilltop dining room has sweeping views and offers prime rib, steak, chicken, and chops with a salad bar.

In Whalan, the **Overland Inn**, 800/240-4162 or 507/467-2623, wins raves for its pies; try a slice of caramel apple pie. Downtown Wykoff's **Gateway Inn**, 507/352-4205, serves hearty breakfasts and lunch. Rushford eateries include the **Mill Street Inn**, 100 W. Jessie St., 507/864-2929. In Harmony, **Country Bread Basket**, 350 Main Ave. N., 507/886-6277, is a good breakfast and lunch place.

LODGING

There are bed-and-breakfasts everywhere. Historic Bluff Country, 800/944-2670, and Lanesboro Visitor Center, 800/944-2670, maintain a vacancy list.
At **Mrs. B's Historic Lanesboro Inn**, 101 Parkway Ave. N., 800/657-4710 or 507/467-2154, you can sleep in a cozy sleigh-bed or a four-poster. Guests enjoy a decanter of sherry and other thoughtful touches plus a full breakfast. Rates are $58 and $75 weekdays, $85 or $95 weekends and holidays. Rates at **Carrolton Country Inn**, out in the country near Lanesboro, 507/467-2257, start at $65 midweek and $85 on weekends for bed-and-breakfast accommodations. At **Historic Lodge Inn**, 105½ Parkway Ave. N., Lanesboro, 507/467-2257, rooms go for $55 to $80 and include a continental breakfast. **Historic Scanlon House**, 708 Parkway Ave. S., 800/944-2158, has rooms for $65 to $130, a full breakfast, and bike rentals. The **Cady Hayes House Bed-and-Breakfast**, 500 Calhoun Ave., 507/467-2621, offers rooms in a century-old Queen Anne–style house for $80 to $115.

Wenneson Hotel in Peterson, on the Root River Trail at 425 Prospect, 507/875-2587, was built in 1904 and charges from $60 (midweek, no breakfast) to $100 (weekend, continental breakfast).

The handsome, restored Italianate 1869 **JailHouse Historic Inn**, 109 Houston St., Preston, 507/765-2181, offers antiques, 12 rooms and whirlpool suites, fireplaces, and a full breakfast for $42 to $149. In Wykoff, the **Historic Wykoff Jail Haus**, 219 N. Main, 507/352-4205, offers jail-cell lodging for two for $55, which includes a breakfast voucher for a nearby café. In Harmony, the 1910 Victorian **Selvig House Bed-and-Breakfast**, 140 Center St. E., 888/887-2922 or 507/886-2200, www.means.net/~selvig, offers evening snacks and rooms from $50 to $75.

Motels include the **Country Lodge Motel**, 525 Main Ave. N., Harmony, 800/870-1710 or 507/886-2515, ctrylodg@means.net. It's a delight, with a hearty continental breakfast and rooms from $46 to $66. There's also the **AmericInn Motel**, 800/634-3444, in Stewartville, with rooms from $60 to $65; and **Green Gables Inn**, 303 W. Sheridan, MN 16 W., Lanesboro, 800/818-4225, with rooms from $55 to $75.

CAMPING

Beaver Creek Valley State Park, five miles west of Caledonia on Highway 1, 507/724-2107, has 42 drive-in sites, showers, vault toilets, and 16 electric and 6 walk-in sites. **Forestville State Park**, four miles south of State 16 on Highway 5 and two miles east on Highway 12, 507/352-5111, offers 73 drive-in campsites with showers and flush toilets, and 23 sites with electricity. **Sylvan Park** and **Riverview Campground**, two pretty city park campgrounds in Lanesboro, 507/467-3722, have 43 sites with hookups and water, 60 tent sites, and showers. Sites range from $8 to $15. **Eagle Cliff Campground**, about three miles east of Lanesboro via MN 16, 507/467-2598, has 20 full-hookup sites and 30 tent sites for $10 to $15. The **Old Barn Resort, Hostel and Campground**, north of Preston via County 17, 800/552-2512 or 507/467-2512, has 200 campsites, 51 hostel beds, showers, a dining room, gift shop, and pool; rates are $12 to $24. At **DunRomin' Park**, four and a half miles south of Caledonia on MN 76, 800/822-2514, there are 106 campsites, flush toilets, free hot showers, and a heated pool. Base rates are $17 to $21. **Supersaw Valley Campground**, about three miles north of Spring Grove on County 4, then two and a half miles west on Highway 19, 507/498-5880, has 106 sites, a swimming pool, and hiking trails. **Maple Springs**, next to Forestville State Park, 507/352-2056, has electric hookups and primitive sites.

NIGHTLIFE AND SPECIAL EVENTS

The towns on the Root River Trail sponsor **Sykkle Tur**, a bike tour the third weekend in May, 888/845-2100. Lanesboro has **Art in the Park** on Father's Day and **Buffalo Bill Days** the first weekend in July, 800/944-2670. Historic Forestville celebrates **Independence Day at Forestville** on July 4, 507/765-2785. There's the **Fillmore County Fair** in Preston in July, 507/765-2100; and **Western Days** in Chatfield in August, 507/867-3966. In September, Wykoff holds its **German Fall Festival**, 507/352-4205, and Harmony celebrates with **Fall Foliage Fest**, 800/247-MINN. The **Commonweal Theatre Company** in Lanesboro stages performances February through December, 800/657-7025.

County Highway 4 from Spring Grove to Houston

While almost every drive in this part of Minnesota turns out to be scenic, one of my favorites is County Highway 4, a partly paved, partly gravel road leading from Spring Grove to Houston. To get to Spring Grove from Harmony, take MN 44 east about 20 miles. If you have time, stop in downtown Spring Grove and browse the **Ballard House's** three floors of antiques and local memorabilia, plus a small ice-cream parlor and restaurant. Then go north on Highway 4. You'll pass a 125-year-old church with a black steeple in the town of Black Hammer. The road winds along a bluff with views of farms; nearby lie the **Winnebago Indian Catacombs** of Yucatan. You'll pass Yucatan and arrive in Houston (about 20 minutes in all), ending up on MN 16, 29 miles east of Lanesboro. You can follow MN 16 to Lanesboro or catch MN 76 and go south about eight miles to visit **Beaver Creek Valley State Park**, picnic on the banks of Beaver Creek, and hike wooded trails.

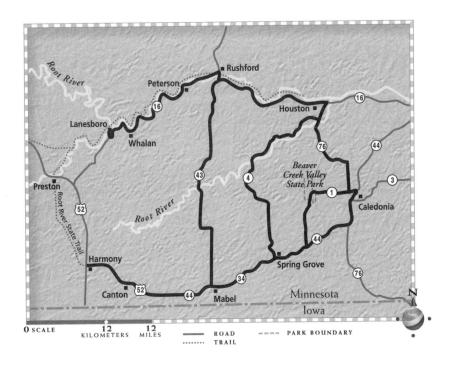

Still in the mood for exploring? Then go south for two miles from the park entrance on MN 76, then head west about 15 miles on MN 44 to Mabel (you'll pass through Spring Grove again on the way). In South Mabel, stop at the **Steam Engine Museum** to view old tractors and equipment, then take MN 43 north. You'll pass through a peaceful, lush green valley in which the tiny town of Choice is located—indeed, a choice location. After 22 miles you'll arrive at Rushford Village, where you'll connect with MN 16 again. From there it's about 14 miles via MN 16 southwest to Lanesboro.

GREAT RIVER ROAD

Marked by green and white pilot's wheel signs, Minnesota's U.S. Highway 61 and Wisconsin's State Highway 35 are among the most scenic of the Great River Road highways that follow the Mississippi River for 3,000 miles to the Gulf of Mexico. Highways 35 and 61 climb and wind to the top of steep, wooded river bluffs, then dip down to hug the river's banks. The Mississippi River Valley occupies the heart of the unglaciated region, where meltwaters cut deep gorges and river channels in sandstone and limestone.

The Wisconsin side of the road is less developed, with river hamlets scattered here and there; the Minnesota side is notable for its string of river towns—some sleepy and serene, others alive with activity. This guide covers a selected handful of attractions on both sides of the river between Minnesota's La Crescent and Red Wing. There are river crossings at La Crescent, Minnesota/La Crosse, Wisconsin; Winona, Minnesota; Wabasha, Minnesota/Nelson, Wisconsin; and Red Wing. You can drive north on one state's Great River Road and then cross the Mississippi to go south on the other state's side. Or you can zigzag back and forth, driving portions of each.

A PERFECT DAY ON THE GREAT RIVER ROAD

Start in La Crescent and drive the scenic Apple Blossom Highway. Then head north to Winona. Do the downtown walking tour and visit the Armory

Museum. Cross the river and drive to Trempealeau to visit Perrot State Park and Trempealeau National Wildlife Refuge. Drive north to Nelson and treat yourself to Nelson Cheese Factory ice cream, then cross the river and check into the historic Anderson House in Wabasha. Explore the quaint town, dine on the inn's Pennsylvania Dutch cooking, then drift off to sleep in an antique bed with a purring cat curled up at your feet.

RED WING ORIENTATION

Surrounded by limestone bluffs, the river city at the foot of Barn Bluff is named for Chief Red Wing. He used red-dyed swans' wings in his headdress—hence the red wing symbol on Red Wing shoes and Red Wing pottery. The best way to get to know the city is on foot: Follow the "Three Walking Tours of Red Wing Architecture" put out by the Red Wing Heritage Preservation Commission, 651/388-6734. Each self-guided tour takes about 45 minutes. And yes, you can buy Red Wing shoes, boots, and work shoes at the Red Wing Shoe Store and visit the Red Wing Shoe Museum in Riverfront Centre (314 Main Street, 651/388-8211). Red Wing is at the junction of U.S. Highways 61 and 63 and MN 58. For additional area information, stop at the visitors center, 418 Levee St., 800/498-3444, www.redwing.org and www.prettyredwing.com.

RED WING SIGHTSEEING HIGHLIGHTS

★★★★ BARN BLUFF
E. Fifth St., Red Wing, 800/498-3444
You haven't really done Red Wing until you've hiked up Barn Bluff in the footsteps of Henry David Thoreau, who walked here and recorded the plant life. The bluff is included in the National Register of Historic Places. Trails offer two routes to the summit.
Details: Free. (1–2 hours)

★★★★ GOODHUE COUNTY MUSEUM
1166 Oak St., Red Wing, 651/388-6024
On a bluff above the city, Goodhue County Museum exhibits Red Wing pottery, a diorama of Chief Red Wing's Dakota village, Dakota artifacts, and more.
Details: Open Tue–Fri 10–5, Sat–Sun 1–5. $2, under 16 free. (30 minutes–1 hour)

★★★ **RED WING POTTERY SALESROOM**
1995 W. Main St., Red Wing, 800/228-0174
In the old pottery district at the Red Wing Pottery Salesroom, you can watch a potter create traditional salt-glazed pottery as it was done in the 1800s. Pottery, dinnerware, and glassware are sold in the main room. The **Historic Pottery Place Mall**, on U.S. 61 at the Withers

RED WING

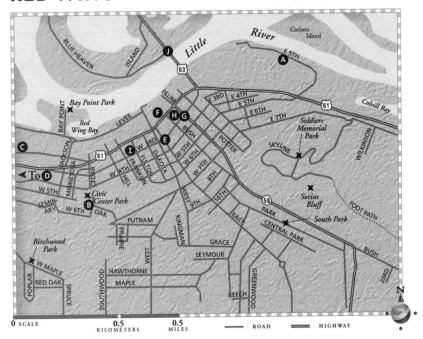

SIGHTS
Ⓐ Barn Bluff
Ⓑ Goodhue County Museum
Ⓒ Red Wing Pottery Sales Room
Ⓓ Red Wing Stoneware Company
Ⓔ Sheldon Performing Arts Theatre

FOOD
Ⓕ Blue Plate Cafe
Ⓖ Liberty's Restaurant and Lounge
Ⓕ Port of Redwing Restaurant
Ⓗ Staghead
Ⓖ Veranda Restaurant

LODGING
Ⓘ Candlelight Inn
Ⓕ St. James Hotel

CAMPING
Ⓙ Island Campground and Marina

Note: Items with the same letter are located in the same place.

Drive exit, occupies the original Red Wing pottery factory. *Details: Open daily. Free. (30 minutes–1 hour)*

★★★ RED WING STONEWARE COMPANY
4909 Moundview Dr., Red Wing, 651/388-4610
This company makes Red Wing stoneware and has a viewing window. *Details: Tours weekdays at 1. Salesroom open daily 10–5. Free. (15 minutes–1 hour)*

★★ SHELDON PERFORMING ARTS THEATRE
Third St. and East Ave., 800/899-5759 or 651/385-3667
Performing arts and events happen in this grandly restored historic 1904 theater. Catch the multimedia show and tour. *Details: Tours offered June–Oct Thu–Sat 1, Nov–May Sat 1. $1–$2.50, under 5 free. (1 hour)*

GREAT RIVER ROAD SIGHTSEEING HIGHLIGHTS

★★★★ ALMA AREA
WI 35, 608/658-3330 or 608/658-4975
All of Alma—two streets wide and seven miles long—is a historic district. There are several restored historic bed-and-breakfasts, terraced rock gardens and stairs connecting streets, antique shops, a viewing tower at Lock and Dam #4, and a museum on Second Street. You can get a good view of the lock, dam, dike, river islands, and the Upper and Lower Wiggle Waggle Sloughs from **Buena Vista Park**: Take County Highway E from WI 35 in Alma. Migrating tundra swans by the thousands stop to feed at **Rieck's Lake Park** on their fall migration from mid-October through early November. Bald eagles winter here, and blue herons and egrets live here in the summer. The park is on the east side of WI 35 on Buffalo Slough, about three miles north of Alma.

The nine-mile drive from Alma to Nelson is especially scenic. Tour the **Nelson Cheese Factory**, 715/673-4725, on WI 35, sample the cheese, and treat yourself to one of their generous ice-cream cones. If you haven't experienced Wisconsin cheese curds, this is the place to try them.

North of Nelson about seven miles on WI 35, the town of Pepin overlooks Lake Pepin, a 22-mile-long lake in the Mississippi, and is the birthplace of Laura Ingalls Wilder. A log cabin has been erected at her birth site, seven miles from Pepin on County Highway CC. Stop at the **Pepin Historical Museum**, 306 Third St., Pepin, 715/442-3161, for local history and Wilder memorabilia.

Details: Alma is on WI 35, nine miles south of Nelson and 16 miles south of Pepin. (1–4 hours)

★★★★ TREMPEALEAU

Chamber of Commerce: 24436 Third St., 608/534-6780

Walk Trempealeau's downtown historic district, then go to **Perrot State Park**, 608/534-6409, the site of French explorer Nicholas Perrot's 1665 trading post, and hike the steep trails for panoramic views. There are burial/ceremonial mounds in the 1,400-acre park and views of Trempealeau Mountain from the swimming and camping area. **Trempealeau National Wildlife Refuge**, 608/539-2311, is north of Perrot State Park on 5,700 acres and offers a five-mile auto tour, half-mile nature trail, an observation deck overlooking the marsh, and a wheelchair-accessible interpretive prairie trail.

Details: WI 35, north and west of Onalaska and north of I-90, at the confluence of the Trempealeau and Mississippi Rivers. (half–full day)

BLUFF TRAIL OVERLOOKING TREMPEALEAU

Alice Vollmar

★★★ STOCKHOLM
WI 35, 715/442-2015

This artists' community, west of Pepin seven miles on WI 35, uses the well-preserved buildings of western Wisconsin's oldest Swedish settlement. You can stay in the restored 1867 **Merchants Hotel**; buy quilts at the **Amish Country Store**, 800/247-7657; see Swedish settlers' memorabilia at the **Stockholm Institute Museum** in the old post office; and eat lunch at the tiny hamlet's Bogus Creek, Star, or Stockholm cafés. Or pack lunch and picnic in the gardens with river views and a rose arbor at **Rush River Produce**, 715/594-3648, where you can pick fat blueberries or black raspberries. A short drive away, pick your own wildflower bouquet on 16 blooming acres at **Blossom Hill Wildflowers**, 715/448-2817, and stock up on seeds.
Details: (Half–full day)

★★★★ WABASHA
U.S. 61 and MN 60, Chamber of Commerce: 800/565-4158

In this venerable river city, most of the brick buildings downtown date prior to 1900. Once home to fur traders, the city's economic history includes lumber, milling, and boat-building. A historic downtown walking-tour booklet is available at the city library, 168 Allegheny Ave., 651/565-3927. At the **Eagle Watch Observatory**, City Deck off MN 60E on the riverbank, 800/565-4158 or 651/565-4989, bundle up and watch for the bald eagles that winter in the Wabasha/Reads Landing area. A short drive away, near Kellogg, is **L.A.R.K. Toys and the Meadowlark Shops** (Lark Ln., north of the junction of U.S. 61 and MN 42; 507/767-3387; www.larktoys.com). Owner Dan Kreofsky started carving toys in his garage back in 1983, and his passion eventually grew into a fantastically successful business. Take a ride on a hand-carved moose and other critters on the L.A.R.K. carousel.
Details: (3–4 hours)

★★★ WINONA
U.S. 61/14, Convention and Visitors Bureau: 67 Main St. 800/657-4972

Between 500-foot-high bluffs and the Mississippi River, this city of 25,000 presents an architecturally intriguing face: elaborate Victorian mansions and quaint houses, church spires and domes, and imposing

GREAT RIVER ROAD

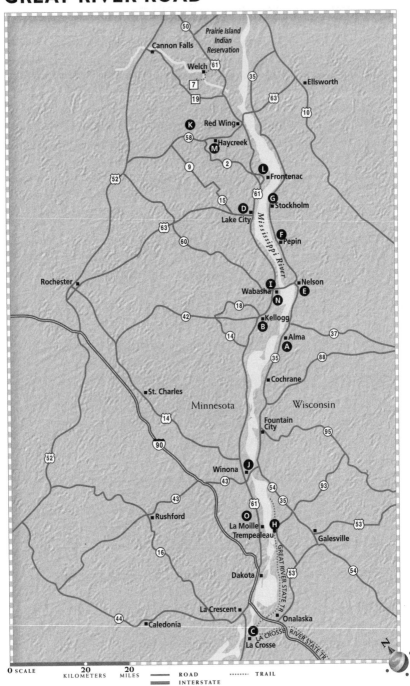

Prairie Island Indian Reservation

50

Cannon Falls

Welch 61

7

19

Ellsworth

35

63

10

K Red Wing

58

M Haycreek

9

2

52

L Frontenac

61

15 G Stockholm

D

Lake City

63

60

F Pepin

Rochester

Wabasha I Nelson

N E

42

18

14

Kellogg

B

37

Alma

A

88

Cochrane

St. Charles

Minnesota   Wisconsin

Fountain
City

14

95

90

52

Winona J

43

54

43

93

61

35

Rushford

O H

53

La Moille
Trempealeau   Galesville

16

Dakota

53

54

La Crescent

Onalaska

44 Caledonia

C

La Crosse

LA CROSSE RIVER STATE TR.

GREAT RIVER STATE TR.

Mississippi River

N

O SCALE   20   20
        KILOMETERS   MILES   ——— ROAD   ········ TRAIL
                        ═══ INTERSTATE

business-district edifices including a Richardsonian Romanesque courthouse and a Beaux Arts Exchange Building.

Hike the trails in **Garvin Heights Park**, Huff St. past U.S. 14/61, for a grand view of the city and river. To see more than 500 plants in bloom, go to **C. A. Rohrer Rose Garden**, east of the band shell in Lake Park, between Huff Street and Mankato Avenue. The fortresslike 1915 **Winona Armory Museum**, 160 Johnson St., 800/657-4972 or 507/454-2723, holds a stained-glass exhibit, carriages, wagons, sleighs, and local historical displays. In **Great River Bluffs State Park**, 16 miles southeast of Winona on U.S. 14/61, 507/643-6849, blackberries are ripe for picking in August. King's Bluff Nature Trail leads through prairie to a scenic overlook in the 3,000-acre park.

Details: (3–4 hours)

★★ **LA CROSSE**
I-90/U.S. 53/WI 35, Convention and Visitors Bureau: 410 E. Veterans Memorial Dr., 800/658-9424 or 608/782-2366
In this bustling crossroads city of 51,000, the *La Crosse Queen* sternwheeler, 608/784-2893 or 608/784-8523, gives river rides and weekend dinner cruises. **Heilman Brewery**, 1111 S. Third St.,

SIGHTS
Ⓐ Alma
Ⓑ Kellogg
Ⓒ La Crosse
Ⓓ Lake City
Ⓔ Nelson
Ⓕ Pepin
Ⓖ Stockholm
Ⓗ Trempealeau
Ⓘ Wabasha
Ⓙ Winona

FOOD
Ⓘ Anderson House
Ⓗ Ed Sullivan's
Ⓗ Historic Trempealeau Hotel
Ⓙ Hot Fish Shop

FOOD (continued)
Ⓙ Natural Habitat Coffee House
Ⓖ Stockholm Café

LODGING
Ⓙ AmericInn Winona
Ⓘ Anderson House
Ⓘ Bridgewaters Bed and Breakfast
Ⓘ Carriage House Bed and Breakfast
Ⓙ Days Inn Winona
Ⓗ Historic Trempealeau Hotel
Ⓚ Hungry Point Inn
Ⓗ Pleasant Knoll Motel

CAMPING
Ⓛ Frontenac State Park
Ⓜ Hay Creek Valley Campground
Ⓗ Perrot State Park
Ⓝ Pioneer Campsite
Ⓞ Winona KOA

Note: Items with the same letter are located in the same place.

800/433-BEER or 608/782-BEER, easily identified by its giant six-pack, offers hourly tours and tasting; and the **Swarthout Museum** (112 Main St., 608/782-1980) preserves local history.

Details: *(2 hours)*

★★ LAKE CITY
U.S. 61/63, Chamber of Commerce: 212 S. Washington St., 800/369-4123

In 1922 Ralph Samuelson invented the sport of waterskiing when he lashed boards to his feet and got a motorboat to pull him across Lake Pepin. In the town named for this lake you'll find a large marina, golf, yacht excursions, and charters. Get a "Historic Walking Tour" guide from the Chamber of Commerce. Take time to stop at **Wild Wings,** two miles south of Lake City on U.S. 61, 800/248-7312, a gallery and catalog showroom featuring wildlife art, sculpture, and carvings. A short drive away, in **Frontenac State Park**, U.S. 61, 10 miles southeast of Red Wing on Lake Pepin, 651/345-3401, the Havana Ridge Sites date from the Hopewellian Indian culture (400 B.C. to A.D. 300). The picturesque park has highlands, lowlands, and 15 miles of hiking trails.

Details: *(1–2 hours)*

FITNESS AND RECREATION

Head for the plentiful state parks to hike, ski, and bike; or jog and walk in the town and city parks. Winona has a five-mile walking/biking path around Lake Winona. And Red Wing's walking tours are exercise! Near Red Wing, the **Cannon Valley Trail** is a 19.7-mile recreational trail for biking, skiing, hiking, in-line skating, and skateboarding; a $2 wheel pass or ski pass is required, except for wheelchair users and pedestrians (507/263-3954). Access the trail near the corner of Bench and Old West Main Streets in Red Wing or from lower A. P. Anderson Park off U.S. 61.

Two Wisconsin state bicycle trails intersect in La Crosse: the **Great River State Trail**, 608/534-6409, running north to Trempealeau and Perrot State Park; and **La Crosse River State Trail**, 608/337-4775, going east along the La Crosse River to Sparta.

You can explore the river via **Great River Houseboat Rental**, 1009 E. Main St., Wabasha, 651/565-3376. If golf is more your style, try the 18 holes at **Mount Frontenac Golf Course** off U.S. 61, 651/388-5826, or the 27 holes at Red Wing's scenic **Mississippi National Golf Links**, 651/388-

1874. In winter, go downhill skiing at **Mount Frontenac**, 800/488-5826 or 651/345-3504.

Red Wing's **Ole Miss Marina**, Bay Point Park, 651/388-8643 or 651/388/9703, has electricity, water, security, and showers. The marina in Lake City, 800/369-4123, moors 600 boats and includes shower facilities, electricity, and water on all docks; a launching ramp; crane; and night security. There are also boat charters, yacht cruises, and fish-cleaning facilities.

FOOD

Walleye fried in a secret batter is the big seller at Winona's **Hot Fish Shop**, 965 Mankato Ave., 507/452-5002, with meals from $8 to $15. **Natural Habitat Coffee House**, 451 Huff St., Winona, 507/452-7020, serves gourmet coffee and espresso, soups, salads, and vegetarian food. Wabasha's **Anderson House**, 333 W. Main, 800/535-5467, serves Pennsylvania Dutch fare from $7 to $15—try the chicken and dumplings, double Dutch fudge pie, or breakfast scrapple. In Stockholm, the **Stockholm Café**, 151 WI 35, 715/442-5162, features catfish cheeks, Swedish potato sausage, and other regional delicacies for $4 to $10, and serves lunch daily.

The **Historic Trempealeau Hotel**, 608/534-6898, dates to the 1800s and has large salads, homemade bread, and good vegetarian walnut burgers for $5 to $11. Between Trempealeau and Perrot State Park, **Ed Sullivan's**, on the Mississippi on Sullivan Rd., 608/534-7775, has river views, an Irish theme, brown-bread muffins, and lots of fish, steamed or batter-fried, from $8 to $15.

Port of Red Wing Restaurant, in Red Wing's historic, classy St. James Hotel, 406 Main St., 800/252-1875 or 651/388-2846, serves well-prepared food in the $19 to $24 range. There's outdoor summer dining in the hotel's more casual **Veranda Restaurant**. The town's **Liberty's Restaurant and Lounge** is a lively gathering place on Third and Plum Streets, 612/388-8877, with meals from $6 to $17. For informal dining, try Red Wing's **Blue Plate Cafe**, 416 Third St., 651/388-7573. Local folks have good things to say about the food at **Staghead**, 219 Bush St., 651/388-6581. The restaurant features a changing menu, fresh fish daily, plus pastas, sirloin, and chicken from $7 to $18.

LODGING

In Red Wing, the **St. James Hotel**, 406 Main St., 800/252-1875, has antique-furnished rooms, the morning newspaper and coffee at your door, and rates from $80 to $170. The **Candlelight Inn**, at 818 W. Third, 651/388-8034, pampers guests and offers rates from $85 to $145.

BARGAIN TOWBOATS

Towboats on the Mississippi River push rather than pull their tows. Tows are made up of barges: Each barge can carry 1,500 tons, equal to the cargo of 58 trucks. You'll see tows of 12 to 15 barges (up to 22,500 tons!) on the Mississippi, often hauling grain downriver to be shipped abroad from New Orleans.

You'll stay in a house built 1750s-Colonial-style at **Hungry Point Inn**, 1 Olde Deerfield Rd., Welch, MN, 651/388-7857 or 651/437-3660. The inn comes with authentic furnishings and woolen bed covers, and serves a great breakfast with homemade bread and hash browns. Rates are $75 to $145.

Wabasha's **Anderson House**, 333 W. Main St., 800/535-5467, has antique furnishings, a cat for your room, and rates from $50 to $139. Reserve the cat, as well as the room. Or stay at Wabasha's **Bridgewaters Bed-and-Breakfast**, 136 Bridge Ave., 800/684-6813, in a 1903 Queen Anne–style house with a wrap-around porch and leaded glass. Rates are $70 to $145.

In Winona, the **Carriage House Bed-and-Breakfast**, 420 Main St., 507/452-8256, is an authentic three-story carriage house. Rates range from $70 to $110. Winona motels include the **Days Inn**, 420 Cottonwood Dr., 800/329-7466; **AmericInn Winona**, 60 Riverview, 800/634-3444, with river views, indoor pool, and continental breakfast for $65 to $95.

In Trempealeau, try the **Historic Trempealeau Hotel,** 150 Main St., 608/534-6898. A European-style small hotel, it has spartan furnishings and a bath down the hall. Its no-frills rooms cost $30 to $35 per night. There are also two whirlpool suites in a historic house on the property which go for $100 to $120. Unfortunately, an active railroad track hugs the riverbank nearby. For less train clatter and rooms for $40 to $59, stay at **Pleasant Knoll Motel**, 11451 Main St., 608/534-6615. Or try the **Sonic Motel** in nearby Coalesville, 608/582-2281. Rates run $36 to $43.

CAMPING

Perrot State Park, near Trempealeau, 608/534-6409, has 96 sites (36 with electricity), showers, a nature center, and more than six miles of hiking trails. **Frontenac State Park**, 651/345-3401, seven miles northwest of Lake City on U.S. 61/63, has 58 drive-in sites, electricity hookups, showers, and flush toilets. Reservations are advised. **Winona KOA**, six miles southeast of Winona on U.S. 14/61, 507/454-2851, has 70 sites, an outdoor pool, free hot showers, hiking trails, and organized weekend activities from April 15 to October 31. **Hay Creek Valley Campground**, six miles south of Red Wing on Highway 58, 888/388-3998 or 651/388-3998, has 100 sites, electricity and water, flush toilets, and laundry for $15 per night. **Island Campground and Marina**, 2361 Hallquist Ave., 715/792-2502, is on the Mississippi River opposite downtown Red Wing, under the Eisenhower Bridge off U.S. 63. It has 50 RV and tent sites for $16 to $19, showers, 70 boat slips, and a boat launch. **Pioneer Campsite** in Wabasha, 651/565-2242, offers 200 sites, showers, organized activities, and a pool.

NIGHTLIFE AND SPECIAL EVENTS

Festivals include **Water Ski Days** at Lake City in June, 800/369-4123; **Riverboat Days Festival** in Wabasha in July, 800/565-4158; **Mark Twain Festival** over the Labor Day weekend in Alma, 608/685-3330; and **Polish Heritage Days** in May and **Steamboat Days** on the July Fourth weekend in Winona, 800/657-4972. Vendors sell Red Wing pottery and much more during the **Antique Rendezvous** in Red Wing in July, 800/498-3444. Also in Red Wing, the Prairie Island Dakota community invites the public to the July **Prairie Island Powwow**, 651/385-2554.

Winona has band concerts in Lake Park every Wednesday evening in summer. Wabasha has a **Meet Me Under the Bridge** summer concert series at seven on Friday evenings in Heritage Square Park. In Red Wing, July concerts take place in Central Park on Wednesday evenings at seven; and the **Sheldon Theatre**, 800/899-5759 or 651/385-3667, hosts events throughout the year.

Apple Blossom Drive

La Crescent offers an eight-mile drive of spectacular beauty on the bluffs above the Mississippi. For the best in blossoms, make the drive around the Mother's Day weekend. Late September brings views of trees heavy with red fruit. Pull off the road to fully enjoy the view—you'll see horses and cattle grazing in lush green pastures, with the meandering Mississippi River visible in the distance.

If you are coming from the Bluff Country, follow MN 16 east from Lanesboro. It will bring you to La Crescent. Head west into town on North Fourth Street, then turn north on Elm Street/County Highway 29, which becomes the Apple Blossom Drive. To get back to U.S. 61, turn east at the junction with County Highway 12. To cross the river into La Crosse, take U.S. 61 south and follow it east across the river.

If you happen to be here in mid-September, you might catch festivities related to La Crescent's annual **Apple Festival**, 800/926-9480. Some of the orchards offer tours, and Apple Fest officials wearing red blazers greet visitors at the beer tent next to the midway. Other tents sell freshly baked apple pies with homemade sugar-sprinkled tan crusts peaked high over mounds of cinnamon-laced fruit. And, of course, there are apples—roadside stands overflow with baskets of them.

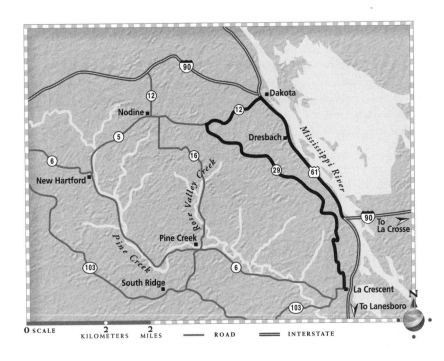

INDIANHEAD COUNTRY

Northwestern Wisconsin's Indianhead Country embraces forested ridges and valleys, gently rolling farmlands, and lakes of all sizes. The region's lakes and rivers are noted for good fishing and for their scenic beauty. Thankfully, Indianhead has escaped heavy tourism; even the resort areas retain a community identity. Artists and rugged individualists squirrel away here, carving, firing their kilns, and painting. This chapter highlights a handful of smaller communities in the Indianhead region that fit nicely into a circle tour starting in Rice Lake and heading northeast to Birchwood; north to Stone Lake; west to Spooner; south to Shell Lake, Barronett, and Cumberland; and finally east to Rice Lake.

If you are coming from Red Wing, take U.S. 63 for 74 miles to Turtle Lake. Go east on U.S 8 for 20 miles to U.S. 53. Follow U.S. 53 about nine miles north to Rice Lake. An enjoyable route from the Twin Cities follows I-35W or I-35E north to U.S. 8 at Forest Lake. Take U.S. 8 east to Taylors Falls/Interstate Park, cross the Mississippi to St. Croix Falls, and continue on U.S. 8 for about 36 miles to U.S. 53. Go north to Rice Lake.

A PERFECT DAY IN INDIANHEAD COUNTRY
Start the day early with pancakes at Maxine's in Rice Lake. Pick up Wisconsin cheeses and accompaniments at Miller's Cheese House or Tuscobia Cheese,

INDIANHEAD COUNTRY

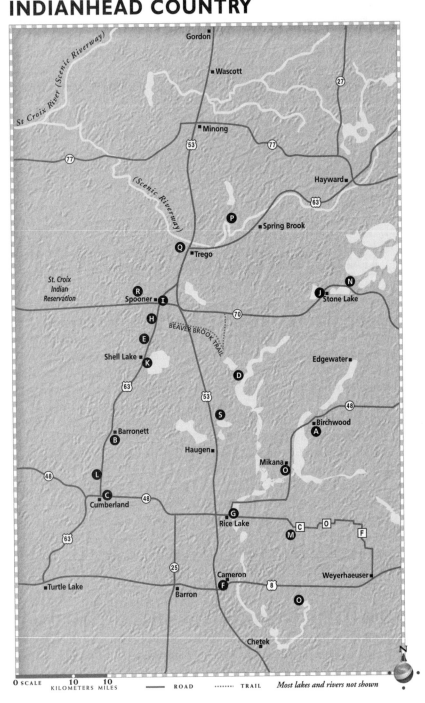

St Croix River (Scenic Riverway)

Gordon

Wascott

27

Minong

53

77

77

Hayward

63

(Scenic Riverway)

P

Spring Brook

Q

Trego

St. Croix
Indian
Reservation

R

Spooner

I

N

J

Stone Lake

70

H

BEAVER BROOK TRAIL

E

Shell Lake

K

Edgewater

63

D

53

48

S

Birchwood

A

Barronett

B

Haugen

Mikana

O

48

L

C

Cumberland

48

G

Rice Lake

63

C

O

F

M

25

Cameron

Weyerhaeuser

Turtle Lake

F

8

Barron

O

Chetek

N

0 SCALE   10   10
       KILOMETERS MILES   —— ROAD   ········ TRAIL   *Most lakes and rivers not shown*

pack a knapsack with food and water, and head for the Blue Hills. Hike the trail leading from Murphy Dam, then stop for a picnic lunch before returning to your car. Browse a few antique shops in Rice Lake. Eat dinner at Lehman's Supper Club and go to the Red Barn for Hardscrabble Players summer theater or, if it's Thursday, catch the free concert in Rice Lake City Park.

RICE LAKE SIGHTSEEING HIGHLIGHTS

★★★★ HUNT HILL AUDUBON SANCTUARY
Audubon Rd., 715/635-6543

In the Sarona/Long Lake area, visit a 500-acre sanctuary with a mature maple, basswood, and oak forest; groves of pines; meadows; black spruce and tamarack bogs; and two lakes. Sundew and pitcher plants grow in Dory's Bog. There are nature trails and environmental education programs.

Details: *Follow U.S. 53 north from Rice Lake, go east .7 mile on*

SIGHTS
- **A** Birchwood
- **B** Brickyard Pottery and Glassworks
- **B** Carousel Creations
- **C** Cumberland
- **D** Hunt Hill Audubon Sanctuary
- **E** Museum of Woodcarving
- **B** Odden's Norsk Husflid
- **F** Pioneer Village Museum
- **G** Rice Lake Antique Shops
- **G** Rice Lake Cheese Houses
- **H** Schaefer Apiaries
- **I** Spooner
- **J** Stone Lake
- **K** Washburn County Historical Museum Complex

FOOD
- **L** 5 O'clock Club
- **M** Blue Hills Inn Supper Club
- **B** Carousel Café
- **C** Coffee Cup Café
- **B** Lehman's Supper Club & Cocktail Lounge
- **N** Maximilian Inn
- **G** Maxine's Family Restaurant
- **B** Spanky's Supper Club
- **N** Stout's Restaurant
- **C** Tower House

LODGING
- **I** American Heritage Inn
- **K** Aqua Vista Resort/Motel
- **O** Canoe Bay Inn & Cottages
- **G** Currier's Lakeview Resort Motel

LODGING (continued)
- **C** Island Inn Motel
- **J** Lake House Bed and Breakfast
- **C** Rectory Bed and Breakfast
- **N** Stout's Lodge, Island of the Happy Days
- **P** Stout Trout Bed and Breakfast
- **G** Super 8 Motel, Rice Lake

CAMPING
- **Q** Bay Park Resort & Campground
- **R** Highland Park Campground
- **S** Rice Lake-Haugen KOA
- **K** Shell Lake Municipal Campground

Note: Items with the same letter are located in the same place.

County Hwy. D to the "T" at Pavlas Lake. Turn left on County Hwy. P, go .2 mile, then right 3.4 miles on Audubon Rd. Open daily dawn–dusk. Donation. (1 hour minimum)

★★★ PIONEER VILLAGE MUSEUM
Cameron, 800/523-6318

Among the 21 furnished pioneer buildings, you'll encounter a "whistle stop" depot, blacksmith shop, and farmstead. There's also a machinery building and three display buildings.

Details: 1½ miles west of Cameron, on Museum Rd. and County Hwy. W. Open June–Labor Day Thu–Sun 1–5. (30 minutes–1 hour)

★★★ RICE LAKE CHEESE HOUSES

At the edge of town, **Miller's Cheese House** carries 70 varieties of Wisconsin cheese, plus honey, fudge, rag rugs, and more. At **Tuscobia Cheese** you can walk into the chilly "cold room" of this 1906 former cheese factory to sample slices cut from wheels of a variety of cheeses.

Details: Miller's Cheese House: One mile north of Rice Lake on WI 48E, 800/677-4144 or 715/234-4144. Tuscobia Cheese: About five miles north on U.S. 53 or County Hwy. SS, then west on 26th Ave.; 715/234-2506. (30 minutes–1 hour)

★★ RICE LAKE ANTIQUE SHOPS

There are a number of shops in the area that specialize in antiques. See cookie cutters, furniture, and more at **Portals to the Past**, 613 N. Main St., 715/234-7530. In a restored 1893 home, **Nutmeg**, 120 W. Messenger, 715/234-4840, overflows with a mix of antique furniture, household items, quilts, dolls, and such.

Details: (45 minutes–1½ hours)

BIRCHWOOD/STONE LAKE SIGHTSEEING HIGHLIGHTS

★★★★ BIRCHWOOD/STONE LAKE
WI 48/WI 70, 800/236-2252

Quiet little Birchwood lies about 18 miles northeast of Rice Lake via WI 48. The small-town atmosphere and the people are the attractions in this town refreshingly short on upscale diversions. Long, shop-lined

Main Street leads to the **Birch Lane Inn** restaurant on Little Birch Lake at one end and to **The Porch** at the other. At The Porch, 715/354-7087, you can sip a cappuccino or order a Reuben pizza or a hearty sandwich. The menu is imaginative and the restaurant sometimes hosts musicians. The knotty-pine building is also home to an eclectic collection of wares: imported gourmet condiments, Mary Engelbreit cards, handmade regional crafts, and fun clothing. Nearby, at **Murly's Sports Hut**, the ultimate mom-and-pop resort-area shop, you'll find everything from minnows and tackle to moccasins and shirts. Also in town, and worth visiting, are the **Log Museum** and **Howard Morey Homestead**.

When you've finished touring Birchwood, head to Stone Lake. With a population of almost 300, Stone Lake courts a distinctly different resort community. Instead of a funky sports shop, you'll find quality antiques in quaint shops, a café or two, and a store specializing in custom-designed settings for precious gems and diamonds.

Details: (2 hours)

SPOONER AREA SIGHTSEEING HIGHLIGHTS

★★★★ SPOONER
U.S. 63/WI 70, Chamber of Commerce: 122 River St. 715/635-2168

Richly endowed with water, the Spooner area splashes in 300 lakes and unspoiled Namekagon River, part of the St. Croix National Scenic Riverway. Bass, walleye, and muskie fishing bring droves of anglers; canoeing, tubing, and other water-based activities also take center stage. Abundant waterfowl translate into upland and big-game hunting. There's also winter skiing and snowmobiling, and a state-of-the-art fish hatchery. Wisconsin Great Northern Railroad Excursions, 715/635-3200, offers a one-and-a-half-hour trip from the Spooner C&NW Depot to Trego Junction and back. Appropriately housed in the old C&NW depot, once the largest depot in northern Wisconsin, **Railroad Memories Museum**, Front St. behind the post office, 715/635-3325 or 715/635-2752, displays original passenger train cars, uniforms, hand tools, switch lights, watches, a model railroad display, and a video. Friendly retired railroad buffs lead the tours.

Details: (2¹/₂ hours)

SHELL LAKE/BARRONETT AREA SIGHTSEEING HIGHLIGHTS

★★★★ MUSEUM OF WOODCARVING
U.S. 63 N., Shell Lake, 715/468-7100

People come from around the world to this one-of-a-kind museum exhibiting life-size wooden figures. They show the life of Christ, and were carved by the late Joseph T. Barta.

Details: Open May–Oct daily 9–6. $2–$4. (30 minutes–1 hour)

★★★ BRICKYARD POTTERY AND GLASSWORKS
Barronett, 715/468-7341

This renovated 1921 brick school building has a pottery studio, a glass studio, and a sales gallery. The building houses the work of Brian and Mary Dosch and Pamela Savas, as well as that of other regional artists.

Details: One mile north of Barronett, just west of U.S. 63. Open Memorial Day–Dec daily 10–5. Free. (30–45 minutes)

★★★ CAROUSEL CREATIONS
Barronett, 715/822-4189

Here, in tiny downtown Barronett, Ron Helstern carves carousel animals complete with his trademark heart and other custom carving work. His wife, Sue Helstern, does the painting. There's a viewing window in the studio. The Helsterns' carousel horses also cavort next door in the Carousel Café.

Details: (10–30 minutes)

★★★ ODDEN'S NORSK HUSFLID
Barronett, 715/822-8747 or 715/468-7624

Across the road from Carousel Creations, a troll grins outside a store selling Scandinavian and European imports such as Brio toys; knits by Selbu, In-Wild, and Norstrikk; and crystal, pewter, linens, and lace. It's also the showroom for Norsk Woodwork's handcarved furniture, including *kubbestul* chairs carved out of solid pieces of basswood.

Details: Open June–Jan Mon–Sat 9:30–5, Fri until 8, Sun 12:30–4; Jan–June 10–4, Fri until 8. Free. (15–45 minutes)

★★★ WASHBURN COUNTY HISTORICAL MUSEUM COMPLEX

120 W. Second St., Shell Lake, 715/468-2982

You'll find a wealth of area history in this museum complex set in an 1888 church. See logging equipment and boats, and learn how practical pioneers turned dried corn husks into mattress stuffing and flour sacks into dishtowels. You can also reacquaint yourself with potato mashers and other kitchen/farm tools.

Details: *Open Memorial Day–Aug Wed–Sat 10–4. Free. (30 minutes–1 hour)*

★★ SCHAEFER APIARIES
U.S. 63, 715/468-7484

Schaefer sells Wisconsin honey, maple syrup, and beeswax candles, and has beekeeping exhibits.

Details: *Three to four miles south of Spooner on U.S. 63. Open mid-April–Dec Mon–Fri 10–5, Sat 10–5. Free. (20 minutes)*

CUMBERLAND SIGHTSEEING HIGHLIGHTS

★★★★ CUMBERLAND
Chamber of Commerce: 1277 Second Ave.
715/822-3378

Surrounded by water, Cumberland (population 2,163) bills itself as Island City. You'll find a delightful, unhurried atmosphere and walkable downtown streets with fun shops—it's quasi-tourist but small-town enough to be charming. The noon whistle still blows in this town, and **Louie's Finer Meats**, U.S. Hwy. 63 N., 715/822-4728, sells a remarkable variety of sausages perfect for lunch. All the meats, from hot and spicy Cajun sausage to award-winning *cotto* salami and Wisconsin sausage, are made on the premises from the market's own recipes. There are also meat loaves, salads, and pickles, plus Wisconsin products such as honey and wild rice, cherry mustard, and other condiments. Sausage samples are available if you can't make up your mind.

Details: *(10–45 minutes)*

FITNESS AND RECREATION

Hike the **Blue Hills Trails** and **Ice Age National Trail** east of Rice Lake in the undeveloped, hilly, and well-forested Blue Hills. The land is teeming with

WISCONSIN'S BLUE HILLS

Bring sturdy shoes and a day pack to experience the Blue Hills east of Rice Lake. The hills are actually isolated remnants of ancient mountains known as monadnocks. Once part of an extensive mountain range, the wooded hills cover more than 60,000 acres.

goldfinches and all manner of wildlife, including herons on the ponds and deer at dusk. Call Rusk County Information Center, 800/535-RUSK, for detailed maps of the region; or go to their Web site at www. wi.centuryinter.net/bluehills/index.htm.

Tuscobia State Trail, 715/634-6513 or 715/635-2101, longest of the state trails at 74 miles, winds through portions of Barron, Washburn, Sawyer, and Price Counties. A 12-mile section of the trail from Tuscobia to Birchwood is part of the Ice Age Scenic Trail and leads through mostly open farmland with a few pothole lakes. Along the trail, monarch butterflies flit above pink clover and sweet-scented wild roses. To walk or bike a segment of the cinder trail from the Rice Lake Area, follow County Highway SS north from WI 48. Drive out of town a few miles and watch for the Tuscobia Trail sign. Other hiking/cross-country ski trails include **Beaver Brook**, south of Spooner off Highway 53; **Nordic Woods**, east of Spooner off Highway 70; and **College Street Park** in Spooner.

Hay Lake Ranch Riding Stable, 715/766-2305, has horseback riding from $20 for one hour to $45 all day. It's north of Spooner off U.S. 63 and County Highway F, and is open daily from late April to mid-October.

For downhill skiing, drive to **Christie Mountain Ski Area**, 18 miles east of Rice Lake in the Blue Hills; 800/373-SNOW for ski conditions or 715/868-7800.

Golfers can try **Tagalong Golf Course** on Red Cedar Lake, 800/657-4843, with an 18-hole course and a nine-hole course patterned after St. Andrew's in Scotland. Other options are the 18-hole **Cumberland Golf Course**, two miles west of town off WI 48, 715/822-4333; and **Butternut Hills Golf Course** in Sarona/Long Lake, 715/635-8563, with 18 holes. **Bulik's Amusement Center**, a half mile north of Spooner on U.S. Highway 63, 715/635-7111, has waterslides, golf, a go-kart track, and a picnic area.

FOOD

Rice Lake's **Lehman's Supper Club & Cocktail Lounge,** 2911 S. Main St., 715/234-9911, features hand-cut steaks, hot popovers, and homemade soups. **Maxine's Family Restaurant,** 1721 S. Main St., 715/234-1662, is a pleasant restaurant with good buckwheat pancakes. Go to **Blue Hills Inn Supper Club,** County Hwy. C, 13 miles east of Rice Lake, 715/353-2326, for the woodland setting, homemade soups and bread, well-prepared food, and a North Woods fish boil.

Maximilian Inn, on WI 27/70 in Stone Lake, 715/865-2080, specializes in Continental-American cuisine. Order Wisconsin roast duck German style and four variations on schnitzel, for $10 to $20.

In Barronett on U.S. 63, **Spanky's Supper Club,** 715/822-2475, is a real find. Behind the unassuming exterior is a fine restaurant with a menu including filet mignon, walleye, and raspberry-braised chicken breast. Wonderful cheesecake is served with a dollop of whipped cream. Prices range from $5 to $30. Also in Barronett on U.S. 63, the **Carousel Café,** 715/822-4189, has soup, sandwiches, and light meals.

The **Coffee Cup Café,** 715/822-3858, in downtown Cumberland, has four tables, seats 20, and is open weekdays from early morning to three in the afternoon. Go there for good-natured banter between local customers, lunch platters for $4.50, and luscious blueberry pie. The **Tower House,** an 1882 mansion on Main Street in Cumberland, 715/822-8457, is a family-dining place with Italian food. For gourmet dining, go to **Stout's Restaurant** near Mikana, 715/354-3646; or try the **5 O'clock Club,** 715/822-2924, just over two miles north of Cumberland off U.S. 63.

LODGING

Canoe Bay Inn & Cottages, 800/568-1995 or 715/924-4594, on 280 acres of hardwood forest near Chetek, has been rated "one of the Midwest's top country inns" by the *Chicago Sun-Times.* Owners Dan and Lisa Dobrowolski pay careful attention to detail—from the room furnishings to the menu's breakfast croissants, egg soufflés, and other gourmet dishes. Rates range from $260 to $450. One friend of mine calls this "the ultimate bed-and-breakfast." In Stone Lake, the **Lake House Bed-and-Breakfast,** N5793 Division Ave., 715/865-6803, has four rooms and offers a full breakfast for $55 to $75. Near Springbrook, the **Stout Trout Bed-and-Breakfast,** 715/466-2790, has rooms for $65 on a quiet lake with adjacent woods, berry-picking, hiking, boating, and biking. They also offer free use of their boats and bicycles. The **Rectory Bed-and-Breakfast,** 1575 Second

COUDERAY

For an interesting taste of 1920s gangster life, visit Al Capone's Couderay estate known as the Hideout. The retreat's grounds overlook a lake at Couderay, Wisconsin, about 12 miles east of Stone Lake. To get there from Stone Lake, take WI 70/27 to County Highway E. Drive north to County Highway N, then east to County Highway CC. Continue east a block and a half to the estate entrance. Tours ($3.50 to $7.50, under 6 free) take in the main lodge, as well as a tower once manned by machine gun–toting guards. Lots of bus tours stop here, so chances are you'll have plenty of company. You'll also find museum displays about the 1920s, a restaurant, a gift shop, and an ice-cream parlor. Before setting out to discover Wisconsin's shadier side, call 715/945-2746 for more detailed information.

Ave., Cumberland, 715/822-3151, in a 1905 rectory, has an extensive library and rooms furnished with antiques; rates are $55 to $65. **Stout's Lodge, Island of the Happy Days**, one mile north of Mikana via WI 48, 715/354-3646, was lumber-wealth heir Frank Stout's family retreat, built with red cedar logs in 1903. There are perennial flower beds, hiking trails, and meals based on vegetables and herbs from the resort gardens. Rates range from $109 to $199.

At Rice Lake's **Super 8 Motel**, 2401 S. Main St., 800/800-8000 or 715/234-6956, double rooms range from $65 to $83. Also in town, **Currier's Lakeview Resort Motel**, 2010 E. Sawyer St., 800/433-5253 or 715/234-7474, is a Swiss chalet–style motel in a pleasant location, with rates from $49 to $69. In Shell Lake, **Aqua Vista Resort/Motel**, U.S. 63N and County Hwy. B, 800/889-2256 or 715/468-2256, has rooms from $69 to $100. At **Island Inn Motel**, U.S. 63N, Cumberland, 715/822-8540, rates are $47 to $57. **American Heritage Inn**, 101 Maple St., Spooner, 800/356-8018, has a pool, whirlpool, and sauna, and offers double rooms for $55 to $95.

CAMPING

Just west of Spooner is **Highland Park Campground**, 715/635-2462. It has 45 sites, a sandy beach, and rental boats. Thirty of the sites come with full hookups, while 15 include electricity and water. The campground is on Cyclone Lake and is open May through September 30. Rates are $19 to $20. **Shell Lake Municipal Campground**, on Shell Lake, 715/468-7846 or 715/468-7679, has a beach, 40 sites with electrical hookups and water, four tent sites, and showers. It's open Memorial Day through Labor Day and sites go for $16 each. Trego's **Bay Park Resort & Campground**, 715/635-2840, has 70 wooded campsites, including many with full hookups. **Rice Lake-Haugen KOA**, 715/234-2360, is on Devil's Lake, 10 minutes north of Rice Lake on U.S. 53. The campground has 104 sites, full hookups, water and electricity, a swimming pool, hiking trails, and boat and canoe rentals. Rates range from $19 to $25.

NIGHTLIFE AND SPECIAL EVENTS

Red Barn Theatre, two miles east of Rice Lake on WI 48, 715/234-8301, is home to the Hardscrabble Players and hosts summer-stock theater productions. **Music in the Parks,** 800/523-6318, sponsors free summer concerts on Thursday evenings in the band shell in Rice Lake City Park.

At the **Cranberry Festival**, 715/865-3302, held the first weekend in October in Stone Lake, contestants race down a steep hill in cranberry crates. You can see cranberries being harvested in the bogs; watch a parade; eat cranberry-laced ice cream, pancakes, or crandogs; and, naturally, buy cranberries by the pound.

Spooner celebrates **Jack Pine Savage Days**, 800/367-3306, in August with music, arts, carnival rides, horseshoes, and other competitions. The **Spooner Rodeo**, 800/367-3306, happens in July with a rodeo parade and competition, chicken barbecue, and a cowboy church service.

Indianhead Arts Center at the University of Wisconsin-Shell Lake, 715/468-2414, has a full summer concert schedule ranging from jazz and symphony concerts to keyboard and horn recitals. Also in Shell Lake, in September, **Town and Country Days**, 715/468-4477, is a five-day celebration with a street dance, sailboat regatta, parade, chainsaw woodcarving, a horse pull, a play, and musical concerts.

Cumberland hosts the **Rutabaga Festival**, 715/822-3378, the weekend before Labor Day. The festivities include a carnival, food, and well-known bands.

10
BAYFIELD AND
MADELINE ISLAND

On a forested Lake Superior peninsula, the quaint coastal town of Bayfield sits across a deepwater harbor from Madeline Island, the largest in the chain of 22 Apostle Islands. The area tolerates—and welcomes—a boisterous influx of summer tourists, but somehow maintains its relaxed, laid-back attitude.

Madeline Island Ferry Line transports people and cars back and forth between Bayfield and Madeline Island. On the island are sea caves to explore via canoe or kayak, a sandy beach, a historical museum, a few shops and lodging places, and a smattering of restaurants. You can unwind, hike, bike, picnic, and camp in Big Bay State Park or the town of LaPointe's Big Bay Town Park.

Madeline Island and Bayfield are part of the Apostle Islands National Lakeshore, which encompasses 21 islands and 12 miles of mainland shoreline with more lighthouses than any other U.S. coastline. You can explore Madeline Island along both north and south shore drives and via County Highway H. Other islands are accessible by water, and tours and a water-taxi service are available.

A PERFECT DAY IN BAYFIELD AND MADELINE ISLAND

Arrive in Bayfield, eat breakfast at the Egg Toss Cafe, and take a ferry to Madeline Island. Rent a kayak or canoe and paddle Big Bay, explore sea caves, then visit the Madeline Island Historical Museum. After a hike in Big Bay State Park, dine at the Inn on Madeline Island, watch the boats come in, and catch the sunset show. After a little lake watching, head for one of the best bargains in town: the well-tended Madeline Island Motel. Or pitch a tent in the island's city or state park campground and sleep under the star-filled night sky.

FERRY INFORMATION

To get to and from Madeline Island, you must take a 20-minute ferry ride between downtown Bayfield and downtown LaPointe. From spring ice breakup to fall freeze-up, the ferry runs daily beginning around seven in the morning. Trips run every hour or half hour from late June to early September, and take 20 minutes each way. One-way rates range from $1.75 (for a bike) to $9.25 (motor home) per vehicle and $2 to $3.50 per passenger. Contact Madeline Island Ferry Line, Bayfield/La Pointe, 715/747-2051, www.madferry.com.

APOSTLE ISLANDS NATIONAL LAKESHORE SIGHTSEEING HIGHLIGHTS

★★★★ APOSTLE ISLANDS CRUISE SERVICE
Bayfield City Dock, 800/323-7619 or 715/779-3925
www.apostleisland.com
This is a long-established cruise service with a range of options including a narrated grand tour of all 22 Apostle Islands, a taxi and shuttle service, kayak rentals, and sailing trips aboard the 54-foot historic wooden schooner, *ZEETO*.
Details: *Open May–Oct daily, reservations recommended. Prices vary with cruise; Grand Tour, $12–$23; trips on ZEETO, $45. (3 hours)*

★★★★ OTHER TOURS AND CRUISES
Trek and Trail, 800/354-8735, has guided kayak trips, sailing, biking, fly-fishing, and dogsledding. **Catchun-Sun Charters**, 888/724-5494 or 715/779-3111, has half- and full-day trips on a classic yacht sailing from Bayfield City Dock. Narrated **Madeline Island Bus Tours** out of LaPointe visit historic sites, Big Bay State Park, and more. Board the bus a half-block from the ferry landing (tours daily at 10:30 and 1, 715/747-2051). **Motion To Go**, 715/747-6585, rents mopeds, mountain bikes, and more in the blue building near the ferry dock.
Details: *(full day)*

BAYFIELD AREA SIGHTSEEING HIGHLIGHTS

★★★ APPLE ORCHARDS

More than 15 apple orchards are in the area. The farms also sell strawberries, raspberries, cherries, and blueberries. To go orchard-hopping,

BAYFIELD AREA

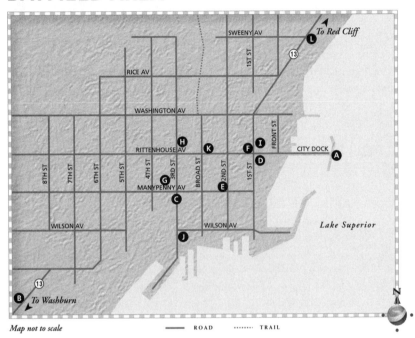

Map not to scale — ROAD ········ TRAIL

SIGHTS
Ⓐ Apostle Islands
   Cruise Service
Ⓑ Eckel's Pottery
Ⓒ Farmers Market

FOOD
Ⓓ Bayfield Inn
Ⓔ Egg Toss Cafe
Ⓕ Greunke's Restaurant

FOOD (continued)
Ⓖ Maggie's
Ⓗ Old Rittenhouse Inn

LODGING
Ⓓ Bayfield Inn
Ⓕ Greunke's First
   Street Inn
Ⓘ Hidden Cottage
Ⓗ Old Rittenhouse Inn

Ⓙ Reiten Boatyard
   Condominiums
Ⓚ Silvernail Guest House
Ⓛ Winfield Inn

Note: Items with the same letter are located in the same place.

follow County Highway I west from the Bayfield ferry dock, then turn right on County Highway J. A fun stop is **Hauser's Superior View Farm**, 715/779-5404, with pick-your-own apples, jams and jellies galore, luscious apple pies, and Jim Hauser's collection of 500-plus caps displayed in a 1928 Sears and Roebuck barn loft. You can also buy fruits, vegetables, herbs, and flowers on Saturdays at the Farmer's Market in town (corner of Manypenny and Third Street).

Details: *Contact the Bayfield Chamber of Commerce, 800/447-4094, for a map and complete listing of orchards. (2–3 hours)*

★★ ECKEL'S POTTERY
Hwy. 13, Bayfield, 715/779-5617

Painters, photographers, and other artists gravitate to this scenic region. Fine galleries display and sell their work, much of which is devoted to capturing the essence of the island and mainland. Visit Eckel's Pottery for handcrafted stoneware and porcelain.

Details: *Open daily year-round. Free. (20 minutes)*

★★ GOOD EARTH GARDENS
County Hwy. J, 715/779-5564

A field of flowers yields dried flowers available by the bunch, custom arrangements, and designer bouquets. You can also buy herbs and pick strawberries, blueberries, blackberries, and gooseberries in season.

Details: *Open summer Mon–Sat 8–5, winter by appointment. You can pick your own berries for $.95–$1.30 per pound. (15 minutes–1 hour)*

MADELINE ISLAND SIGHTSEEING HIGHLIGHTS

★★★★ BIG BAY STATE PARK
Madeline Island, County Hwy. H, 715/747-6425 or 715/779-4020

Wisconsin's northernmost state park contains sandstone bluffs with hollowed-out caves, nearly seven miles of hiking trails, picnic areas, and a sandy beach that stretches for more than a mile along Lake Superior. White-tailed deer live here, as do eagles. Reservations are recommended for the 60 primitive campsites.

Details: *Open daily 6–11. Park sticker required. (1 hour minimum)*

MADELINE ISLAND AND BAYFIELD AREA

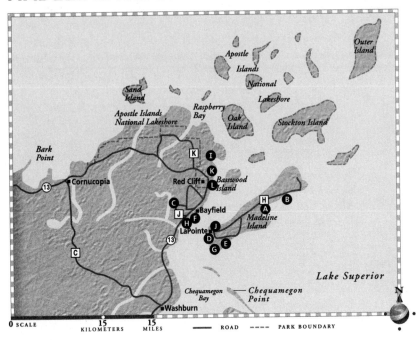

SIGHTS

- Ⓐ Big Bay State Park
- Ⓑ Big Bay Town Park
- Ⓒ Apple Orchards
- Ⓒ Good Earth Gardens
- Ⓓ Madeline Island Historical Museum
- Ⓓ Woods Hall Crafts Shop

FOOD

- Ⓔ The Clubhouse on Madeline Island
- Ⓓ Grandpa Tony's

FOOD (continued)

- Ⓕ Portside Bar and Restaurant
- Ⓖ Pub Bar & Restaurant
- Ⓓ Thirsty Sturgeon

LODGING

- Ⓗ Apostle View Inn
- Ⓓ Madeline Island Motel
- Ⓗ Pinehurst Inn on Pike's Creek
- Ⓘ Thimbleberry Inn
- Ⓙ Woods Manor

CAMPING

- Ⓗ Apostle Island Area Campground
- Ⓐ Big Bay State Park
- Ⓑ Big Bay Town Park
- Ⓚ Buffalo Bay Campground and Marina
- Ⓛ Dalrymple Campground

Note: Items with the same letter are located in the same place.

★★★★ BIG BAY TOWN PARK
Madeline Island, 888/475-3386 or 715/747-2685

This wooded park is operated by the town of LaPointe. You'll find a footbridge across the lagoon, a sandy beach, fishing and canoeing in the lagoon, and rustic campsites. Canoes, paddleboats, and rowboats are for rent at the park. From Big Bay you can paddle or row south to Long Island—a curved, elongated strip of land facing Chequamegon Bay—for blueberry-picking or fishing for smallmouth bass in the warm, shallow waters. The only building on Long Island is a lighthouse.

Details: Across the bay from Big Bay State Park. Boat rentals: $7.50 per hour, $25 half day, $35 full day. Rent by calling Bog Lake Outfitters, 715/747-2685. No fee for daily park use. (30 minutes minimum)

★★★ MADELINE ISLAND HISTORICAL MUSEUM
Colonel Woods Ave., La Pointe, 715/747-2415

Displays track three centuries of Madeline Island history—from ancient Ojibwa culture, fur trade, and missionaries to logging and maritime industries. Watch the 25-minute multimedia show for colorful historical details. Not far away, you can do a little historical "sleuthing" on your own, too. Near Ojibway Memorial Park is an old Indian burial ground (five blocks to the right of the ferry landing, behind the Madeline Island Yacht Club), part of an 1830s Catholic mission, with tombstones dated from 1840 to 1981. Quiet visitors are welcome.

Details: Open Memorial Day–early Oct daily 10–4, July 4–late Aug 10–6. $2–$4, under 6 free. (1–2 hours)

★★ WOODS HALL CRAFT SHOP
La Pointe, 715/747-3943

The craft shop is noted for handwoven rugs, handcrafted jewelry, pottery, and "rock people." The shop displays and sells the work of 50 craftspeople. It also provides a loom room, mudroom (with a kiln), and wood shop in which artisans can work.

Details: Three blocks south of the ferry landing, next to St. John's Church. Memorial Day–early Oct Mon–Sat 10–4, Sun 11–2. Free. (30 minutes)

FITNESS AND RECREATION

You can hike and bike in Big Bay State Park and Big Bay Town Park. You'll also find trails in the Madeline Island Wilderness Preserve/LaPointe inland woods, but first get yourself a map from the Chamber of Commerce. Other popular activities in the area are sailing, fishing, canoeing, kayaking, and swimming.

In winter, try skiing at **Mount Ashwabay Ski Area**, 715/779-3227. The resort has 13 downhill runs and 40 kilometers of cross-country trails. ATV trails and snowmobile trails abound throughout Bayfield County; call 800/GRAND-FUN for maps. Bayfield also has a pool and recreation facility, 715/779-5408, with a swimming pool, a whirlpool, and racquetball courts.

The **Madeline Island Golf Course**, 715/747-3212, on Madeline Island just south of the ferry landing, is an 18-hole Robert Trent Jones–designed Scottish links–style course. If you prefer to spend your days on the water, **Roberta's Sport Fishing**, 715/779-5744 or 612/462-8866, provides all the gear and light tackle you'll need for sportfishing.

FOOD

The restaurants in the area, offering a wide variety of foods, range from the award-winning to the funky and unusual. While most of the best dinners fall in the $8 to $24 range, there are exceptions: Try the renowned **Old Rittenhouse Inn**, 301 Rittenhouse Ave., Bayfield, 715/779-5111, which serves wonderful chilled fruit soups and a delicious hot Burgundy-raspberry soup. The cuisine is gourmet—local ingredients with a French touch—and dinner is offered for a set price of $45. A place to go for very special events is the **Clubhouse on Madeline Island**, 715/747-2612, overlooking the Madeline Island Golf Club and Yacht Club south of the ferry dock. It's expensive, but the food is gourmet, the menu is creative, and the wine list is outstanding.

The redone **Bayfield Inn**, 20 Rittenhouse Ave., Bayfield, 715/779-3363, has harbor views to compliment its good food. Nearby, **Greunke's Restaurant**, 17 Rittenhouse Ave., Bayfield, 715/779-5480, abounds in 1940s memorabilia. Try their Bayfield fruit desserts and Lake Superior whitefish. At **Maggie's**, 257 Manypenny Ave., Bayfield, 715/779-5641, you can dine on the area's prized whitefish livers in the company of pink flamingoes. They also serve delectable fried beets and summer squash cakes, and a good black beans-and-rice dish. Well-prepared food is standard at **Portside Bar & Restaurant**, Port Superior Marina, Bayfield, 715/779-5380. Go to **Egg Toss Cafe**, 41 Manypenny, 715/779-5181, for breakfast in Bayfield.

On Madeline Island, **Grampa Tony's**, a half block from the ferry on Main Street in LaPointe, 715/747-3911, has deli foods, gourmet coffee, salads, and limited entreés. Also in LaPointe, the **Thirsty Sturgeon**,

715/747-5777, serves creatively seasoned dishes and fresh seafood in a funky, tacked-together building. The Inn on Madeline Island's **Pub Bar & Restaurant**, four blocks south of the ferry landing, 715/747-6315, has good food and sunset views.

LODGING

The area's lodging options are bountiful and interesting. In the Bayfield area you'll find the **Old Rittenhouse Inn**, 301 Rittenhouse Ave., 715/779-5111. The restored 1890s Victorian mansion includes working fireplaces, Jacuzzis, and rates from $99 to $229. An 1880s restaurant/photo gallery is now **Silvernail Guest House**, 249½ Rittenhouse Ave., 715/779-5575. It comes with a Victorian ambiance and rooms ranging from $75 to $109. At the historic **Greunke's First Street Inn**, 17 Rittenhouse Ave., 800/245-3072 or 715/779-0200, guests enjoy a full breakfast and antiques-filled rooms for a moderate price (up to $110). On the Bayfield waterfront, **Reiten Boatyard Condominiums**, 800/842-1199, occupies the site of the old Halvor Reiten Boatyard. The bright and airy studios and suites range from $55 to $150. **Bayfield Inn**, 20 Rittenhouse Ave., 715/779-3363, is on the waterfront, with moderately priced rooms from $30 to $85. **Thimbleberry Inn**, on the Lake Superior shore, 715/779-5757, has island views, fireplaces, and rooms from $75 to $135. Tucked behind an antiques shop, **Hidden Cottage**, 20 N. First St., Bayfield, 715/779-3488, offers "a slice of paradise from the cake of heaven," according to an entry in the guest book. Rooms are $75 or more. On Highway 13 at the north edge of town, you'll find good, affordable rooms at the **Winfield Inn**, 715/799-3252. Another charming and well-priced find along the highway is **Apostle View Inn**, 715/779-3385, three miles south of town. In the same area, the Queen Anne–style **Pinehurst Inn at Pike's Creek**, 715/779-3676, has a full breakfast and rooms for $70 to $138.

Alice Vollmar

On Madeline Island, **Woods Manor**, two and a half miles from the ferry landing in LaPointe, 715/747-3102, is a grand summer home turned bed-and-breakfast with a tennis court, bikes, sauna, canoes, and a sandy beach on the lake. Rooms range from $119 to $209. Or try the **Madeline Island Motel**, 715/747-3000, two blocks east of the ferry landing in LaPointe. It's a pleasant, well-kept place with rooms for $40 to $80.

CAMPING

You can camp in the Apostle Islands' backcountry with a permit from the Apostle Islands National Lakeshore headquarters (Apostle Islands National Lakeshore, Rt. 1, Box 4, Bayfield, WI 54814; 715/779-3397). **Big Bay State Park**, 715/779-4020 or 715/747-6425, has 60 campsites, backpacking, a wheelchair-accessible picnic and camping area, swimming, boating, and hiking and cross-country skiing trails. **Big Bay Town Park**, 715/747-2801, across the bay from the state park, has a sandy beach and 45 rustic campsites for tents or RVs. No reservations are accepted, and rates are $9 to $13 per night. **Apostle Island Area Campground**, 715/779-5524, a half mile south of Bayfield on Highway 13 and County Road J, is a private area with 55 sites, a separate tenting area, two cabins, and pay showers. It's open from Memorial Day weekend to October 10, and rates are $12 to $22. **Dalrymple Campground**, one mile north of Bayfield on Highway 13, 715/779-5712, is a lovely, wooded campground with 30 rustic tent and RV sites. It's open from mid-May to mid-October. **Buffalo Bay Campground and Marina**, three miles north of Bayfield on Highway 13, 715/779-3743, offers 42 sites for $15 each.

NIGHTLIFE AND SPECIAL EVENTS

The **Lake Superior Big Top Chautauqua**, three miles south of Bayfield on Mount Ashwabay, 715/373-5552, hosts a variety of entertaining events including concerts, public radio programs, and musicals about the Apostle Islands region. Past celebrity guests at these summer events have included Emmylou Harris and Johnny Cash. In Bayfield, the 1870 Christ Church, 715/779-3401, hosts free chamber music concerts (with hors d'oeuvres and sherry on the lawn) every July and August on Thursday evenings at five. In late July the **Bayfield Festival of the Arts**, 800/447-4094, showcases the work of local metalsmiths, potters, painters, weavers, and woodworkers. It's held in Memorial Park or at the waterfront pavilion. **Red Cliff's Annual Powwow**, 715/779-3700, draws visitors to the Red Cliff Tribal Grounds on July Fourth. Other Independence Day celebrations include

Fireworks in Bayfield Harbor and Madeline Island's **Annual Parade and Fireworks**.

In September, the **Apostle Islands Lighthouse Celebration**, 715/779-5619 or 715/779-3925, features displays, lectures, and cruises with access to all of the lighthouses. The **Bayfield Wooden Boat and Maritime Heritage Fest** in mid-August and the **Annual Apple Festival** in early October are also great fun. Call the Bayfield Chamber of Commerce, 800/447-4094, for information on these and other festivals.

For gaming action, try the **Isle Vista Casino**, three miles north of Bayfield on Highway 13, 715/779-3712. Check a current issue of *Bayfield Scene* magazine for other happenings.

11
WISCONSIN'S
NORTH WOODS

Wisconsin's North Woods, in the state's northern midsection, has a color-ful history. About 62 miles southeast of Bayfield (via WI 13 and U.S. 2) lies Hurley, a once-bawdy and brawling town in mining and logging country. (See the Scenic Route at the end of this chapter.) Hard-drinking, rough-edged miners and loggers gave the town a reputation as one of the toughest places on earth. During Prohibition, 200 thinly disguised saloons in Hurley were fre-quented by big-name gangsters. South of Hurley about 30 miles, just off U.S. 51 on Little Star Lake in Manitowish Waters, bullet holes remain in the win-dows of Little Bohemia Lodge, remnants of a 1934 John Dillinger–FBI gun battle.

Before all this, in 1745, the Lac du Flambeau (Lake of the Torches) band of Ojibwe established a permanent settlement on the banks of Lac du Flambeau. Named by French explorers who saw the Ojibwe fishing by torchlight from birch-bark canoes, the lake and town bearing the same name (about 15 miles southeast of Manitowish on WI 47) are at the center of the contemporary Lac du Flambeau Indian Reservation. Forests and lakes make the area popular for skiing, hunting, fishing, snowmobiling, camping, and boating. Just 13 miles south-east of Lac du Flambeau, Minocqua sits at one end of the Bearskin State Trail. Northeast of Minocqua five miles, Arbor Vitae is in 222,000-acre Northern Highland–American Legion State Forest, which borders Minocqua and neigh-boring Woodruff.

NORTH WOODS AREA

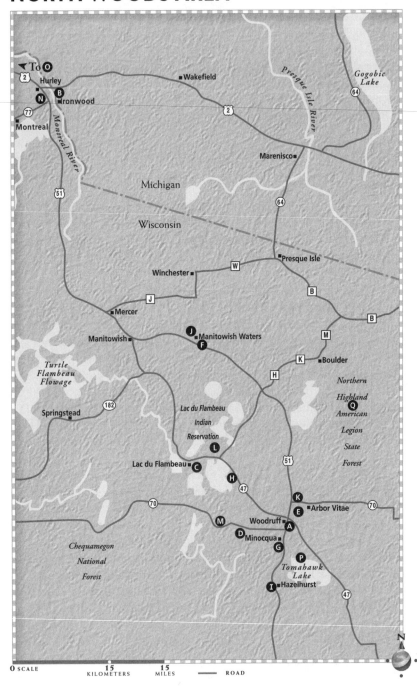

To **O**
Hurley
B Ironwood
N
Montreal
Montreal River
Wakefield
Presque Isle River
Gogobic Lake
Marenisco
Michigan
Wisconsin
Presque Isle
Winchester **W**
J
Mercer
J Manitowish Waters
F
Manitowish
B
B
M
Turtle Flambeau Flowage
K Boulder
H
Northern
Highland
Q
American
Legion
State
Forest
Lac du Flambeau Indian Reservation
Springstead
L
Lac du Flambeau **C**
H
47
51
70
K
E Arbor Vitae
70
Chequamegon National Forest
M
D Minocqua
Woodruff **A**
G
P
Tomahawk Lake
I Hazelhurst
47

O SCALE   **15** KILOMETERS   **15** MILES   —— ROAD

N

A PERFECT DAY IN THE NORTH WOODS

Start the day with a lumberjack breakfast at Paul Bunyan's Northwoods Cook Shanty, between Minocqua and Woodruff on U.S. 51; then head for Northern Highland–American Legion State Forest for some serious hiking or biking. Have a trailside picnic, then visit the Dr. Kate Pelham Newcomb Museum in Woodruff. Drive to Lac du Flambeau to visit the Ojibwe Museum and check out the action at the trout hatchery. Go to Hazelhurst and treat yourself to dinner at Jacobi's, then follow up your meal with a Northern Lights Playhouse production.

MINOCQUA-ARBOR VITAE-WOODRUFF SIGHTSEEING HIGHLIGHTS

★★★★ DR. KATE PELHAM NEWCOMB MUSEUM
923 Second Ave., Woodruff, 715/356-6896

SIGHTS

- **A** Dr. Kate Pelham Newcomb Museum
- **B** Iron County Historical Museum
- **C** George W. Brown Museum and Cultural Center
- **C** Lac du Flambeau Fish Hatchery
- **D** Northwoods Wildlife Center
- **A** Scheer's Lumberjack Show
- **E** Woodruff State Fish Hatchery
- **C** Waswagoning Ojibwe Village

FOOD

- **F** Blue Bayou Inn
- **G** Bosacki's Boathouse
- **H** Fence Lake Lodge

FOOD *(continued)*

- **G** Gaslight Cafe
- **I** Jacobi's
- **J** Little Bohemia Restaurant
- **A** Paul Bunyan's Cook Shanty
- **K** Plantation Supper Club
- **G** Polecat and Lace
- **A** S.A. Loons
- **G** Spangs Italian Restaurant

LODGING

- **G** AmericInn Motel Minocqua
- **G** Beacons of Minocqua
- **G** Best Western Lakeview Motor Lodge
- **L** Dillman's Sand Lake Lodge
- **M** Dream Catcher's Resort, L.L.C.

LODGING *(continued)*

- **N** Eagle Bluff Condo Rentals
- **H** Fence Lake Lodge Resort
- **N** The Inn
- **C** Lake of the Torches Casino Hotel
- **G** The Pointe Resort Hotel and Conference Center

CAMPING

- **O** Copper Falls State Park
- **M** Dream Catcher's Resort, L.L.C.
- **P** Indian Shores
- **C** Lac du Flambeau Tribal Campground
- **Q** Northern Highland-American Legion State Forest

Note: Items with the same letter are located in the same place.

This delightful museum tells the story of Woodruff's "Angel on Snowshoes," a doctor who reached her North Woods patients by snowshoe and snowplow. Displays include photos, her medical equipment and snowshoes, and a recount of the heartwarming million-penny collection launched by schoolchildren to help Dr. Kate build a hospital. Ralph Edwards heard about Dr. Kate and brought attention to her dedicated work on his television program, *This Is Your Life*. As a result, donations came and the hospital was built.

Details: *Mid-June–Labor Day Mon–Fri 11–4; special tours by appointment. Donation. (30 minutes–1 hour)*

★★★ NORTHWOODS WILDLIFE CENTER
8683 Blumstein Rd., Minocqua, 715/356-7400
This wildlife hospital and rehab facility cares for injured wildlife then returns them to the wild. Tours pass baby animals being fed in the nursery and follow outdoor trails to see permanently disabled animals including a bald eagle, a snowy owl, and hawks. Tours leave every half hour during summer. You can take impromptu tours in winter.

Details: *Off WI 70 W, across from Trig's shopping center. Open Memorial Day–Labor Day Mon–Sat 10–4, winter 10–2. Donation. (20 minutes–1 hour)*

★★★★ SCHEER'S LUMBERJACK SHOW
WI 47, Woodruff, 715/356-4050 or 715/654-5010
You'll learn about life during the lumberjack era at lakeside shows.

Details: *Shows starting in June Tue, Thu, Sat 7:30 p.m.; matinees Tue–Thu. $4.25–$6.50. (1¼ hour)*

OTHER NORTHWOODS SIGHTSEEING HIGHLIGHTS

★★★★ GEORGE W. BROWN JR. OJIBWE MUSEUM AND CULTURAL CENTER
603 Peace Pipe, Lac du Flambeau, 715/588-3333
Featuring Ojibwe customs, traditions, and arts, the museum includes an excellent collection of Native American artifacts, such as a 100-year-old dugout canoe and a four-season diorama. Take

time to see the fine video presentation created by tribal member Nick Hockings.

Details: *Open May–Oct daily 10–4, Nov–Apr Tue–Thu 10–2 or by appointment. $1–$2, under 5 free. (45 minutes–1 hour)*

★★★ IRON COUNTY HISTORICAL MUSEUM
303 Iron St., Hurley, 715/561-2244

"There are three of us weaving rugs at the museum and we can't keep up," relates rug-maker Doris Morello. The rug-makers do a brisk business at the museum, which preserves colorful logging and mining history in Hurley's National Historic Registry courthouse. The weavers' rugs are displayed and sold here. The museum has working looms from the nineteenth century, the old courthouse clock, and cultural artifacts. Guides offer daily tours; there are also demonstration workshops.

Details: *Open year-round Mon, Wed, Fri, Sat 10–2. Free. (30 minutes–1 hour)*

★★★ WASWAGONING OJIBWE VILLAGE
Hwy. H, Lac du Flambeau, 715/588-2617

Visit a re-created traditional Ojibwe village on the Lac du Flambeau Reservation and learn about Ojibwe customs and culture on tours.

Details: *Open mid-June–late Sept Tue–Sat 10–4. Tours $5–$7, under 5 free. (1 hour)*

★★ LAC DU FLAMBEAU FISH HATCHERY
WI 47 N, 715/588-9603 or 715/588-3303

This state-of-the-art hatchery raises more than 30 million walleye, muskie, and northern pike yearly. You can fish for trout in a hatchery fishing pond (no license required).

Details: *Open Memorial Day–Labor Day 8–5. Free, except $2 per fish caught. (30 minutes)*

★★ WOODRUFF STATE FISH HATCHERY
8770 County Hwy. J, Woodruff, 715/356-5211

This hatchery produces muskie fingerlings as well as northern pike and walleye. Catch a guided tour at 11 or 2 to learn about how the hatchery works.

Details: *Open Memorial Day–Labor Day 7:45–4:30 Mon–Fri. Closed holidays. Free. (45 minutes–1 hour)*

FITNESS AND RECREATION

Outdoor recreation is the backbone of this region. **Northern Highland–American Legion State Forest**, 715/356-5211, offers hiking and nature trails, fishing, swimming, picnicking, winter recreation, backpacking, and canoe campsites. The forest's **Madeline Trail** southeast of Woodruff leads through more than nine miles of rolling terrain, while aspen and birch shade the two-mile **Schlect Trail**, just over a mile south of Minocqua. Also in this wilderness are the 10-mile **Raven Trail**, the seven-mile **McNaughton Trail**, and the **Bearskin State Trail**, among others. These add up to hundreds of miles of hiking, biking, and cross-country skiing, and snowmobiling. Call 715/385-2727 or 715/356-5211 for more information. **Copper Falls State Park**, 715/274-5123, contains seven miles of hiking and off-road biking trails and nearly 14 miles of ski trails on 2,483 acres.

Lac du Flambeau Tribal Campground and Marina, 715/558-3303 (ask for campground), has boat and motor rentals for $30 to $35 per day and canoe rentals for $12 per day. If you're intent on catching that really big one, **Greg Biggs Guide Service**, 715/385-2611, specializes in trophy muskie and walleye.

Golfers can play three courses, including an 18-hole championship course at **Pinewood Country Club**, 715/282-5500. **Circle M Corral Family Fun Park**, 10295 Highway 70 W, Minocqua, 715/356-4441, specializes in recreational fun with a water slide, go-karts, train rides, and more. It's open mid-May through mid-October. For more information on recreation in the area, call 800/446-6784.

FOOD

The garlic-stuffed tenderloin with cognac mustard sauce warrants applause at Hazelhurst's **Jacobi's**, 9820 Cedar Falls Rd., 715/356-5591. The restaurant opens for dinner at 4:30, and meals cost $13 to $26. At the lively, Old World–style pub **Polecat and Lace**, 427 Oneida St., Minocqua, 715/356-3335, sautéed veal and chicken are the specialties, and dinners range from $12 to $15. Meaty barbecued ribs bring rib-lovers to the **Plantation Supper Club**, 715/356-9000, in Arbor Vitae. It's located one and a half miles north of Woodruff at the junction of U.S. 51 and WI 70 E, and meals range from $12 to $18. Busy **Bosacki's Boathouse**, 715/356-5292, at the Minocqua bridge, dates to 1917 and has a hand-carved bar and casual dining. You'll eat family-style at long tables and drink from tin cups at **Paul Bunyan's Northwoods Cook Shanty**, 715/356-6270, on U.S. 51 between Minocqua and Woodruff. Their all-you-can-eat breakfast costs $7, while dinner costs from $9 to $11. For casual, fun dining go to **S. A. Loons**, 715/356-1700, on Highway 51N in Woodruff; or to **Spangs Italian Restaurant**, 715/356-4401. **Gaslight Cafe**, 415 Oneida, Minocqua, 715/358-7482, serves specialty coffees and deserts. At **Little Bohemia Restaurant**, 715/543-8433, in Manitowish Waters, you can view the John Dillinger-FBI bullet holes as you dine. Liver dumpling soup and roast duck are the specialties. Go to the highly praised **Blue Bayou Inn** on U.S. 51 in Manitowish Waters, 800/533-9671, for catfish en papillote, Louisiana seafood gumbo, and shrimp étouffée for $16 to $25. There's also excellent dining at upscale **Fence Lake Lodge** in Lac du Flambeau, 888/588-3255.

LODGING

Dillman's Sand Lake Lodge has become **Dillman's Bay Properties/ White Sand Lake Condo Association/Dillman's Creative Arts Foundation**, a condo/cabin rental resort on White Sand Lake, 715/588-3143. It includes tennis courts, retreats and workshops, sandy beaches, and water sports, and rooms are $89 to $130 per night. Opened in 1996, **Lake of the Torches Casino Hotel**, 800/25-TORCH, on WI 47 in Lac du Flambeau, carries out a North Woods theme. **Fence Lake Lodge**, 12919 Frying Pan Camp Ln., 888/588-3255 or 715/588-3255, offers log-walled suites with whirlpools and fireplaces and motel-style rooms on the Flambeau Chain of Lakes. Rooms are $80 to $140, suites range from $168 to $240. The **Beacons of Minocqua**, 8250 Northern Rd., 800/236-3225, rents upscale vacation condominiums and has a wide range of activities. Rooms there go for $115 to $160. **Dream Catcher's Resort, L.L.C.**, 8940 E. Minch Rd., Minocqua, 715/356-5609, is set on the shores of Lake Shishebogama. The resort has cabins, a sandy shoreline, and a trading post and lodge, and rates range from $125 to $175.

There are also a few motels to choose from. Try the **AmericInn Motel**, 700 WI 70, Minocqua, 800/634-3444, with rooms starting at $89; or the **Best Western Lakeview Motor Lodge**, 311 E. Park Ave. off U.S. 51, Minocqua, 800/852-1021, with rooms from $71 to $111. The **Pointe Resort Hotel and Conference Center**, Hwy. 51 in Minocqua, 715/356-4431, has attractive rooms and condo-suites for $64 to $139. **Eagle Bluff Condo Rentals**, 990 10th Ave. N., Hurley, 800/336-0973, has rooms ranging from $49 to $125. A short drive southwest of Hurley you'll find **The Inn**, 104 Wisconsin Ave., Montreal, 715/561-5180. It's located in the 1913 Montreal Mining Company office building and has mining memorabilia, private baths, and a full breakfast for $50 to $85.

WISCONSIN CONCRETE PARK, PHILLIPS

Wisconsin Concrete Park must be seen to be believed. As you drive south from Phillips on Highway 13 you'll suddenly come face-to-face with gigantic concrete people and animals. Among the characters and scenes depicted are Paul Bunyan, Ben Hur, Abe Lincoln, and Sacajawea. Logger, tavern-owner, and farmer Fred Smith starting sculpting in concrete embellished with metal, stone, wood, and glass (those beer bottles from the tavern came in handy) when he was in his 60s. When he died in 1976 he left a legacy of more than 200 historical and mythological larger-than-life figures on his farm—a head turner, indeed. Today Phillips honors Smith at an annual Wisconsin Concrete Park celebration in August with a puppet parade, a musical production, guided tours, and a slide show on the park's history. Phillips is 52 miles southwest of Minocqua via WI 70 west and WI 13 south. Continue south on WI 13 to reach the park. It's free and open daily during daylight hours. Call 800/269-4505 or 715/339-7505 for more information.

CAMPING

Lac du Flambeau Tribal Campground, on WI 47 N across from the fish hatchery in Lac du Flambeau, 715/588-3303 (ask for campground), has 70 paved sites with water and electricity, 17 sites with full hookups, tent camping, and free showers. Sites cost $12 to $16. North of Mellen, **Copper Falls State Park**, Hwy. 169, 715/274-5123, has 55 sites. Thirteen of the sites have electricity, but there are no showers. **Northern Highland-American Legion State Forest**, north and east of Minocqua and Woodruff, offers a total of 886 family backpacking and canoe campsites. To reach the forest's Clear Lake Campground from the intersection of U.S. 51 and WI 47, follow WI 47 south 2.4 miles then turn left on Woodruff Road. Clear Lake will be on your right. For detailed maps and information on campgrounds, call the camping hotline at 715/385-2704. Bring fishing gear to take advantage of the abundance of lakes in the forest, and your binoculars to spot eagles, osprey, and hawks. Check with the Woodruff DNR headquarters, 715/356-5211, for canoe route and trail maps, and for information on summer programs.

Private campgrounds include **Indian Shores**, off Highway 47E in Woodruff, 715/356-5552. It has 210 wooded RV sites, most of which offer full hookups, as well as showers, a recreation room, swimming pool, store, boat rentals, and more. Rates range from $26 to $30, with a 20-percent discount in spring and fall. **Dream Catcher's Resort, L.L.C.**, 8940 E. Minch Rd., Minocqua, 715/356-5609, has 14 campsites with water and electricity, and charges $20 per night.

NIGHTLIFE AND SPECIAL EVENTS

Witness authentic Ojibwe dances at the **Lac du Flambeau Indian Bowl Powwow**, 715/588-3333, in downtown Lac du Flambeau. The powwow takes place Tuesday evenings late June through late August. Indian Bowl also hosts a July Fourth powwow and parade. **Lake of the Torches Casino**, 800/25-TORCH, has gaming and dining and is open all the time. Crowds gather for the area's annual **Beef-A-Rama** and **Colorama** in September. **Bear River Powwow**, 715/588-3333, takes place during the second weekend in July at the Bear River Powwow grounds on Old Indian Village Road. **Wisconsin Native American Annual Art Show and Sale** events in July and August feature authentic cultural and contemporary Native American art—painting, carving, birch-bark, and bead- and yarn-work—in downtown Lac du Flambeau. Call 715/588-3333 for information. Folks celebrate winter at **Snowfest** in February and Minocqua Winter Park hosts **Ski Jumping Championships** in March. People come from near and far to attend the summer productions at **Northern Lights Playhouse**, U.S. 51 in Hazelhurst. Call 715/356-7173 for reservations and ticket prices.

To Hurley via Copper Falls State Park

Be prepared to be surprised on this scenic route to Hurley. To find the hidden trea-sure—waterfalls tucked away in the woodlands—turn south onto WI 169 from U.S. 2 between Ashland and Hurley, then drive three miles to tiny Gurney. At the south edge of Gurney, Rowe Farm Road leads west to a small park overlooking **Potato River Falls**. It's a pleasant place to linger, and picnic facilities are available.

Continue southwest on WI 169 about 11 miles to 2,483-acre **Copper Falls State Park**, and you'll enter a world of canyons, streams, and waterfalls. The park's aptly named **Bad River** includes two 30-plus-foot waterfalls, as well as seven miles of hiking trails that lead through stands of hemlock, cedar, birch, basswood, and white pine. A self-guided nature trail offers excellent views of both falls. Other trails lead to **Red Granite Falls** and **Murphy** and **Loon Lakes**. You can also cross the Tyler's Forks footbridge and follow the river to sandstone ledges; or hike the segment of the **North Country National Scenic Trail** that runs through the park. Wildlife is plentiful, and you may encounter deer, porcupine, or pileated woodpeckers. Anglers fish the Bad River for trout; Loon Lake is a good place to swim, and has a sandy

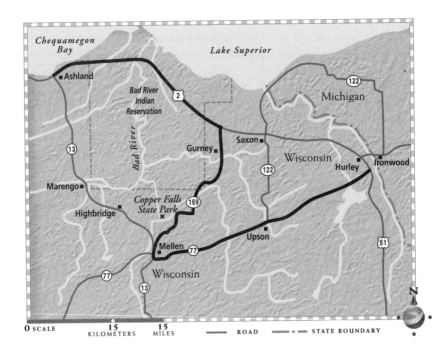

beach and a boat landing. There are also off-road bike trails, cross-country ski trails, and campsites (715/274-5123).

To get to Hurley from the park, take WI 169 south a short distance to the junction with WI 13, then follow WI 13 south to Mellen. Hurley is about 26 miles northeast of Mellen on WI 77.

12
DOOR PENINSULA

In far northeastern Wisconsin, Door Peninsula juts out into the water between the bay of Green Bay, Wisconsin, and Lake Michigan. Its mix of rugged limestone bluffs overlooking the shore, coastal fishing villages with white Victorian houses, woodlands, stone fences, fields of mustard and Queen Anne's lace, and lighthouses gives the peninsula a coastal Maine flavor beloved by locals and throngs of tourists in summer and fall.

Two counties—Door and Kewaunee—share the 75-mile-long peninsula; Door occupies the more dramatically scenic northern end. At the tip lies "Death's Door" (Porte des Mortes), a six-mile-wide tempestuous strait between the peninsula and Washington Island, where many ships sank. The region's rich maritime history is chronicled in a Sturgeon Bay maritime museum.

To explore the top half of the peninsula, you can drive north through Sturgeon Bay—a major shipbuilding port on the Great Lakes—and follow WI 57 along the Lake Michigan side of the peninsula until it merges with WI 42. Follow WI 42 north to the tip of the peninsula then, after backtracking a short distance, follow 42 south along the Green Bay side. A must is the ferry ride from the tip of the peninsula to Washington Island. From there, take another ferry to Rock Island, a wooded promontory with a lighthouse and a primitive state park—the one place in the area you are likely to find genuine solitude.

A PERFECT DAY IN DOOR PENINSULA

Fortify yourself with breakfast and unforgettable pecan rolls at Grandma's Swedish Restaurant/Wagon Trail Resort on Rowleys Bay. Pack a lunch and water bottles and drive to Northport Pier to board the Washington Island Ferry. Drive across Washington Island and catch the Rock Island Ferry, *Karfi*. Spend the day hiking and exploring Rock Island. Visit the 1920s Viking Hall, take a lunch break on the beach, and hike to Potawatomie Lighthouse. Ride the two ferries back to the mainland, then stop for a fish-boil dinner (The White Gull Inn in Fish Creek is my first choice). Later in the evening go to a Peninsula Players play.

ELLISON BAY-GILLS ROCK-WASHINGTON ISLAND SIGHTSEEING HIGHLIGHTS

★★★★ WASHINGTON ISLAND FERRY
Northport Pier, Gills Rock, 800/223-2094

Take the 30-minute ferry trip from the mainland to explore Wahington Island and/or connect with the ferry to Rock Island. Harbor Bike Rental rents bikes at the ferry dock.

Details: *End of WI 42. Open May–June 8–6, July–Aug 7:15–6:15 (every half hour), Sept–Oct 8–6; reduced service other times of the year. $17 round-trip for a car, $4–$7.50 for passengers, under 6 free, $3 per bicycle, $10 per motorcycle. (1 hour round-trip)*

★★★★ NEWPORT STATE PARK
475 County Hwy. NP, Ellison Bay, 920/854-2500

East of Ellison Bay, this 2,200-acre wooded, rugged, and mostly undeveloped park overlooks the Lake Michigan shoreline and contains 30 miles of hiking trails through remnant boreal forest and virgin white pine. The park has a naturalist program and guided hikes. Follow the European Bay trail for views of Pilot Island Lighthouse. In the park, hikers may encounter the foundations of old logging camps and lilac bushes marking the former settlement of Newport. You'll find wild strawberries in early summer.

Details: *Open year-round daily. State park sticker required. (2 hours minimum)*

★★★ DOOR COUNTY MARITIME MUSEUM
12724 Hwy. 42, Gills Rock, Wisconsin Bay Rd.
920/854-1844

DOOR PENINSULA

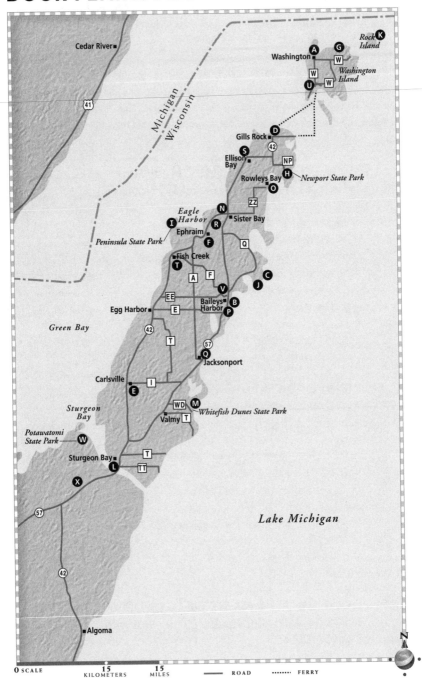

The story of commercial fishing, shipwrecks, and navigation unfolds at this maritime museum.

Details: *Open Memorial Day–Oct Mon–Sat 10–4, Sun 1–4. $1–$2.50, under 5 free; $5 family rate. (30 minutes–1 hour)*

★★★ **ISLAND CRUISES**

Island Clipper Cruises/Viking Tour Train (920/854-2972) and C. G. Richter Passenger Cruises/Cherry Tour Train (920/847-2546) are narrated cruises that depart from Gills Rock. They connect with open-air trains offering 90-minute narrated tours of Washington Island. The Clipper also has bikes and mopeds available for rent.

Details: *Island Clipper/Viking Train: Operates May–mid-Oct; combo ticket $7–$13.50. C.G. Richter/Cherry Train: Operates July–Aug; $7.50–$13.50. Train tours alone cost $3.50–$6. Cruises without the train tour cost $3.50–$7.50. (half–full day)*

SIGHTS

- **A** Art and Nature Center
- **B** Bailey's Harbor
- **C** Cana Island Lighthouse
- **D** Door County Maritime Museum
- **E** Door Peninsula Winery
- **F** Ephraim
- **D** Island Cruises (Gills Rock)
- **G** Jackson Harbor Maritime Museum
- **H** Newport State Park
- **I** Peninsula State Park
- **J** Ridges Sanctuary
- **K** Rock Island
- **L** Sturgeon Bay
- **D** Washington Island Ferry
- **M** Whitefish Dunes State Park

FOOD

- **N** Al Johnson's Swedish Restaurant
- **O** Grandma's Swedish Restaurant
- **I** Inn at Cedar Crossing
- **P** Sandpiper Restaurant
- **Q** Square Rigger Galley
- **R** Summer Kitchen
- **S** The Viking
- **F** Wilson's Restaurant & Ice Cream Parlor
- **T** White Gull Inn

LODGING

- **N** Church Hill Inn
- **F** Eagle Harbor Inn
- **U** Findlay's Holiday Inn
- **F** French Country Inn of Ephraim
- **S** Grand View Motel
- **I** Inn at Cedar Crossing
- **L** Scofield House Bed and Breakfast

LODGING (continued)

- **O** Wagon Trail Resort
- **T** Whistling Swan Inn
- **T** White Gull Inn
- **L** White Lace Inn

CAMPING

- **V** Bailey's Grove Travel Park & Campground
- **H** Newport State Park
- **I** Peninsula State Park
- **W** Potawatomi State Park
- **X** Quiet Woods North Camping Resort
- **U** Rock Island State Park
- **O** Wagon Trail Campground

Note: Items with the same letter are located in the same place.

★★★ JACKSON HARBOR MARITIME MUSEUM
Jackson Harbor Rd., Washington Island, 920/847-2179

This museum has indoor and outdoor maritime exhibits and offers visitors a fascinating look at Great Lakes history and wildlife.

Details: *Open Memorial Day–late June weekends, late June–Labor Day daily, and Labor Day–Columbus Day weekends 10:30–4:30. $1. (20 minutes–1 hour)*

★★ ART AND NATURE CENTER
Main Rd. and Jackson Harbor, Washington Island, 920/847-2025

The center features the work of island artists, a nature room, an observation beehive, island history, nature hikes, and art classes.

Details: *Open Mid-June–Labor Day Mon–Sat 10:30–4:30, Sun 11–4:30; Labor Day–Sept daily 11–3. $1, under 12 free. (20 minutes–1 hour)*

OTHER DOOR PENINSULA SIGHTSEEING HIGHLIGHTS

★★★★ ROCK ISLAND
920/847-2235 or 920/854-2500

The island is contained in 912-acre Rock Island State Park. No motorized vehicles are allowed. From the peninsula, go to Washington Island via the Washington Island Ferry, drive across the island, and catch the Rock Island Ferry from Jackson Harbor on Washington Island. Or leave your car on the mainland and rent a bike on Washington Island to ride to Jackson Harbor. A day on the island removes you from the tourist traffic of popular Door County. Attractions include more than nine miles of hiking trails, a sandy beach, cliff carvings, a lighthouse on the north shore, campsites, and the stone Viking Hall boathouse and other buildings built by Icelanders in the early 1900s, when inventor Chester Thorardson owned the island. The craggy island reminded him of his native Iceland. The boathouse now houses the park's nature center. *Karfi*, the Rock Island ferry, departs Washington Island from Jackson Harbor. It's wise to reserve ferry space and campsites in advance.

Details: *For information, write Rock Island State Park, Rte. 1, Box 118A, Washington Island, WI 54246. Open May–mid-Oct. Rock Island ferry: Jackson Harbor, Washington Island, 920/847-2252. July–*

September daily 10–4 (hourly); late May–June and early Sept–mid-Oct daily 10:30, 1, and 3:30, with additional trips on weekends and Memorial Day. $4–$8 round-trip. (3 hours minimum)

★★★★ WHITEFISH DUNES STATE PARK
Valmy, WI 57, 920/743-4456

Northeast of Valmy, between Lake Michigan and Clark Lake, 90-foot sand dunes are the main attraction in 863-acre Whitefish Dunes State Park. There are more than 14 miles of hiking and skiing trails, a long beach, and two miles of rocky shoreline. In the northeastern section cliffs rise 20 feet above the shore. At the northern end of the park, waves boom against undercut limestone cliffs at Cave Point County Park. This side of the peninsula is wilder than the Green Bay side, and the park has few visitors in early morning or late afternoon.

Details: East on Clark Lake Rd. off WI 57, 920/823-2400. Day-use only. State park sticker required. (2 hours minimum)

★★★ BAILEY'S HARBOR
2392 County Hwy. F (Visitors Center), 920/839-2366 or 920/743-4456

On the shores of Lake Michigan north of Jacksonport, wetlands and wilderness surround Bailey's Harbor. Privately owned **Ridges Sanctuary** offers bird-watching and guided hikes. The 1,000-acre wildflower preserve contains rare plant communities and 23 species of orchids native to Wisconsin. Trails are open year-round dawn to dusk. Northeast of Bailey's Harbor stands the 1869 **Cana Island Lighthouse**. You can reach the lighthouse by a causeway when the lake is low, or by wading.

Details: Ridges Sanctuary: Off WI 57 N, a quarter mile east on County Hwy. Q; 920/839-2802. $2 trail fee. (2½ hours)

★★★ PENINSULA STATE PARK
Fish Creek, WI 42, north of Egg Harbor, 920/868-3258

The entrance to Peninsula State Park lies a short distance from the heart of the historic village of Fish Creek, noted for its professional summer theater. The 3,775-acre park has 20 miles of hiking trails, a nature center with guided tours, a seven-mile bikeway, and kayaks and canoes for rent at Nicollet Beach. Sunset Trail passes **Eagle Bluff Lighthouse,** built in 1868, now restored, furnished, and open for summer tours. Some campsites here are open for winter camping.

This scenic and popular park can be extremely crowded in summer.

Details: *Open year-round daily 7–11. State park sticker required.* (2 hours minimum)

★★★ STURGEON BAY
WI 57/42, 920/743-3924

With a population of 9,000 people, Sturgeon Bay qualifies as the only real city on the peninsula. It's also one of the largest Great Lakes shipbuilding ports and gateway to the upper peninsula. Go to the downtown farmer's market for Door County produce and crafts Saturdays, June through October. The **Door County Maritime Museum** features shipbuilding history and maritime trades. The city's **Door County Museum** also has exhibits on local history. And at **Cherryland Brewery and Pub**, you can watch the brewer at work in an old railroad station.

Details: *Door County Maritime Museum: 120 N. Madison Ave.; 920/743-5958. Door County Museum: 18 N. Fourth Ave.; 920/743-5809. Cherryland Brewery and Pub: 341 N. Third Ave.; 920/743-1945.* (2 hours)

★★ DOOR PENINSULA WINERY
5806 Highway 42, Carlsville, 920/743-7431.

Orchards thrive on Door Peninsula. You'll see cherry and apple trees in blossom in May. Come summer and early fall, plump strawberries, tart cherries, and ruby-red apples fill produce stands on Highway 42 between Egg Harbor and Fish Creek. Door Peninsula Winery in Carlsville, south of Egg Harbor, produces wines from locally grown cherries, apples, cranberries, and plums. Stop for a tour and tasting.

Details: *Winery open Apr–Oct daily 9–6, Oct–May 9–5. $1.50, children free.* (30 minutes)

★★ EPHRAIM
WI 42, 920/854-4989 (Door County Chamber of Commerce)

Memorable for tiers of white wooden houses and churches overlooking Eagle Harbor on the Green Bay side of the peninsula, this picturesque hamlet was founded in 1853 by Moravians who came here from Norway. It's a favored spot for windsurfing and sailing. If you're yearning to try either, **Ephraim Sailing and Windsurfing Center** offers lessons and rentals at South Shore Pier, 920/854-4336. The town is also the northern entrance to Peninsula State Park. Stop at the information center, 920/854-4989, in a small stone building at the north end of downtown. Ephraim's history is preserved at **Anderson Barn Museum**, a barn with a square silo, open during the resort season. There's also a restored and furnished pioneer school and the **Anderson Store**, built by Aslag Anderson in 1858.

Details: (*30 minutes–4 hours*)

FITNESS AND RECREATION

Diverse recreational options include fishing charters, such as **Dawiduk's Fishing Team** in Sturgeon Bay, 920/746-9916 (promising salmon, trout and more); and **Lynn's Charter Fishing** (with a zoologist as your guide) at Bailey's Harbor Yacht Club, 920/854-5109. There are also sailing cruises, horse stables, boat rentals, scuba diving (**Shoreline Resort Charters** at Gills Rock/Ellison Bay, 920/854-2606), and parasailing (**Wisconsin Water Wings** in Ephraim, 920/854-9000).

You can hike in any of the five Door County state parks, bike in most of them, and golf on seven courses. **Peninsula Golf Course** in Peninsula State Park, 920/854-5791, is majestically situated above Green Bay. Bike rental shops are plentiful: **Bailey's Harbor Yacht Club Resort** in Bailey's Harbor, 920/839-2336, rents 12-speeds for up to a full day and kid carts for $5 to $15. A 100-mile **Backroad Bicycle Route**

Ask for the Door County Official Vacation Guidebook, *available free from the village information centers or from the Door County Chamber of Commerce, 920/743-4456.*

traverses the fields and forests between small towns; pick up a map from the Door County Chamber of Commerce on WI 42/57, just south of Sturgeon Bay, 920/743-4456, or in any village information center.

FOOD

Fish boil is a Door County tradition handed down from Scandinavian settlers and lumberjacks and served nearly everywhere. Whitefish steaks, potatoes, and onions are boiled in an open pot over an outdoor fire. The meal is served along with melted butter and, if you're lucky, a slab of fresh cherry pie. Dinner rates are a moderate $8 to $20 in most restaurants, with a few costing up to $25.

The Viking, Hwy. 42, Ellison Bay, 920/854-2998, serves boiled fish nightly, as well as steaks and other seafood. In Sister Bay, goats graze on the roof of **Al Johnson's Swedish Restaurant**, 920/854-2626, a good breakfast spot with Swedish pancakes. Landmark **Wilson's Restaurant and Ice-Cream Parlor**, 9990 Water St., 920/854-2041, has been dishing up malts and sundaes since 1906 in Ephraim. The cherry and four-berry pie rate compliments at the **Summer Kitchen**, 920/854-2131, north of Ephraim on WI 42. The pecan rolls have been rated best in the state at **Grandma's Swedish Restaurant** at Wagon Trail Resort, Restaurant, and Conference Center on Rowleys Bay, 1041 Hwy. ZZ, 800/99-WAGON. There's also a nightly Swedish smorgasbord. The **Inn at Cedar Crossing**, 336 Louisiana St., Sturgeon Bay, 920/743-4200 or 920/743-4249, gets raves for its cherry pie and other homemade fare. **Square Rigger Galley**, 6332 WI 57, on the lakeshore in Jacksonport, 920/823-2408, has a nightly fish boil and breakfast daily July through August. **Sandpiper Restaurant** on WI 57, Baileys Harbor, 920/839-2528, serves a traditional fish boil May through October in a family-friendly atmosphere. The **White Gull Inn**, Door 4225, Main St., Fish Creek, 920/868-3517, serves wonderful food and a fish boil Wednesday, Friday, Saturday, and Sunday evenings.

LODGING

Choosing among the fine lodging places can be difficult. Among the best bed-and-breakfasts is the **White Gull Inn**, 4225 Main St., Fish Creek, 920/868-3517, a historic country establishment with rooms and cottages for $99 to $195. There's also the **Whistling Swan Inn**, 4192 Main St., Fish Creek, 920/868-3442, with rooms from $99 to $139. **Church Hill Inn**, 425 Gateway Dr., Sister Bay, 800/422-4906 or 920/854-4885, has country antiques in 34 rooms, a heated outdoor pool, and a breakfast buffet for $65 to $174 per night.

Area motels include **Grand View Motel**, Hwy. 42 S., Ellison Bay, 800/258-8208, with rooms for $77; and **Findlay's Holiday Inn**, Detroit Harbor, Washington Island, 920/847-2526, with a Scandinavian theme and rooms from $75 to $110. Overlooking Rowleys Bay south of Newport State Park, **Wagon Trail Resort**, 1041 Hwy. ZZ, 800/99-WAGON, has lodge rooms and rental homes. In Ephraim, **Eagle Harbor Inn**, 9914 Water St., 920/854-2121, is a nine-room inn with guest houses and rates from $95 to $155. **French Country Inn of Ephraim**, 3052 Spruce Ln., 920/854-4001, has seven guest rooms in a 1912 summer cottage for $62 to $89. You'll find excellent lodging in Sturgeon Bay at the **White Lace Inn**, 16 N. Fifth Ave., 920/743-1105, with rooms from $58 to $179; the **Scoffield House Bed-and-Breakfast**, 908

NAMUR

If you're in the vicinity, drive through Namur, a large ethnic settlement with Belgian-style red-brick farmhouses. It's located about 14 miles south of Sturgeon Bay on WI 57. Back in 1871 a fire destroyed the Belgian community, but the farmers rebuilt the log structures and fire-proofed with brick. You can see a monument honoring the fire victims in Tornado Park north of Brussels on WI 57.

Michigan St., 888/463-0204, with rooms from $93 to $196; and **Inn at Cedar Crossing**, 336 Louisiana St., 920/743-4200, with rates of $95 to $155.

CAMPING

State parks offer public camping. On Sturgeon Bay, **Potawatomi State Park**, 920/746-2890 or 920/746-2891, has 1,225 acres and 123 sites. The Ice Age National Trail starts here. From the city of Sturgeon Bay, take U.S. 42/57 south, go north on County Highway S and west on County C, then turn right on Park Road. **Peninsula State Park** has 469 sites (100 with electricity) and showers; **Newport State Park** has 16 sites but no electricity or showers; **Rock Island State Park** has 40 backpacking sites, no electricity or showers. (See Sightseeing Highlights for details on these parks.) Private campgrounds include excellent **Wagon Trail Campground**, 1190 Hwy. ZZ, six miles northeast of Sister Bay on County ZZ, 920/854-4818, with 140 sites, free showers, cabins, and a separate tent area. Rates are about $20 to $31. **Bailey's Grove Travel Park and Campground**, left on County Hwy. F from Bailey's Harbor, 920/839-2559, has 68 shaded sites and a grassy tent area with trees, electricity, and pay showers. Rates are about $20 to $26. Next to Potawatomie State Park, **Quiet Woods North Camping Resort**, two miles southwest of Sturgeon Bay off County Hwy. C, 800/9TO-CAMP, has 258 mostly wooded sites, a heated swimming pool, and showers. Rates range from $20 to $28.

NIGHTLIFE AND SPECIAL EVENTS

Birch Creek Music Center, 920/868-3763, a noted music academy east of Egg Harbor, hosts summer evening concerts in a barn. The **Peninsula Players**,

920/868-3287, a venerable and respected professional resident theater company, performs plays and musicals in a bayside pavilion in Fish Creek. **American Folklore Theatre**, 920/869-9999, mixes musical comedy with history with entertaining results in Fish Creek's Peninsula State Park amphitheater. Ephraim's **Midsummer's Music**, 920/854-1833, an 11-concert chamber music festival, celebrates the summer solstice in June. Annual events include a May **Door County Lighthouse Walk**, 920/743-5958; and Ephraim's June **Fyr-Bal** Scandinavian festival, 920/854-5919. For more information call the Door County Arts Hotline, 920/746-ARTS; or the area's information hotline, 920/743-4456, ext. 3.

13
LAKE WINNEBAGO

Lake Winnebago's 215-square-mile glacially crafted bed makes it the largest lake in Wisconsin. Lake Michigan and Lake Superior, both Great Lakes, aren't contenders since Wisconsin shares their shorelines with other states. Winnebago, inland from Lake Michigan about 35 miles and 60 miles northwest of Milwaukee, measures 28 miles long, 10 miles wide, and a shallow 20 feet deep.

Fed by the Fox and Wolf Rivers, the lake attracted a variety of Native American tribes, including Fox, Menominee, Winnebago, Macouten, Ottawa, and Sauk. A settlement named for Menominee Chief Oshkosh grew into the city of Oshkosh. Its 61,800 or so residents populate Lake Winnebago's west shore. In the 1870s Oshkosh took on the nickname "Sawdust City" when lumber-era mills on the Fox River transformed it into the largest wood-manufacturing city in the country.

Today only a handful of mills remain, and the city's contemporary claim to fame lies in overalls: first, the heavy-duty bibbed variety and, more recently, upscale kids' duds labeled Oshkosh B'Gosh. Oshkosh has a lovely lakeside park, as does Fond du Lac, a city of nearly 38,000, 21 miles south of Oshkosh on the southern end of Lake Winnebago. Both cities abound in water sports activities and have interesting historic buildings. Fond du Lac's location makes it a handy base for outings to waterfowl haven Horicon Marsh and the Kettle Moraine State Forest's Northern Unit.

A PERFECT DAY IN LAKE WINNEBAGO

Head out to Horicon Marsh to glimpse some of the thousands of geese, egrets, herons, and other migratory and resident water-loving birds. Then set off for the Kettle Moraine State Forest; bring hiking boots, a camera, and a picnic lunch. Visit the Ice Age Center to bone up on moraine characteristics, then hike the wooded trails and eat lunch under a tree. Drive to Greenbush to tour the historic Wade House Stagecoach Inn and Wesley Jung Carriage Museum, built in 1850, then head back to Fond du Lac for a lakeside stroll and dinner at the elegant Rosewood Dining Room.

FOND DU LAC SIGHTSEEING HIGHLIGHTS

★★★★ GALLOWAY HOUSE AND VILLAGE
336 Old Pioneer Rd., Fond du Lac, 920/922-6390

In Fond du Lac you can tour a restored 30-room Victorian mansion surrounded by 23 turn-of-the-century buildings, including the Blakely Museum, the Adams House Resource Center, a photographer's shop, and more.

Details: Open Memorial Day–Labor Day and Sept weekends daily 10–5; gates close at 4. $3–$5.50, preschoolers free. (1–3 hours)

★★★★ LARSEN'S RANCH CLYDESDALES
W12654 Reeds Corner, Fond du Lac, 920/748-5466

Larsen's ranch visits include a 90-minute guided tour, a museum, antique hitch wagons, harnesses, and a Clydesdale horse show—plus a Clydesdale foal to pet.

Details: 17 miles west of Fond du Lac—take WI 23 west to County Hwy. KK, turn left on KK, left on Meadow Vale Rd., and right on Reeds Corner. Open May–Oct Mon–Sat; shows at 1. Reservations recommended. $4–$8. (2 hours)

★★ SILVER WHEEL MANOR MUSEUM AND SHOPPES
N6221 County Hwy. K, Fond du Lac
920/922-1608
www.marlenesinternational.com

If you're in search of vintage wedding gowns, there are 3,000 of them to buy or to rent in this "collections-gone-wild" place featuring "rentable history." Marlene Hansen fills a 30-room mansion with her family's 87-year collection of antique furnishings, 2,000 dolls, 38 doll carriages, 300 trains, and more. Many exhibits have items that can be rented or bought.

Details: *Southeast of Fond du Lac—from U.S. 41, follow WI 23 east five miles to County Hwy. K, then go south about one mile. Open year-round by appointment or chance. $5–$8. (1 hour minimum)*

FOND DU LAC

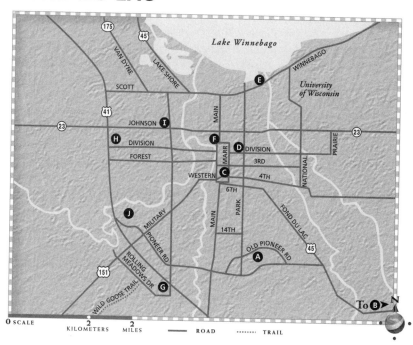

SIGHTS

Ⓐ Galloway House and Village
Ⓑ Silver Wheel Manor Museum and Shoppes

FOOD

Ⓒ Main Exchange
Ⓓ Rosewood Dining Room
Ⓔ Salty's Seafood and Spirits
Ⓕ Theo's Supper Club

LODGING

Ⓖ Budgetel Inn BudgetDome
Ⓗ Days Inn
Ⓘ EconoLodge
Ⓙ Northway Motel
Ⓓ Ramada Plaza Hotel

Note: Items with the same letter are located in the same place.

OSHKOSH SIGHTSEEING HIGHLIGHTS

★★★★ **EXPERIMENTAL AIRCRAFT ASSOCIATION (EAA) AIR ADVENTURE MUSEUM**
3000 Poberezny Dr., Oshkosh, 920/426-4818, www.eaa.org
The EAA Museum preserves aviation history and has the world's largest private aircraft collection. The Eagle Hangar features WWII displays. There are five theaters including the Air Adventure Theater with a 12-by-30-foot screen, photo and art galleries, and docents to answer questions. The Pioneer Airport revives the barnstorming era and offers rides May through October for a fee. Held near the museum, the annual **EAA Fly-In Convention**, 920/426-4800, is a major aviation event, with educational forums, workshops, seminars, evening programs, and 12,000 airplanes, from antiques to homebuilts to ultralights. Acrobatic performers give daily air shows. The seven-day convention at the end of July draws 800,000-plus people.
Details: East of U.S. 41, off WI 44. Open year-round Mon–Sat 8:30–5, Sun 11–5. $6–$7.50, under 8 free, $20 family. (1–3 hours)

★★★ **PAINE ART CENTER AND ARBORETUM**
1410 Algoma Blvd., Oshkosh, 920/235-4530
The center occupies an impressive 1920s Tudor Revival house designed for lumber baron Nathan Paine and his wife, Jessie. In addition to period rooms, nineteenth-century French and American paintings, sculpture, Oriental rugs, and decorative arts, the center has an arboretum with six display gardens. Ask about musical performances and family events.
Details: Open year-round Tue–Sun 11–4, Fri 11–7; guided tours by appointment, 920/235-6903. Art Center $2–$3, under 12 free. Arboretum free. (1 hour)

★★ **OSHKOSH PUBLIC MUSEUM**
1331 Algoma Blvd., Oshkosh, 920/424-4730
www.publicmuseum.oshkosh.net
Tiffany studios–designed interiors are preserved in a 1907 English Tudor–style mansion built for lumber baron and banker Edgar Sawyer. Displays include the Wisconsin folk art Apostles Clock and exhibits on regional history.
Details: Open year-round Tue–Sat 9–5, Sun 1–5. Donation. (30 minutes–1 hour)

★ OSHKOSH B'GOSH STORES
Prime Outlet Center, 3001 S. Washburn, 920/426-5817 and 920/426-9707

Based in Oshkosh since 1895, the company now has two stores here: **Oshkosh B'Gosh Menswear Store** and **Oshkosh B'Gosh Super Store**, which sells general merchandise.

OSHKOSH

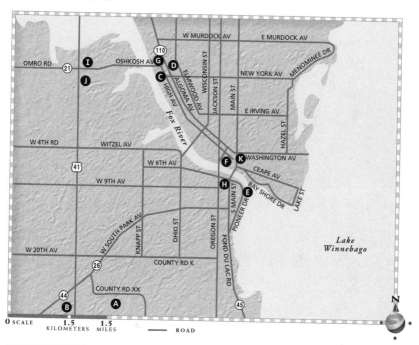

SIGHTS

- **A** Experimental Aircraft Association (EAA) Air Adventure Museum
- **B** Oshkosh B'Gosh Stores
- **C** Oshkosh Public Museum
- **D** Paine Art Center and Arboretum

FOOD

- **E** Bellvue Dining Room
- **F** Esprit Restaurant
- **G** Fratellos Italian Cafe
- **H** Granary Restaurant

LODGING

- **I** Budgetel Motor Inn
- **J** Howard Johnson
- **K** Oshkosh Hilton and Convention Center
- **E** Pioneer Inn and Marina

Note: Items with the same letter are located in the same place.

LAKE WINNEBAGO REGION

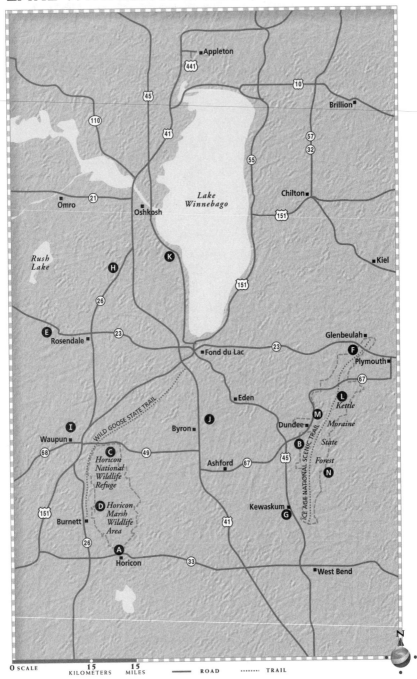

Details: Open year-round Mon–Sat 10–9, Sun 11–6. (10 minutes–1 hour)

HORICON MARSH SIGHTSEEING HIGHLIGHTS

★★★★ HORICON MARSH WILDLIFE AREA
Hwy. 28 (DNR office), 920/387-7860

Stop at the main DNR Headquarters office on Highway 28, about two miles north of Horicon, for views of the marsh and hiking and program information. A short drive away, the DNR Field Station on North Palmatory Street in Horicon has marked trails.

Details: Open Mon–Fri 7:45–4:30. Free. (1 hour minimum)

★★★★ HORICON NATIONAL WILDLIFE REFUGE
W4279 Headquarters Rd., Mayville, 920/387-2658

The Horicon National Wildlife Refuge has two hiking trails and a floating boardwalk, and offers informative goose talks. There are also exhibits and a gift shop, and visitors are free to use the spotting scope on the deck.

Details: From Fond du Lac take U.S. 151 south, WI 49 east, and Country Z south to the visitor center. Open year-round Mon–Fri 7:30–4, early Sept–early Nov also open Sat and Sun 9–6. Goose talks late Sept–Oct Sat 4 p.m. Free. (1 hour minimum)

SIGHTS

Ⓐ Blue Heron Tours
Ⓑ Henry S. Reuss Ice Age Visitor Center
Ⓒ Horicon Marsh Wildlife Area
Ⓓ Horicon National Wildlife Refuge
Ⓔ Larsen's Ranch Clydesdales
Ⓕ Wade House Stagecoach Inn and Wesley Jung Carriage Museum

FOOD

Ⓐ Ice Cream Station

LODGING

Ⓖ Country Ridge Inn

CAMPING

Ⓗ Circle R Campground
Ⓘ Fond du Lac County Park
Ⓙ Fond du Lac KOA Campground
Ⓚ Kalbus Country Harbor
Ⓛ Kettle Moraine State Forest
Ⓜ Long Lake Recreation Area
Ⓝ Mauthe Lake Recreation Area

Note: Items with the same letter are located in the same place.

★★★★ BLUE HERON TOURS
WI 33 at Blue Heron Landing, Horicon
920/485-4663
Take a one-hour lecture tour or the two-hour "Strictly Birding" tour. Or rent a canoe and explore on your own.

    Details: Open May–October weekdays 10 a.m., weekends 9 a.m.; tours daily 1 p.m. One-hour tour $3.50–$8, under 4 free. "Strictly Birding" tour $7–$15, under 4 free. Canoe rental $15–$22.50 a day. (1¹/₂ hour minimum)

KETTLE MORAINE AREA SIGHTSEEING HIGHLIGHTS

★★★★ HENRY S. REUSS ICE AGE VISITOR CENTER
WI 67, Dundee, 920/533-8322
The Ice Age Center interprets by film and panorama the drumlins, kettles, kames, and other dramatic characteristics left by receding glaciers 18,000-plus years ago. You can also hike more than 66 miles of trails, including 36 miles of the **Ice Age National Scenic Trail** that runs north-south through the **Kettle Moraine State Forest Northern Unit**.

    Details: About 18 miles southeast of Fond du Lac. Take U.S. 45 southeast, then follow WI 67 northeast to the center. Open year-round weekdays 8:30–4, weekends 9:30–5. Hourly, daily, or annual park sticker required. Kettle Moraine State Forest Northern Unit headquarters: 414/626-2116. (half–full day)

★★★ WADE HOUSE STAGECOACH INN AND WESLEY JUNG CARRIAGE MUSEUM
W7747 Plank Rd., Greenbush, 920/526-3271
At the Wade House you'll meet the costumed innkeepers, tour the rooms, and speak with inn "patrons"—all of whom are caught up in talk about a civil war. The Wisconsin State Historical Society operates this 1850s stagecoach inn, built alongside a plank walk in the village of Greenbush. A horse-drawn carriage takes you to view more than 100 restored hand- and horse-drawn carriages at the carriage museum.

    Details: 23 miles east of Fond du Lac, off WI 23. Open May–October daily 9–5. $3.50–$7. Carriage rides $1. (1–2 hours)

FITNESS AND RECREATION

In Oshkosh, access to the **WIOUWASH Recreational Trail**, 920/232-1960, offering 20 miles of backcountry for hiking or biking, is at Westwind Road in the Sunset Point area off WI 110. **Wild Goose State Biking and Hiking Trail**, 920/929-3135, can be accessed in Fond du Lac from Rolling Meadows Drive just south of the intersection of U.S. 41 and 151. Families enjoy 400-acre **Lakeside Park on Lake Winnebago**, 800/937-9123, in Fond du Lac with picnic grounds, floral displays, an amusement park, a lighthouse with an observation deck open daily until dusk, a miniature train, and bumper-boats. The park is open year-round.

There are six public boat-launch sites in Oshkosh and four in Fond du Lac, and both cities have a number of marinas. In Oshkosh, three businesses offer boat rentals: Try **Fox River Marina**, 501 S. Main St., 920/236-4220. Canoes can be rented at **Blue Heron Landing**, WI 33 in Horicon, 920/485-4663. With lots of water, windsurfing is popular in Fond du Lac: **Wind Power**, across from the Roosevelt Park area at U.S. 151 N., N7351 Winnebago Dr., 920/922-2550, offers lessons and rentals Memorial Day through Labor Day. Among the plentiful fishing guides and charters are **4 Seasons Guide Service**, 920/922-6982, in Fond du Lac; and **Captain Walleye Guide Service**, 920/233-3209, in Oshkosh.

Oshkosh's golf courses include **Westhaven Golf Club**, 1400 Westhaven Dr., 920/233-4640 (18 holes). The Fond du Lac area's four courses include **Camelot Country Club Golf Course** on WI 67, one mile east of U.S. 41, 920/269-4949. For more information on Fond du Lac recreation, call 800/937-9123; for that in Oshkosh, call 800/876-5250.

FOOD

Dinner at the best restaurants here will usually cost less than $25. In Oshkosh: In addition to steak and prime rib, historic **Granary Restaurant**, 50 W. Sixth Ave., 920/233-3929, offers a healthy steamed-vegetable platter; prices range from $10 to $20. The cold strawberry soup and the Sunday brunch both elicit praise at **Esprit Restaurant** in the Hilton Hotel, 1 N. Main St., 920/231-5000. Dinner prices there are $8 to $15. Go to **Fratellos Italian Cafe**, 1501 Arboretum Dr., 920/232-2337, for casual dining on the Fox River. The highly rated **Bellvue Dining Room** at Pioneer Inn and Marina, 1000 Pioneer Dr., 800/683-1980, specializes in baby-back ribs, with meals from $14 to $18.

You'll find a formal dining atmosphere in Fond du Lac's **Rosewood Dining Room**, 1 N. Main St. at Division St., 920/923-3000. It's located in a renovated

KOHLER

Take WI 23 east from Fond du Lac about 33 miles to visit Kohler, a village built around bathroom fixtures. The hub of the charming town, complete with walking paths and championship golf courses, is the Kohler Company, a leading manufacturer of bathtubs, whirlpools, lavatories, and toilets. Tour the **Kohler Design Center**, *101 Upper Rd., 920/457-3699 (reservations required), to see "the Great Wall of China"—an artistically arranged wall of vitreous china fixtures weighing some 23,000 pounds. You can track bathroom-design changes since 1873 in the center's museum and admire Kohler-made RV and marine generators. There's also* **Artspace**, *920/452-8602, a gallery of the John Michael Kohler Arts Center, featuring contemporary American painting, sculpture, photography, and more. You can also tour* **Waelderhaus**, *a replica of the Kohler home in Vorarlberg, Austria, offering free daily tours each afternoon.*

When you're through touring, you'll probably want a place to stay and eat. This rather unlikely company town boasts the exclusive (and very expensive) **American Club**, *Highland Dr., 800/344-2838. The club, originally a company-owned hotel for workers, is now a resort hotel listed on the National Register of Historic Places. While there are many excellent places to dine, among the best is the resort's informal* **Wisconsin Room**, *920/457-8888, where you'll find regional fare at around $21. Take a free tour of the resort hotel and stay for a bit less at the* **Inn on Woodlake**, *800/919-3600, with your own private beach and rooms for $144 to $214. The Village Information Center, 444 Highland Dr., has maps and details; or call 920/457-4441.*

1920s hotel that's now a Ramada Plaza Hotel, and offers dinner for $8 to $15. The **Main Exchange**, 161 S. Main St., 920/923-8181, offers casual dining in a turn-of-the-century tavern with steaks, sandwiches, and specialty drinks; meals are an affordable $4 to $16. **Salty's Seafood and Spirits**, 503 N. Park Ave., 920/922-9940, is popular and crowded on weekends, with dinner from $9 to $28. Another recommended restaurant is **Theo's Supper Club**, 24 N. Main St., 920/922-8899; meals cost $7 to $20.

In Horicon, the **Ice Cream Station**, 518 E. Lake St., 920/485-2311, is a tiny joint open May through October. The honey almond yogurt and coconut chocolate-chip ice cream—huge double dips in waffle cones—are pure bliss.

LODGING

There are many hotels to choose from in Fond du Lac. Try the **EconoLodge**, 649 W. Johnson St., 800/553-2666, with a complimentary continental breakfast and rooms for $69 to $90. Or go to **Budgetel Inn BudgetDome**, 77 Holiday Ln., 920/921-4000, also with continental breakfast and rooms from $74 to $83. The **Days Inn**, 107 N. Pioneer Rd., U.S. 41 and WI 23, 920/923-6790, has rooms from $46 to $61; and the historic **Ramada Plaza Hotel**, 1 N. Main St. at Division St., 800/2-RAMADA, has an indoor pool, whirlpool, and rooms from $89 to $179. Another possibility is the **Northway Motel**, 301 S. Pioneer Dr., 920/921-7975, with rooms from $38 to $46.

Oshkosh choices are equally plentiful. The **Pioneer Inn and Marina**, 1000 Pioneer Dr., 800/683-1980, has lake views and rates of $109 to $139, $299 for a suite. **Budgetel Motor Inn**, 1950 Omro Rd., 920/233-4190, has doubles for $55 to $59. **Oshkosh Hilton and Convention Center**, 1 N. Main, 800/HILTONS, has rooms for $85 to $125. **Howard Johnsons**, 1919 Omro Rd., 800/446-4656 or 920/233-1200, has rooms for $55 to $70.

A good nearby bed-and-breakfast is the **Country Ridge Inn**, 414/626-4853, a renovated 1800s brick farmhouse in the Kettle Moraine hills at 4134 Ridge Road in Kewaskum (at the south end of the Kettle Moraine State Forest Northern Unit). The inn offers rooms for less than $100 per night.

CAMPING

Private campgrounds in the Oshkosh area include **Circle R Campground**, 1185 Old Knapp Rd., 920/235-8909, with 110 sites and 44 full hookups from $13 to $17. There's a grocery store, firewood, showers, and a playground. South of Oshkosh, **Kalbus Country Harbor**, 5309 Lake Rd., 920/426-0062, has 35 tent sites and eight full-hookup pull-throughs, plus flush toilets, showers, boat rentals, ice, and wood for $13 to $24 per night. The **Fond du Lac KOA Kampground**, W. 5099 County Hwy. B, 920/477-2300, has a spring-fed pond for fishing, a pool, hot tub, hot showers, and 84 tent and full-hookup sites from $19 to $25; camping cabins cost about $36. **Fond du Lac County Park**, County Hwy. MMM off WI 49 in Waupun, 920/324-2769, has 38 sites. **Kettle Moraine State Forest**, 414/626-2116, offers camping east of Dundee at **Long Lake Recreation Area**, 920/533-8612; and at

Mauthe Lake Recreation Area, 414/626-4305. There are 337 sites, 49 with electricity.

NIGHTLIFE AND SPECIAL EVENTS

Oshkosh's 1883 **Grand Opera House** has been restored to its former glory and now hosts diverse programs, including national and international touring companies. Performers have included the Peking Acrobats and Jack Daniel's Original Silver Cornet Band. For information, call 920/424-2355; for ticket availability, call 920/424-2350. The town also hosts concerts in Riverside Park Thursday evening June through August and the **Winnebago County Fair** in August.

In Fond du Lac, the **Buttermilk Performance Center** on South Park Avenue at Old Pioneer Road holds summer open-air concerts by the Fond du Lac Symphonic Band on Wednesday evenings, and **Music Under the Stars** performances on Monday evenings. For 1950s and 1960s nostalgia, there's **Jukebox Charlie's**, 248 N. Hickory St., 920/926-1950, with a Wurlitzer jukebox, DJ dancing, and waitresses in poodle skirts. Town events include the **Annual Walleye Weekend Festival and Tournament** in June, and a July Fourth concert and fireworks in Lakeside Park.

In Greenbush, the **Historic Wade House Draft Horse Expo**, 920/526-3271, with giant Belgians, Percherons, and Clydesdales in competition, takes place in June. Pick up the Fond du Lac visitor's guide for lodging and current happenings or call 800/937-9123.

14
MILWAUKEE

The onion domes and cathedral spires of Milwaukee's gracious old churches and the eclectic mix of architectural styles bespeak a city of diverse cultures and traditions. Native Americans once occupied this spot where three rivers feed into Lake Michigan. Then came the hard-working German, British, Norwegian, and Irish immigrants, who shaped an industrial, manufacturing city. New immigrants arrived to work in the factories—Poles, Bohemians, Bavarians, Russians, Ukrainians, and others.

Today the grand mansions, ethnic working-class neighborhoods, and elaborate churches bring texture to this city of 643,000. Settled first, the eastern section's historic structures include the Mitchell Building, with lion-head keystones. North of downtown stand the industrial barons' mansions. To the south lie the old industrial area and ethnic communities.

The Milwaukee County Transit System's Milwaukee Loop sightseeing tours (414/344-6711) are a good way to meet the city that's been called the Beer Capital of the World. The only big-name active brewery in Milwaukee now is Miller, but microbreweries keep the tradition alive.

A PERFECT DAY IN MILWAUKEE
Start the day visiting churches. View Polish-heritage St. Josaphat's Basilica and Old St. Mary's Church dating to 1846. Tour St. Joan of Arc Chapel and the

Cathedral of St. John the Evangelist. Go to the Milwaukee Art Museum for a look at the work of Degas, O'Keeffe, and Picasso. Have lunch at a custard shop. Tour the elaborate Pabst Mansion, then follow Old World Third Street to Usinger's Famous Sausage in the old German business district. Stroll the RiverWalk to work up an appetite. Eat red cabbage and sauerbraten at Mader's German Restaurant and top off the day with jazz at a pub.

ORIENTATION

In this bustling city of stately old buildings and ornate churches, major streets angle toward the downtown district on Lake Michigan. U.S. 45/I-894 and I-43/I-94 carry traffic north-south through the city. I-94 feeds into downtown from the west, then turns south to parallel Lake Michigan's shore. I-894 has an east-west leg south of downtown creating a loop with I-94. I-794 carries traffic east into downtown then runs south along the lakefront. The downtown area's main east-west city arteries are Wisconsin Avenue and State, Wells, and Michigan Streets. Primary north-south routes are Water and Milwaukee Streets, Broadway, and Martin Luther King, Jr. Drive/Old World Third Street. Water Street skirts the Milwaukee River downtown, and Lincoln Memorial Drive runs along Lake Michigan north of downtown. To really meet Milwaukee, tour the 10 historic neighborhoods outlined in the "Visitors Guide," available from Greater Milwaukee Convention and Visitors Bureau, 510 W. Kilbourne Ave., 800/554-1448 or 414/273-7222, www.milwaukee .org/visit.htm.

DOWNTOWN MILWAUKEE SIGHTSEEING HIGHLIGHTS

★★★★ **MILWAUKEE ART MUSEUM**
750 N. Lincoln Memorial Dr., 414/224-3200
Housed in the striking Eero Saarinen–designed War Memorial Building overlooking Lake Michigan, the museum includes exhibits of significant artworks by Picasso, Georgia O'Keeffe, Warhol, other greats, and lesser-knowns. There are also special exhibits.

Details: Open Tue, Wed, Fri, and Sat 10–5, Thu noon–9, Sun noon–5. $3–$5, under 12 free. (1–2 hours)

★★★★ **MILWAUKEE PUBLIC MUSEUM**
800 W. Wells St., 414/278-2700

Follow a dirt path through bamboo and trees and encounter real thorn bushes in this exceptional museum. Natural habitat reconstructions bring the world's cultures and natural sciences to life in exhibits such *as The Streets of Milwaukee* and *Tropical Rainforest*. Also housed in the

DOWNTOWN MILWAUKEE

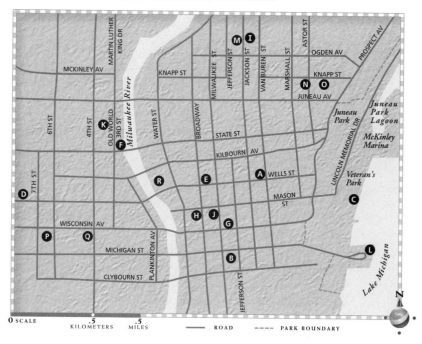

SIGHTS

- **A** Cathedral of St. John the Evangelist
- **B** Mackie Building
- **C** Milwaukee Art Museum/War Memorial Building
- **D** Milwaukee Public Museum
- **E** Old St. Mary's Church
- **F** Usinger's Famous Sausage

FOOD

- **G** English Room
- **H** Grenadier's
- **I** John Ernst
- **J** Karl Ratzsch's Restaurant
- **K** Mader's German Restaurant
- **K** Historic Turner Restaurant
- **L** Pieces of Eight
- **M** Sanford Restaurant

LODGING

- **N** Astor Hotel
- **O** County Clare
- **P** Holiday Inn Milwaukee City Centre
- **J** Hotel Metro
- **Q** Milwaukee Hilton
- **G** Pfister Hotel
- **R** Wyndham Milwaukee Center

Note: Items with the same letter are located in the same place.

museum complex are the Humphrey IMAX Dome Theater, 414/319-4629; and Discovery World—The James Lovell Museum of Science, Economics, and Technology, 414/765-9966. The latter has hands-on exhibits.

Details: Open daily 9–5; $3.50–$5.50, under 4 free; stroller rental $2; wheelchairs $1. Wheelchair-accessible. IMAX Dome Theater and James Lovell Museum are located at 815 N. James Lovell St. (1–2 hours)

★★★★ **ST. JOAN OF ARC CHAPEL**
14th St. and Wisconsin Ave., 414/288-6873

On the Marquette University campus, this small, fifteenth-century Gothic chapel sits amid lovely gardens. Built in France, the chapel was reconstructed on the campus in 1965 and offers tours.

Details: Open Mon–Sat 10–4, Sun noon–4. Free. (15 minutes–1 hour)

★★★★ **ST. JOSAPHAT'S BASILICA**
2336 S. Sixth St., 414/645-5623

More than 90 years old, this National Landmark's stained glass and murals pay tribute to Milwaukee's cultural history and heritage. The basilica was built by Polish immigrants and was designed after St. Peter's in Rome.

Details: Tours Sun 11, after the mass at 10; meet guides in the front pews in the sanctuary. Donation. (45 minutes–1 hour)

★★★ **CATHEDRAL OF ST. JOHN THE EVANGELIST**
802 N. Jackson St., 414/276-9814

This Romanesque Greco-style church, seat of the Archdiocese of Milwaukee, offers self-guided tours. Pick up the tour booklet in the vestibule or office.

Details: Mon–Fri 9–11:30 a.m. and 1–4:30 p.m. Free. (30 minutes–1 hour)

★★★ **OLD ST. MARY'S CHURCH**
836 N. Broadway, 414/271-6180

The oldest Catholic church in the city has been a downtown landmark since 1846 and is beautifully restored. Pick up a brochure on church history from the pamphlet rack.

Details: Open daily 11–1 p.m. Free. (30 minutes–1 hour)

FIRESIDE DINNER THEATRE

If your travels take you near Fort Atkinson, eat dinner and catch a musical at the Fireside Dinner Theatre. It's understandably a big tour-bus draw: This is quality entertainment. The performers are professional and put on excellent shows—from Joseph and the Amazing Technicolor Dreamcoat to Nunsense and Fiddler on the Roof.

The dinner theater started as a small restaurant run by two relocated bar-and-grill owners from Milwaukee, Dick and Betty Klopcic. Dick helped out a university theater group, letting them use the restaurant banquet room to put on some performances. The shows were a hit with diners—so the Klopcic's decided to make it a permanent addition. Their son Rick Klopcic runs the Fireside now and holds auditions for directors, choreographers, and actors in New York. Family members are directly involved with the business, and walk around and shake hands with folks after the show.

You'll find lodging nearby at the Best Western Courtyard Inn on Business 26 South, 800/922-6789. Fort Atkinson is between Milwaukee and Madison via I-94 west and WI 26 south. The Fireside is on Business Highway 26 South in Fort Atkinson, 800/477-9505 or 414/563-9505, www.firesidetheatre.com.

★★★ USINGER'S FAMOUS SAUSAGE
1030 N. Old World Third St., 414/276-9100

This turn-of-the-century store boasts 75 varieties of sausage, as well as brats and Old World ham. The store retains its original decor, from the round center bench and marble counters to panorama murals above windows and doors, and elves cavorting in window dioramas. While you're here, see the vintage architecture in the old German industrial district and stroll on the RiverWalk.

Details: *Open Mon–Sat 8:30–5. Free. (20 minutes–1 ½ hours)*

★★★ WALKING TOUR
Milwaukee Districts, 414/277-7795
www.mixcom.com/histmilw/

Historic Milwaukee, Inc. offers 14 walking tours featuring Milwaukee's early settlements, east-side mansion areas, German/Polish heritage, and more. There's also a SkyWaukee Tour through the skyways.

Details: *Tours June–mid-Oct; starting points and times vary; call for a recorded schedule. SkyWaukee Tour Sat at 1 from Plankinton Arcade Bldg., 161 W. Wisconsin Ave. in the Grand Ave. Mall. No reservations needed for any tours. $2–$5. (1 1/2–2 hours)*

★ **ANNUNCIATION GREEK ORTHODOX CHURCH**
9400 W. Congress, Wauwatosa, 414/461-9400

Frank Lloyd Wright designed this distinctly nontraditional church. The interior is open only to group tours.

Details: *Free. (5–10 minutes)*

★ **MACKIE BUILDING**
225 E. Michigan, Milwaukee, 414/272-6230

If you happen to be near 225 E. Michigan, visit the Grain Exchange Room on the second floor, a trade center when Milwaukee was the largest cash grain market in the world. The building dates to 1879, with a restored Victorian Renaissance interior.

Details: *Open Mon–Fri 9–4. Free. (5–20 minutes)*

GREATER MILWAUKEE SIGHTSEEING HIGHLIGHTS

★★★ **CHARLES ALLIS ART MUSEUM**
1801 N. Prospect Ave. at Royal Pl., 414/278-8295

This elegant 1909 Edwardian-style mansion, designed for the first Allis-Chalmers Company's president, displays collections of art by Whistler, Homer, Corot, and other artists. From this museum it's a picturesque one-mile walk to the Villa Terrace Decorative Arts Museum, another period house museum.

Details: *Open Wed–Sun 1–5. $3, under 12 free. (1–2 hours)*

★★★ **MITCHELL PARK HORTICULTURAL CONSERVATORY**
524 S. Layton Blvd., 414/649-9800

Come to see banana and papaya plants and a chocolate tree. Admire white orchids, or spend time with prickly pear and saguaro cacti in "the domes." Tropical, seasonal, and all kinds of plants thrive under the conservatory's three glass domes.

Details: Open daily 9–5. $2.50–$4. Wheelchair-accessible. (30 minutes–2 hours)

★★★ PABST MANSION
2000 W. Wisconsin Ave., 414/931-0808

The accurately restored Flemish Renaissance–style home built for the Pabst Brewery founder has exquisite wood, glass, and ironwork.

Details: Tours daily Mon–Sat 10–3:30, Sun noon–3:30. $3–$7, under 6 free (1–2 hours)

★★★ SCHLITZ AUDUBON CENTER
1111 E. Brown Deer Rd., 414/352-2880
www.execpc.com/sac/index

This 225-acre lakeshore nature preserve with hiking trails through woodlands, meadows, bluffs, and fields has an interpretive center, natural history bookstore, and gift shop.

Details: Open year-round Tue–Sun 9–5. $2–$4. (1 hour minimum)

★★ MILWAUKEE COUNTY ZOO
10001 W. Blue Mound Rd., 414/771-3040

Animals here live in environments designed to replicate the natural ones they've had to leave behind. You can ride the zoo train, take zoomobile tours, and watch a multimedia show in the Welcome Center. The zoo has a restaurant and gift shop.

Details: Open May–Sept daily 9–5, Sun and holidays 9–6; Oct–Apr daily 9–4:30. $6–$8, under 2 free; parking $5 per car, stroller rental $7. Wheelchair-accessible. (2–4 hours)

★★ MILLER BREWING COMPANY
4251 W. State St., 414/931-BEER

Taste and learn about brewing on a four-block indoor/outdoor walking tour. There's also a gift shop.

Details: Open year-round Mon–Sat 10–3:30. Gift shop open 10–5:30. Closed Sun and holidays. Free. (1 hour)

★★ VILLA TERRACE DECORATIVE ARTS MUSEUM
2220 N. Terrace Ave., 414/271-3656

Decorative arts are showcased in this Italian-style villa overlooking Lake Michigan.

GREATER MILWAUKEE

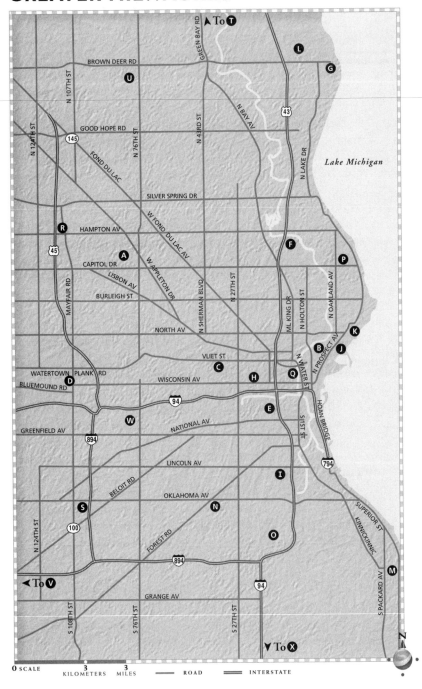

Details: *Open Wed–Sun 1–5. $3, under 12 free. (30 minutes–1 hour)*

FITNESS AND RECREATION

Schlitz Audubon Center (see Sightseeing Highlights) is a wonderful place for walks, as are the 144 parks and parkways in the Milwaukee County Park System. A bicycle trail of 75 miles or so circles around the city (call 414/257-6100 for maps). Head to a city park around Lincoln Memorial Drive for a jog with the locals. At least six companies offer Lake Michigan charter fishing, including **Take Five**, 414/871-FISH; **Captain Jack**, 414/482-2336; and **Maritime Charters**, 414/964-1073. **McKinley Marina**, 1750 N. Lincoln Memorial Dr., 414/273-5224, has rental slips, launching ramps, and marine supplies. **McKinley Beach** on North Lincoln Memorial Drive offers swimming, water-bike rental, and boardsailing. South of McKinley Marina, **Veterans Park** has bike and skate rental as well as kite-flying.

You'll find excellent golf at the courses at **Brown Deer** and **Whitnall Parks**. And there's lawn bowling every afternoon and Monday, Tuesday, and Thursday evenings at Lake and Dineen Parks. Instruction and equipment are available. Seasoned players love to explain the game: You'll learn that the

---

SIGHTS

- Ⓐ Annunciation Greek Orthodox Church
- Ⓑ Charles Allis Art Museum
- Ⓒ Miller Brewing Company
- Ⓓ Milwaukee County Zoo
- Ⓔ Mitchell Park Horticultural Conservatory
- Ⓕ Pabst Mansion
- Ⓖ Schlitz Audubon Center
- Ⓗ St. Joan of Arc Chapel

SIGHTS (continued)

- Ⓘ St. Josaphat's Basilica
- Ⓙ Villa Terrace Decorative Arts Museum

FOOD

- Ⓚ Bartolottas Lake Park Bistro
- Ⓛ Chip and Py's
- Ⓜ Fountain Blue
- Ⓝ Leon's
- Ⓘ Old Town Serbian Gourmet House
- Ⓞ Polish Crocus Restaurant
- Ⓟ Red Rock Cafe
- Ⓠ Water Street Brewery

LODGING

- Ⓡ Budgetel Inn Northwest
- Ⓢ Golden Key Motel
- Ⓣ Stagecoach Inn Bed & Breakfast
- Ⓤ Super 8 Milwaukee Airport

CAMPING

- Ⓥ Kettel Moraine State Forest South Unit
- Ⓦ Wisconsin State Fair RV Park
- Ⓧ Yogi Bear Jellystone Camp Resort

Note: Items with the same letter are located in the same place.

---

lawns are called greens and that the Lake Park club has been around since 1920. Additionally, 34 county parks have free tennis courts. Call 414/257-6100 or 257/4575 for more information about golf, lawn bowling, and other park activities.

FOOD

Food is fun in Milwaukee, whether it's gourmet or down-home. Milwaukee is surely the only city to publish a guide just for beer, Friday night fish-fries, and frozen custard—three of its long-standing traditions. Of course, you'll want to sample the specialties.

Frozen custard is loaded with eggs and heavy cream—alas, not for the cholesterol-conscious. Made fresh daily, it comes in countless flavors, from standard vanilla to Grand Marnier, blueberry crisp, and pineapple caramel pecan. Some custard stands publish a flavor calendar and even have a flavor hotline. Among the numerous places to indulge, **Leon's**, 3131 S. 27th St., 414/383-1784, has been serving custard since 1942.

A Friday night fish-fry meal is usually breaded or batter-fried fish served with coleslaw, a potato (maybe baked, maybe American fries, maybe a pancake), rye bread, and butter. For a real dip into Milwaukee cultural heritage, get your Friday night fish-fry fix at the German-heritage gymnastics club Turner Society's **Historic Turner Restaurant**, 1034 N. Fourth St., 414/276-4844. Here, in cavernous rooms decorated with Old-World German-style panorama paintings, waiters juggle trays piled high with food. For beer, try **Water Street Brewery** brewpub (a watch-the-brewer-work-while-you-drink-and-eat place), 1101 N. Water St., 414/272-1195.

Bartolotta's Lake Park Bistro, 3133 E. Newberry Rd., 414/962-6300, serves up French country-bistro cooking in a renovated pavilion. You can dine formally on French Continental cuisine at **Grenadier's**, 747 N. Broadway, 414/276-0747, with dinner from $19 to $30 (jacket and reservations required). Pfister Hotel's intimate **English Room**, 424 E. Wisconsin Ave., 414/273-8222, is wonderful for special occasions; dinner costs $14 to $32. You'll get German cuisine with all the trappings for $18 to $24 at **Mader's German Restaurant,** 1037-41 N. Old World Third St., 414/271-3377; **Karl Ratzsch's Restaurant**, 320 E. Mason St., 414/276-2720, for $16 to $26; and **John Ernst**, 600 E. Ogden Ave., 414/273-1878, for $16 and up. All three are mainstays of German cooking in Milwaukee.

For a different ethnic adventure, try **Old Town Serbian Gourmet House**, 522 W. Lincoln, 414/672-0206, featuring well-regarded Serbian food and music on weekends, and meals for $10 to $15. **Chip and Py's**, 1340 W.

OLD WORLD WISCONSIN

Old World Wisconsin is a must-see. On 600 acres of Kettle Moraine woods, costumed interpreters do their daily chores and re-create the lives lived by immigrants in more than 65 ethnic farmhouses, barns, village homes, and merchants' and craftsmen's shops. You can visit with a woman baking bread or a farmer pitching hay and see historic breeds of oxen and horses at work. It takes a full day—better yet, two days—to experience everything on this State Historical Society site (S103 W37890 WI Highway 67, 414/594-6300). The site's Clausing Barn Restaurant offers cafeteria-style meals. Old-World Wisconsin is one mile south of Eagle on WI 67. Eagle is 35 miles from Milwaukee: Take I-94 west to 67, then take WI 67 south through Eagle.

Towne Square Rd., just west of U.S. 43 in Mequon, 414/241-9589, has Wednesday-night and weekend jazz and an eclectic menu with meals from $12 to $17. **Polish Crocus Restaurant** at 3577 S. 13th St., 414/643-6383, on Milwaukee's south side, serves Polish food including pierogi, stuffed cabbage, and dill pickle soup. Or go to **Fountain Blue** (complete with running fountain), 5133 S. Lake Dr., 414/481-8222, for Polish/American dishes. **Pieces of Eight** is great for lakefront cocktails or seafood at 550 N. Harbor Dr., 414/271-0597. **Sanford Restaurant** offers excellent food in an elegant, European-style store-front, 1547 N. Jackson St., 414/276-9608. At **Red Rock Cafe**, 4022 N. Oakland Ave., Shorewood, 414/962-4545, expect fantastic fish and seafood and a red crab atop the restaurant during the July Crabfest.

LODGING

The **Pfister Hotel,** 424 E. Wisconsin, 800/558-8222 or 414/273-8222, over 100 years old, remains a grandly elegant hotel; double rooms/suites range from $160 to $284. The **Astor Hotel**, 924 E. Juneau, 800/558-0200 or 414/271-4220, is a nice older hotel with doubles from $113 and suites for $123 to $145. About 20 miles north of Milwaukee, **Stagecoach Inn Bed & Breakfast**, W. 61 N. 520 Washington Ave., Cedarburg, 888/375-0208, offers rooms from $75 to $130 in a historic building dating back to the mid-1800s. The downtown

MOVING UP

The Milwaukee Art Museum is expanding—virtually into the sky—with construction of a winglike roof designed by architect Santiago Calatrava to rise above Milwaukee's lakefront. The expansion will house a lakefront restaurant, an auditorium, and exhibits, and is planned to open by early 2000.

Milwaukee Hilton, 509 W. Wisconsin Ave., 414/271-7250, has rooms for $154 to $174. At the **Wyndham Milwaukee Center**, in the renovated theater district at 139 E. Kilbourne Ave., 800/WYNDHAM, double rooms cost $129.

Motels offering economical lodging are **Super 8 Milwaukee Airport**, 5253 S. Howell Ave., 800/800-8000 or 414/481-8488, with doubles for $70; **Golden Key Motel**, 3600 S. 108th St., 414/543-5300, with doubles for $45 to $65; and **Budgetel Inn Northwest**, 5442 N. Lovers Lane Rd., 800/428-3438, with rates starting around $49. **Holiday Inn Milwaukee City Centre**, 611 W. Wisconsin, 800/HOLIDAY, is a full-service downtown hotel. Its double rooms generally range from $99 to $144 but are subject to seasonal and weekend price changes.

The Irish **County Clare** is an inn, pub, and restaurant near Lake Michigan, 1234 Astor St., 888/94CLARE, with whirlpools and four-poster beds for $100 to $130. Another heart-of-downtown choice is **Hotel Metro** at 411 E. Mason St., 414/272-1937, with suites starting at $165. Milwaukee's lodging and reservation service, 800/554-1448, can help with information and reservations for major hotels or motels.

CAMPING

Reservations are needed—all campgrounds near Milwaukee fill, especially on weekends. You'll find public camping at **Kettle Moraine State Forest South Unit**, 414/594-6200, about 40 miles west of Milwaukee at Eagle (take I-94 west and WI 67 south). The unit has 328 campsites (49 with electricity), showers, and 80 miles of hiking trails. (See Planning Your Trip for reservation/fee details.) **Wisconsin State Fair RV Park**, I-94 and 84th St., 414/266-7000, lacks the fine scenery but is a closer option. It has 88 sites, showers, and electrical hookups, and is open April through October. Or try **Yogi Bear Jellystone Camp Resort**, south of Milwaukee near Caledonia (take I-94 south, exit at Seven Mile Rd., then go east two miles and north a quarter-mile), 414/835-2565. There are 247 sites (51 with full hookups, 168 with electricity and showers), a swimming pool, snack bar, and more. Rates are $24 to $30.

NIGHTLIFE AND SPECIAL EVENTS

Festivals happen nonstop in Milwaukee, where the **Henry W. Maier Festival Park** (HMFP) enjoys a prime waterfront location at 200 North Harbor Drive. Festivities include June's **Polish Fest** at HMFP and **Bavarian VolkFest** in Old Heidelberg Park. July and August bring **Bastille Days** to East Town, the **Great Circus Parade** downtown, **Festa Italiana**, **German Fest**, and **Irish Fest** to the HMFP, plus **Serbian Days** at the St. Sava Cathedral grounds. In September and October, celebrations include **Oktoberfest** in Old Heidelberg Park and **Indian Summer**, a Native American cultural celebration, at HMFP.

For sports fans there's an equivalent bounty, from **Milwaukee Admirals** professional hockey at the Bradley Center, 414/227-0550, to the American League **Milwaukee Brewers'** baseball games at Milwaukee County Stadium, 414/933-4114. The city is also home of the **NBA Milwaukee Bucks**, 414/227-0500, and the **Milwaukee Wave**, 414/962-WAVE, a professional indoor soccer team.

The **Marcus Center for Performing Arts**, 414/273-7121, in the heart of downtown, is home to the Florentine Opera Company, First Stage Milwaukee, the Milwaukee Ballet Company, and the Milwaukee Symphony Orchestra. Additionally, the historic Victorian Baroque **Pabst Theater**, 144 E. Wells, 414/286-3663, and the **Riverside Theater**, 116 W. Wisconsin, 414/224-3000, host touring Broadway shows, symphony, and popular music artists. There's also a fine repertory theater and an opera theater center. There are, of course, lots of lively pubs and clubs in "the beer capital of the world," plus skyline sightseeing cruises on the **Iroquois**, 414/332-4194, and dinner cruises via **Edelweiss Cruise Dining**, 414/272-3625.

15
MADISON

Picturesque Madison sits on a mile-wide isthmus between Lake Mendota to the north and Lake Monona to the south. Centered on the isthmus is the white-domed state capitol, a scaled-down replica of our country's capitol in Washington, D.C. With a population of around 201,000, the city is home to the top-ranked University of Wisconsin and its more than 40,000 students. The university and the government bring a heady cultural milieu to the city. There is always something going on, and lodging can be scarce. Reservations are a must. The city's heart beats on State Street, a long stretch of shops, bars, and restaurants between the capitol and the university.

Madison has nearly 200 parks as well as Cherokee Marsh, with its herons, ducks, and cranes. Since this is dairy country, you'll encounter rich ice creams, frozen custards, and cheese curds (a dairy by-product popular as an appetizer), plus German-heritage beer and bratwurst ("brats"). Madison is about 90 minutes southwest of Milwaukee via I-94. For current happenings pick up the *Isthmus* newspaper, free at newsstands or visitors centers.

A PERFECT DAY IN MADISON

Start out with a tour of the capitol and a visit to the State Historical Museum. Tour Monona Terrace, then stroll down State Street and check out the action at the open-air mall. Eat lunch at a State Street café or the Memorial Union

Terrace on Lake Mendota. Visit the Elvehjem Museum, then hike the trails at the arboretum. Treat yourself to dinner at L'Etoile, Delaney's, or Coyote Capers; catch a Madison Repertory Theatre play; and stop for a cappuccino at the 544 State Street Steep 'n' Brew.

ORIENTATION

Picture an hourglass slightly tipped to the right: The narrow waist, an isthmus bounded by Lake Mendota above and Monona below, is Madison's downtown. The head of the hourglass is east Madison, the foot is west Madison. I-90 skirts the eastern perimeter of the city, and is joined by I-94 in the northeast quadrant. U.S. 12/14 loops from northwest Madison along the southern edge of the city, becoming the Beltline Highway; U.S. 14 splits off to carry traffic south, while 12 continues east to meet up with I-90. U.S. 151 runs through Madison diagonally. Major city thoroughfares are University Avenue/Campus Drive in western Madison, central Regent, Gorham and Johnson Streets, Washington Avenue, and eastern Williamson/Winnebago Street and Atwood Avenue. Streets angle or curve to accommodate the city's Mendota, Monona, and Wingra Lakes. For a visitors guide and other information, contact the Greater Madison Convention and Visitors Bureau, 615 E. Washington Ave., 800/373-6376 or 608/255-2537, www.visitmadison.com.

SIGHTSEEING HIGHLIGHTS

★★★★ MONONA TERRACE COMMUNITY AND CONVENTION CENTER
One John Nolen Dr., 608/261-4000
Frank Lloyd Wright designed the Monona Terrace with a sweeping curved wall of glass overhanging Lake Monona back in 1938. It took city fathers awhile to give the design a thumbs-up: The structure didn't get built until 1997. Take a tour and enjoy the breathtaking lake vistas. There's also a gift shop with items featuring Frank Lloyd Wright designs. Cafe Kiosk sells sandwiches and desserts, and you can walk in the William T. Evjue Gardens on the rooftop. Inquire about free summer concerts.

   Details: *Open daily 9–5. Tours from the gift shop daily 11 and 1. Rooftop Gardens open Mon–Fri 8 a.m.–10 p.m., Fri–Sun 8–11. Monona Terrance and gardens free; $2 for tours exept free on Mon and Tue. (1 hour)*

★★★★ **WISCONSIN VETERANS MUSEUM**
30 W. Mifflin St., 608/264-6086

An exceptional museum on an unlikely topic. Exhibits range from the Civil War to the present, including military artifacts, full-size aircraft, model ships, and a submarine periscope which visitors may look

MADISON

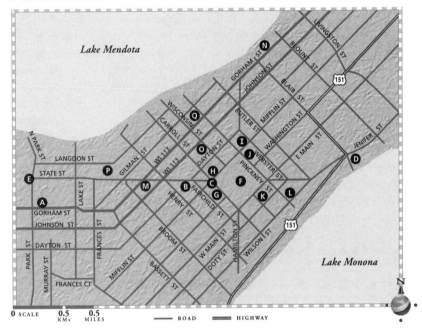

SIGHTS

- Ⓐ Elvehjem Museum of Art
- Ⓑ Madison Art Center
- Ⓒ Madison Children's Museum
- Ⓓ Monona Terrace Community and Convention Center
- Ⓔ State Street
- Ⓕ Wisconsin State Capitol

SIGHTS (continued)

- Ⓖ Wisconsin State Historical Museum
- Ⓗ Wisconsin Veterans Museum

FOOD

- Ⓘ Blue Marlin
- Ⓙ L'Etoile
- Ⓚ Opera House Restaurant & Wine Bar
- Ⓛ Restaurant Magnus

LODGING

- Ⓜ Canterbury Bookstore, Coffee House, and Inn
- Ⓝ Collins House Bed and Breakfast
- Ⓞ Madison Concourse Hotel and Governors Club
- Ⓟ Madison Inn
- Ⓠ Mansion Hill Inn

through. Sound effects add a chilling reality to dioramas depicting military events including World War II's Battle of the Bulge. Displays tell the story of Wisconsin veterans from Civil War to the Persian Gulf War.

Details: *Open year-round Mon–Sat 9:30–4:30, Sun noon–4. Free. (30 minutes–2 hours)*

★★★★ STATE STREET
Downtown (from the capitol to Park St.), 608/255-2537

State Street, that anything-goes stretch of open-air mall between the capitol and the state university, is the best place to experience free-spirited Madison. The street holds a children's museum, galleries, cozy bookstores, eclectic shops and eateries, art vendors and street musicians, and hordes of energetic university students. Give yourself time to browse or sit on a bench and people-watch.

Details: *(1 hour minimum)*

★★★★ WISCONSIN STATE CAPITOL
4 E. State Capitol, 608/266-0382

Madison's unusually beautiful capitol, separating Washington Avenue East and West, is the seat of government in a state that has embraced populist extremes—from progressive "Fighting" Robert LaFollette, who chalked up 5 million votes as a 1924 independent presidential candidate, to the post–World War II anti-Communist fervor of Wisconsin senator Joseph McCarthy. If you're there on a Saturday morning, don't miss the farmer's market on Capitol Square May through October.

Details: *Open daily 6–6, free tours on the hour Mon–Sat 9–11 and 1–3, Sun 1–3; tours also at 4 Memorial Day–Labor Day. Wheelchair-accessible. Free. (1 ½ hours)*

★★★ WISCONSIN STATE HISTORICAL MUSEUM
30 N. Carroll, 608/264-6555

Located on Capitol Square, the museum's displays include an excellent Native American exhibit and four floors of Wisconsin history. The museum collections include a hand-built clock made by Sierra Club founder John Muir when he attended the university. To reinforce study habits, the clock drops books on a student's desk at regular intervals. The clock is displayed in the Wisconsin Historical Society's lobby at 816 State Street.

MADISON AREA

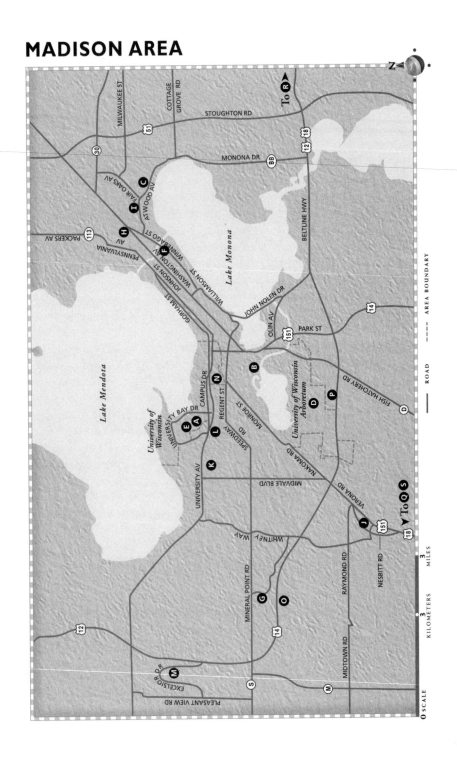

Details: Open Tue–Sat 10–5, Sun noon–5. $1–$2. Wheelchair-accessible. *(30 minutes–1 hour)*

★★★ UNIVERSITY OF WISCONSIN ARBORETUM
1207 Seminole Hwy., 608/262-2746 or 608/263-7888

You can visit a restored prairie, a wetland with orchids, woods with effigy mounds, and spring-fed watercress beds. The McKay Center interprets plant collections and has maps of the arboretum's more than 1,200 acres. Spring-lilac time is glorious here.

Details: Open year-round Mon–Sat 7 a.m.–10 p.m., Sun noon–6. McKay Center open Mon–Fri 9:30–4, Sat–Sun 12:30–4. Free. *(1–3 hours)*

★★ FIRST UNITARIAN SOCIETY MEETING HOUSE
900 University Bay Dr., 608/233-9774

Frank Lloyd Wright designed this 1950 stone and glass church with a soaring peaked roof.

Details: Guided tours May–Sept Mon–Fri 10–4, Sat 9–noon, and following Sunday service. Tours also by appointment. $3 donation. *(30 minutes–1 hour)*

★★ OLBRICH BOTANICAL GARDENS
3330 Atwood Ave., 608/246-4718 or 608/246-4550

SIGHTS
- **A** First Unitarian Society Meeting House
- **B** Henry Vilas Park Zoo
- **C** Olbrich Botanical Gardens
- **D** University of Wisconsin Arboretum
- **E** University of Wisconsin-Madison

FOOD
- **F** Coyote Capers
- **G** Delaney's Charcoal Steaks

FOOD *(continued)*
- **H** Ella's Deli & Ice Cream Parlor
- **E** Memorial Union
- **I** Monty's Blue Plate Diner
- **J** Quivey's Grove
- **K** Smoky's Club

LODGING
- **L** Best Western/ The Inn Tower
- **M** Budgetel Inn BudgetDome
- **N** Ivy Inn Hotel

LODGING *(continued)*
- **O** Radisson Inn of Madison
- **P** Super 8 Motel

CAMPING
- **Q** Blue Mound State Park
- **R** Lake Kegonsa State Park
- **S** Tom's Campground

Note: Items with the same letter are located in the same place.

Herb, rose, rock, and other gardens on 14 acres make this a wonderful place to stroll. A glass pyramid conservatory holds tropical plants. There's also a nice gift shop.

Details: *Conservatory: Open Mon–Sat 10–4, Sun 10–5. $1. Grounds: Open June–August daily 8–8, Sept–May daily 8–5. Free. (30 minutes–1 hour)*

★★ UNIVERSITY OF WISCONSIN-MADISON
170 Peterson Bldg., 750 University Ave., 608/262-3318; UW Visitor Service, 93 Bascom Hall, 500 Lincoln Dr., 608/265-9501

With a lakeside setting complete with an expansive terrace and boat docks, the 1,000-acre university campus has rightly been called one of the prettiest in the country. Highlights include the **Elvehjem Museum of Art** (800 University Ave., 608/263-2246), with a permanent collection of paintings, sculpture, and decorative arts from 2300 B.C. to the present. Kids love the **Geology Museum** (Weeks Hall, 1215 W. Dayton St., 608/262-1412), with its mastodon skeleton and limestone cave that visitors may walk through. In **Babcock Hall** you can watch ice-cream making every morning from a second-floor

WISCONSIN STATE CAPITAL

Alice Vollmar

balcony and buy wonderful, 12-percent-butterfat ice cream from the dairy store (608/262-3045). While you are in this area, stop at the lovely **Allen Centennial Gardens**, Observatory Dr. at Babcock Dr., 608/262-8406, to see the nearly 1,400 plants on the site.

Details: *Great UW-Madison information available from Campus Assistance, 608/263-2400. (30 minutes–1 hour)*

★★ HENRY VILAS PARK ZOO
702 S. Randall Ave., 608/266-4732

This zoo—in a pretty park on the shores of Lake Wingra—has more than 800 animals. You'll find playgrounds, a beach, and picnic areas, as well as free camel rides for kids on Saturday mornings.

Details: *Open June–Labor Day 9:30–8, Sept–May 9:30–5. Free. Wheelchair-accessible. (1 hour minimum)*

★★ MADISON ART CENTER
211 State St., 608/257-0158

The center's local, regional, and national modern and contemporary art displays are housed in a restored movie theater.

Details: *Open Tue–Thu 11–5, Friday 11–9, Sat 10–9, Sun 1–5. Donation. Wheelchair-accessible. (30 minutes–1 hour)*

★ MADISON CHILDREN'S MUSEUM
100 State St., 608/256-6445

This hands-on museum is great for kids and their families. Experience the "Digestion Tunnel" and weave a scab on a wall of skin.

Details: *Tue–Sat 10–5, Sun 1–5. $3, under 2 free. (30 minutes–2 hours)*

FITNESS AND RECREATION

Lots of people bike here, so bike paths are numerous, and busy streets have bike lanes. Madison bike and road maps are available from the Convention and Visitors Bureau, 800/373-6376. You can rent bikes from **Budget Bicycle**, near the lakes and arboretum at 1230 Regent, 608/251-8413; rates are $7 per day, $21 a week. Tandem rentals are $10 to $30 a day. Try the bicycle trail around Lake Monona that includes Olbrich Botanical Gardens. Walking is also great fun here. The city has interesting architecture, plus good coffee shops and bookstores to explore along the way. The several public golf courses include the Robert Trent Jones–designed **University Ridge Golf**

WISCONSIN DELLS

One of the state's extremely popular vacation spots, Wisconsin Dells, is 54 miles north of Madison via I-90/94. A frenzy of tourist shops, water parks, shows, and games detracts significantly from the original attraction, the Wisconsin River's tall sandstone cliffs and rock forma-tions. Fortunately, however, you can see the latter on Dells Boat Tours' (608/254-8555) narrated rides. Call 800/22-DELLS or the Wisconsin Dells Visitor and Convention Bureau, 608/254-4636, to order a travel guide. More information is available at www.dellschamber.com.

Course, 7120 County Hwy. PD, Verona, 608/845-7700. Hike in the arbore-tum or in the city's 3,500 acres of parks. There are several downhill ski areas within an hour's drive.

FOOD

A Madison favorite is **Ella's Deli & Ice Cream Parlor**, 2902 E. Washington Ave., 608/241-5291, an old-fashioned kosher deli with corned beef and great hot-fudge sundaes. In central Madison, **Smoky's Club**, 3005 University Ave., 608/233-2120, has been around for more than 40 years. It's a Wisconsin tradi-tion, serving steaks you'll never forget and meals for $12 to $19. Smoky's is crowded and noisy, with Wisconsin memorabilia hanging everywhere. It's a bit of a trip to dine here; the wait is long on weekends, and it's not low-fat fare.

On the west side, **Delaney's Charcoal Steaks**, 449 Grand Canyon, 608/833-7337, has steaks that are just as good as those at Smoky's. The atmos-phere, however, is much less chaotic. "The place to take your aunt when she comes to visit" is how a friend describes **Quivey's Grove**, 6261 Nesbitt Rd., 608/273-4900, where you can eat lamb shank or trout in the quilt-decorated dining rooms of an 1850s fieldstone mansion for $14 to $22. It's on a four-acre estate, two miles south of the Beltline Highway off U.S. 151/18.

At **Monty's Blue Plate Diner**, on the east side at 2089 Atwood Ave., 608/244-8505, across the street from the old Barrymore Theater, a wall of famous Barrymore musicians/performers smile at you as you enter. The diner specializes in great desserts, and '50s-diner decor with lots of blue neon. You can also dine economically at the University's **Memorial Union**, on Lake

Mendota at Park and Langdon, 608/265-3000; expect fast-food fare cafeteria-style and a chance to mingle with profs and students.

Coyote Capers, 1201 Williamson St., on the near-east side of town, 608/251-1313, has a creative menu and great salads; dinner runs about $15 to $25. In central Madison at the **Opera House Restaurant and Wine Bar**, 117 Martin Luther King Jr. Blvd., 608/284-8466, you'll dine elegantly on regional cuisine for $17 to $25. For European cuisine with a South American touch, go to **Restaurant Magnus**, 120 E. Wilson St., 608/258-8787. Meals there cost $15 to $24. Menus are seasonal at **L'Etoile**, 25 N. Pinckney St., on Capitol Square, 608/251-0500. You can get goat cheese and garlic baked in a squash blossom come summer, and dinner generally costs $45 to $50 per person. Locals recommend the seafood and lobster at the **Blue Marlin**, 101 N. Hamilton St. on Capitol Square, 608/255-2255.

LODGING

The exquisite **Mansion Hill Inn**, 424 N. Pinckney St., 800/798-9070 or 608/255-3999, has complimentary valet parking and afternoon refreshments in the parlor. Guests find the opulence of a small European hotel in this 1858 Romanesque Revival–style mansion: Rates range from $100 to $290. **Collins House Bed and Breakfast**, 704 E. Gorham St., 608/255-4230, is a National Historic Register Prairie School house with a library, home-baked breads, and specialties including Swedish oatmeal pancakes. Rates are $85 to $140. In a historic 1924 building, the **Canterbury Bookstore, Coffee House, and Inn**, 315 W. Gorham at State, 800/838-3850 or 608/258-8899, has rooms named for *Canterbury Tales* travelers and decorated in that theme. Guests enjoy book readings, Sunday storytelling, and live music. Rates are from $117 to $290. In the **Madison Concourse Hotel and Governors Club**, 1 W. Dayton, 800/356-8293 or 608/257-6000, the club occupies the top two floors with views of the capitol and a complimentary bar and breakfast area. Rates range from $89 to $169. Rates at the Governors Club are $109 to $200 per night.

Motels include the **Madison Inn**, 601 Langdon, 608/257-4391, with rooms for $79 per night; **Radisson Inn of Madison**, 517 Grand Canyon Dr., 608/833-0100, at $71 to $119 per night; and the **Super 8 Motel**, 1602 W. Beltline Hwy., 800/800-8000 or 608/258-8882, for $63 to $69 per night. Also in town are the **Best Western/The Inn Towner**, 2424 University Ave., 800/258-8321, for $82 to $129; the **Budgetel Inn Budgetdome**, 8102 Excelsior Dr., 608/831-7711, with sauna, whirlpool, indoor pool, and doubles for $87; and the **Ivy Inn Hotel**, 2355 University Ave., 608/233-9717, with rooms for $66 to $74.

BARABOO

If you have time, visit Baraboo. From Middleton, take U.S. 12 W north then west. Just before Sauk City turn north on WI 188. From there, drive two miles to historic **Wollersheim Winery**, 800/VIP-WINE or 608/643-6515, for free tours and tastings. The winery also hosts the Wine Festival during the first full weekend in October. When you're through tasting, follow WI 188 north to Merrimac and ride the free ferryboat across the Wisconsin River (in operation mid-April through November). Then take WI 78 west (sign says 78 south) and 113 north into Baraboo.

In Baraboo you'll find the colorful **Circus World Museum**, 426 Water St., 608/356-8341 or 608/356-0800, where you can tour the original headquarters of the old Ringling Bros. Circus. The 50-acre establishment presents daily demonstrations, a circus parade, and performances from early May to early September ($6 to $12, under 3 free). The museum, exhibit hall, and visitors center are open daily year-round except holidays.

About five miles west of Baraboo you can visit **Mid-Continent Railway Museum**, E8948 Diamond Hill Rd. (take WI 136 west, then County Highway PF south to North Freedom), 608/522-4261. Steam engines offer 50-minute rides, and the museum is open daily in summer. If you're there over the second weekend in February, the museum offers a wonderful snow-train ride.

Another Baraboo attraction is the **International Crane Foundation**, 10 minutes north of Baraboo via U.S. 12, on Shady Lane Rd., 608/356-9462, where you can see all 15 crane species. The center has a multimedia exhibit, gift shop, and guided or self-guided tours (May–Oct daily 9–5. $2.50–$6, under 5 free).

If you decide to spend a few days in Baraboo, Pinehaven Bed-and-Breakfast, E13083 WI 33, www.dells.com/pinehaven/, offers a room and a full breakfast for $79 to $89, and a cottage for $135. Pinehaven is two and a half miles east of Baraboo on WI 33. You'll find good food in Baraboo at Garden Party Restaurant, 525 Oak St., 608/355-0355; and at the Little Village Cafe, 146 Fourth Ave., 608/356-2800. For more Baraboo information, contact the Baraboo Area Chamber of Commerce, 800/227-2266.

CAMPING

Blue Mound State Park, 608/437-5711, is about 30 miles west of Madison near the town of Blue Mounds, off U.S. Highway 151/18. The park has 78 sites (four with electricity) as well as showers. **Lake Kegonsa State Park**, southeast of Madison near Stoughton, 608/873-9695, has 80 campsites with showers but no electricity. **Tom's Campground**, 608/935-5446, is west of Madison off Highway 151/18, six miles east of Dodgeville. Take County Road BB south from 151/18, then go left 700 feet on State 191. There are 96 sites (50 with electricity), a tent area, and pay showers. Sites cost $8 to $16 per night.

NIGHTLIFE AND SPECIAL EVENTS

The Madison Civic Center, housed along with the Art Center in a restored movie theater at 211 State St., hosts the **Madison Symphony Orchestra**'s winter season, 608/257-3734; the **Madison Opera** in its Oscar Mayer Theatre, 608/238-8085; and the **Madison Repertory Theatre**, 608/266-9055. Broadway shows appear here, as do big-name entertainers (also at the University's Union Theater, 608/262-2201). The **UW Memorial Union Terrace**, 608/265-3000, overlooking Lake Mendota has musical entertainment (usually LOUD) on the terrace at various times. The university also has music and theater productions, 608/262-1500 or 608/263-1900, as well as UW Badger football at **Camp Randall Sports Complex** and hockey games at **Kohl Center** (608/262-1440). You can catch **Mad City Water Ski Team** shows Sunday evenings at seven-thirty from Memorial Day through Labor Day at Law Park on Lake Monona near Monona Terrace.

Michael Feldman's **Whad'Ya Know?** national live radio show is broadcast Saturday mornings from the lecture hall at Monona Terrace, 800/942-5669. You can also attend free Chamber Orchestra concerts on Capitol Square Wednesday nights at seven from late June through late July (608/257-0638). Special events include **Art Fair on the Square**, 608/257-0158, usually the weekend after the Fourth of July, with artists from all over the world. There's a concurrent **Art Fair off the Square**, 608/798-4811, a couple of blocks away, with a more casual and "crafty" orientation. The first Saturday in June, **Cows on the Concourse**, 608/266-6033, offers a chance to milk a cow on Capitol Square, courtesy of the University of Wisconsin farms. Agriculture grabs the limelight the third week in July at the **Dane County Fair**, 608/267-3967.

16
HIDDEN VALLEYS

About 45 minutes northwest of Madison, two men built distinctly different houses in a breathtakingly lovely green valley near Spring Green. One of those men, famed architect Frank Lloyd Wright, was born here in 1867, kept returning, and chose the Wyoming Valley as the site for Taliesin, his "organic" home of native limestone and sandstone. At Hillside School on the 600-acre Taliesin estate are the blocks given to Wright as a toddler by his mother, who wanted him to become an architect. Those wooden blocks evidently worked.

One can only wonder what might have influenced the other man, Alex Jordan, to build a house on top of a rock and fill it with the weird and the strange. On the other hand, there's no doubt about why Norwegian immigrants chose to farm southwestern Wisconsin's rumpled landscape of ravines and valleys near Mount Horeb: It looks like Norway.

This region nurtures unusual creativity. American Players Theatre performs Shakespeare in the woods a few miles from dairy barns; Global View sells Asian textiles, clothing, and art in a country barn; and Barry Levenson opted out of a job as state assistant attorney general to start a museum devoted to mustard.

A PERFECT DAY IN THE HIDDEN VALLEYS
Breakfast in Mount Horeb at Schubert's Old Fashioned Café-Bakery and stock up on their incomparable Swedish rye bread. Visit the Mustard Museum and

Little Norway. Drive to Taliesin. On the way, pull off on the WI 23 scenic over-look to glimpse the House on the Rock. Tour Hillside School—or tour Wright's house if you can part with $35. Take an afternoon hike in Governor Dodge State Park. Dine at the Springs Golf Club Resort's Dining Room or picnic on cheese and fruit and that good Swedish rye on the American Players Theatre grounds before the play.

SPRING GREEN AREA SIGHTSEEING HIGHLIGHTS

★★★★ **FRANK LLOYD WRIGHT'S TALIESIN AND HILLSIDE SCHOOL**
WI 23 and Hwy. C, Spring Green, 608/588-7900
www.TaliesinPreservation.org
Taliesin, Wright's home for 50 years, sits on a hillside overlooking the Wyoming Valley. The entire 600-acre estate and the Wright-designed buildings on it—Taliesin, the Hillside School in which Wright based his Taliesin Fellowship (a training program for young architects still in operation today), Tan-y-deri House, Midway Farm, and Romeo and Juliet Windmill—are a National Historic Landmark.
    Details: Frank Lloyd Wright Visitor Center, WI 23 at the junction with County Hwy. C, three miles south of Spring Green. One- to four-hour tours of the buildings and grounds offered May–Oct daily. $8–$50. (1–4 hours)

★★★★ **HOUSE ON THE ROCK**
WI 23, 608/935-3639
As bizarre a creation as one is likely to encounter anywhere, the original house, built atop a 60-foot-high limestone rock tower, has been all but obscured by the proliferation of additional rooms and warehouses for the expansive exhibits. The House on the Rock is a huge complex today, requiring most of a day to explore in unhur-ried fashion. Inside are the personal collections of the late Alex Jordan, put on display for all to see. He also bought other people's collections, including music machines, the world's largest carousel, antique guns, hundreds of ship models, and on and on. A special Christmas season exhibit features a collection of 6,000 Santas. Jordan built the original house in the early 1940s, sculpting it to fit the towering chimney-rock's surfaces. He died in 1989, and facts

HIDDEN VALLEYS

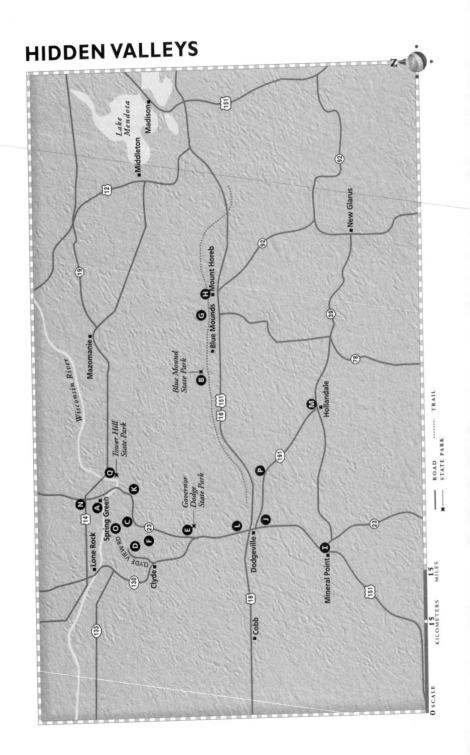

about the mysteriously media-elusive Jordan are now being made available by House on the Rock staff. On the premises are restaurants and vast gardens. It all seems otherworldly and, well, more than a little strange.

Details: *Open mid-March–Memorial Day 9–7, last ticket sold at 6; Memorial Day–Labor Day 9–8, last ticket at 7; Labor Day–late Oct 9–7, last ticket at 6. $3.50–$14.50, under 4 free. Holiday season tour mid-Nov–early Jan daily 10–6; $2–$9. (3 hours–full day)*

★★★ **GLOBAL VIEW**
6593 Clyde Rd., Spring Green, 608/583-5311

It's a surprise to find a foreign bazaar in a barn out in the alfalfa-scented Wisconsin countryside. This unusual enterprise features five levels of folk, tribal, and ritual art and textiles from India, Thailand, Indonesia and Nepal. You'll find ethnographic items, wall hangings, fabrics, and native costumes along with pictures and histories of the foreign-based artisans. If your timing is right, you can attend one of the festivals and special events hosted here, which in the past have included a chanting

---

SIGHTS
- ⓐ American Caliope Center
- ⓑ Cave of the Mounds
- ⓒ Frank Lloyd Wright's Taliesin and Hillside School
- ⓓ Global View
- ⓔ Governor Dodge State Park
- ⓕ House on the Rock
- ⓖ Little Norway
- ⓗ Mount Horeb
- ⓗ Mount Horeb Mustard Museum
- ⓘ Pendarvis
- ⓐ Wisconsin Artists Showcase and Jura Silverman Gallery

FOOD
- ⓙ Courthouse Inn Restaurant
- ⓔ Red Rooster Café
- ⓗ Schubert's Old Fashioned Café-Bakery
- ⓐ Spring Green Cafe & General Store
- ⓚ Springs Golf Club Resort: The Dining Room
- ⓛ Thym's Supper Club

LODGING
- ⓕ Cothren House
- ⓙ Grand View Bed-and-Breakfast
- ⓐ Hill Street Bed-and-Breakfast
- ⓕ House of the Brau-Meister

LODGING (continued)
- ⓗ Karakahl Inn Best Western
- ⓜ Old Granary Inn
- ⓛ Pine Ridge Motel
- ⓝ Prairie House Motel
- ⓝ Round Barn
- ⓞ Silver Star
- ⓚ Springs Golf Club Resort

CAMPING
- ⓑ Blue Mound State Park
- ⓐ Bob's Riverside Camp
- ⓔ Governor Dodge State Park
- ⓟ Tom's Campground
- ⓠ Tower Hill State Park
- ⓝ Valley R.V. Park

Note: Items with the same letter are located in the same place.

---

concert by the Gyuto Monks, the creation of a sand mandala, and a celebration of Tibetan culture.

Details: *Between County Hwy. C and WI 130, eight miles west of Taliesin. May–Oct Mon–Fri 10–5, Sat 10–7. Nov and Dec weekends, call for hours. (30 minutes–2 hours)*

★★★ GOVERNOR DODGE STATE PARK
4175 WI 23 N., Dodgeville, 608/935-2315

Named for Henry Dodge, governor of the Wisconsin Territory from 1836 to 1841, this 5,029-acre park offers a chance to scramble atop the Enee Point rock formations for lovely views of the countryside, especially when fall transforms the hardwood-forested hills into a patchwork quilt of red, orange, and gold. Two hiking trails start at the Enee Point picnic area.

Details: *Open year-round. Park sticker required. (See Fitness and Camping sections for more details.) (30 minutes–full day)*

★ AMERICAN CALLIOPE CENTER
U.S. 14, Spring Green, 608/588-7041

This circus calliope collection includes an intact 43-whistle calliope and a 1929 Model A Ford calliope truck.

Details: *Open Apr–Dec daily 10–8. Free. (15 minutes–1 hour)*

★ WISCONSIN ARTISTS SHOWCASE AND JURA SILVERMAN GALLERY
143 S. Washington St., Spring Green, 608/ 588-7049

More than 100 Wisconsin artists exhibit their work in a restored 1900 cheese warehouse.

Details: *Open July–Oct Tue, Fri–Sun 11–5; May, June, Nov, Dec Fri–Sun 11–5; Jan–Mar weekends by chance. Free. (30 minutes–1 hour)*

OTHER HIDDEN VALLEYS SIGHTSEEING HIGHLIGHTS

★★★★ MOUNT HOREB MUSTARD MUSEUM
109 E. Main St., Mount Horeb, 800/438-6878 or 608/437-3986, www.mustardweb.com

See what is claimed to be the world's largest collection of mustards—

around 3,000 varieties—and an antique mustard pot display. Watch a video about mustard, taste mustards until your tongue goes numb, and take some home. You can choose from more than 500 mustards for sale here.

Details: *Daily 10–5, except closed Wed Jan and Feb. (15 minutes–1 hour)*

★★★ LITTLE NORWAY
County Hwy. JG Mount Horeb, 608/437-8211

This genuine Norwegian pioneer farmstead dates from around 1856. The Norse architecture buildings include a growing sod-roofed cabin, a storage bin and other outbuildings, and the Norway Building, modeled after a twelfth-century *stavkirke* (Norwegian church) and made in Trondheim, Norway, for the 1893 World's Columbian Exposition in Chicago. The farm, originally called Nissedahle (Valley of the Elves), sits in a wooded valley in the foothills of the Blue Mounds.

Details: *Open May–July daily 9–5, July–Aug daily 9–7, Aug–Oct daily 9–5. Guided tours. $2.50–$7, under 6 free. (1 hour)*

★★★ PENDARVIS
114 Shake Rag St., Mineral Point, 608/987-2122

When miners from the Cornwall area of England came to mine the lead in this region between 1830 and 1848, they created a Cornish village of cottages in a ravine. Because the women signaled their miner husbands to come to dinner by shaking a cloth in the doorway, the village was nicknamed Shake-Rag-Under-the-Hill. Costumed interpreters guide tours through the historic site now called Pendarvis. At the edge of the Pendarvis parking lot you can follow trails past crevice mines and lead-miners' badger holes on the 43-acre Merry Christmas Mine site. (In fact, lead-miners' badger holes—dugouts in which early miners lived—are why Wisconsin is called "the Badger State.") The mine trails are self-guided and free.

Details: *U.S. 151, about 10 miles south of U.S. 18. Open May–Oct daily 9–5, last tour at 4. Village tour $2.70–$6.50, under 5 free. (1 hour)*

★★★ CAVE OF THE MOUNDS
Cave of the Mounds Rd., Blue Mounds, 608/437-3038

The architect of Wisconsin's National Landmark Cave, acidic water, took centuries to sculpt delicate stalagmites, stalactites, columns, and other formations. Part of the cave was shaped by the force of an underground stream, a phenomenon which gives visitors a chance to compare the effects of both chemical action and water on sandstone.

Details: Three miles west of Mount Horeb, off U.S. 18/151 on County Hwy. ID. Open mid-Mar–Memorial Day daily 9–5, Memorial Day–Labor Day daily 9–7, Labor Day–mid-Nov daily 9–5, mid-Nov–Mar weekends 9–5. Guided tours every 15 minutes daily Memorial Day–Labor Day; Labor Day–mid-Nov and winter tours weekends hourly. $4.50–$9, under 5 free. (1 hour)

★★ MOUNT HOREB
U.S. 18/151, 888/765-5929

In this Norwegian-heritage town, carved wooden trolls parade on Main Street, standing guard over the precious metals and minerals the troll creatures have buried in the ground (or so the story goes). In the **Mount Horeb Historical Museum** on the corner of Main and Second Streets, exhibits replicating pioneer life include an 1870s Norwegian-American home.

Details: Open Labor Day–Dec Fri–Sat 10–5, Sun 12:30–5. $2 donation. (15–40 minutes)

FITNESS AND RECREATION

Head for state parks for hiking, biking, and ski trails. Some offer snowmobile trails as well. A state permit is required; there's usually an extra fee for off-road bike trails. **Blue Mound State Park**'s (608/437-5711) nine miles of hiking and cross-country ski trails and five miles of off-road bike trails pass through oak and sugar-maple forests. Climb two lookout towers for views. There's also a swimming pool, handicapped accessible via a lift. The 1,200-acre park is about 25 miles west of Madison. Take U.S. Highway 151/18 to Blue Mounds and follow the signs.

Military Ridge State Trail, 608/437-7393, offers 39 miles of hiking and biking on an abandoned railroad bed and can be accessed from Mount Horeb, the town of Blue Mounds, Dodgeville, and from Governor Dodge State Park. Trail fees ($3–$10) must be paid by all bicyclists 16 and older. Bikers can also tour the area via routes recommended in the Spring Green visitor's guide. One route runs from the Frank Lloyd Wright Visitor Center parking lot to Governor Dodge State Park, where it hooks up with the Military Ridge State Trail. This is moderate to challenging biking with some big hills. To get the visitor's guide, call 800/588-2042.

Governor Dodge State Park's (608/935-2315) 5,029 acres include nearly 27 miles of hiking trails, 18 miles of ski trails, 25 miles of horse trails (extra fee), 10 miles of mountain-bike trails, and 15 miles of snowmobile trails, all graced with meadows, wooded bluffs, and ridges. You can also swim, boat, canoe, and fish in the park's scenic lakes. Winter camping is allowed.

Area golf courses include the **Springs Golf Club Resort**'s (800/822-7774) 27-holes, with an original Robert Trent Jones–designed 18-hole championship course. The Club Resort is off WI 23 between Dodgeville and Spring Green: Go east on County Highway C, then follow Golf Course Road.

Doby Stables, across the road from Governor Dodge State Park on WI 23, offers one-hour rides in the state park for $14 plus a $3 trail fee May through October. Two-hour rides cost $27 plus a $3 trail fee. There's also a 45-minute ranch ride for $12. For reservations, call 608/935-5205.

FOOD

Food in this area tends to be standard Midwestern fare, with a few exceptions. One of those is the **Dining Room at the Springs Golf Club Resort**, between Dodgeville and Spring Green, 800/822-7774, where executive chef Chris Bergner creates American regional cuisine and meals cost $18 to $35. The **Spring Green Cafe and General Store**, 137 S. Albany St. in Spring Green, one block west of WI 23 between Jefferson and Madison, 608/588-7070, is very casual and nontraditional. The natural foods café and grocery serves moderately priced homemade soups and sandwiches, weekend breakfasts, specialty beers, and, sometimes, live music. The casual **Courthouse Inn Restaurant,** across from the historic courthouse on WI 23 in downtown Dodgeville, 608/935-3663, has a generous Sunday brunch and good food for $4 to $10. **Thym's Supper Club**, on WI 23 one mile north of Dodgeville, 608/935-3344, offers filet mignon, pork chops, seafood, and chicken in a popular dining room. In delightfully charming (not yet too touristy) Mount Horeb, don't miss **Schubert's Old Fashioned Café-Bakery**, Main St., 608/437-3393, serving wonderful food for breakfast, lunch, and dinner at a reasonable price. At Mineral Point's inexpensive **Red Rooster Café**, 158 High St., 608/987-9936, you can taste Cornish pasty and *figgyhobbin*.

LODGING

For luxurious resort trappings, the **Springs Golf Club Resort,** off WI 23 and County Hwy. C near Spring Green, 800/822-7774, is the place to stay. Guests enjoy two-room suites, chocolate truffles, swimming pools, workout equipment, saunas, racquetball, tennis, and golf. Standard rates range from $125 to $225. **Hill Street Bed-and-Breakfast**, 353 W. Hill St., Spring Green, 608/588-7751, has seven rooms, five with private baths, in a 1904 Queen Anne Victorian with three cats. Rates range from $70 to $80. The **Silver Star**, 3852 Limmex Hill Rd., south of Spring Green and west of Hwy. 23, 608/935-7297, www.silverstarcountryinn.com, has its own café for European-style coffees, pastries, and entrées (for guests or by reservation). The inn has 10 rooms with private baths at $95 to $135. Spring Green motels include the **Prairie House Motel** on U.S. 14, 800/588-2088, with spacious rooms, a recreation area, and exercise room ($45–$75 for doubles); and the **Round Barn**, on U.S. 14 west of WI 23, 608/588-2568, with doubles from $45 to $90, depending on the season.

You might want to stop at the renovated **Karakahl Inn Best Western**, 1405 Business WI 18/151E, 608/437-5545, Mount Horeb, just to experience "Norwegian architecture in the Frank Lloyd Wright tradition"; doubles rates are $80 to $136. In Dodgeville, the **Grand View Bed-and-Breakfast**, 4717 Miess Rd., 608/935-3261, offers rooms in a new house on a 360-acre farm with animals, fishing ponds, and a full breakfast, for $80 to $105. Also in Dodgeville, the modest, one-story mom-and-pop-run **Pine Ridge Motel**, a half-mile east of WI 23 on County Hwy. YZ, 608/935-3386, is a clean, no-frills motel with rates from $48 to $54. (A plus is access to the Military Ridge State Trail across the road for your morning walk.)

In Mineral Point you can choose from ten bed-and-breakfasts and three motels. Try the **House of the Brau-Meister**, 254 Shake Rag St., 608/987-2913, a Queen Anne with two guest rooms and shared baths for $55 to $70 per night. Or stay near historic High Street in the **Cothren House**, 320 Tower, 608/987-2612, with five rooms, fireplaces, and whirlpools from $80 to $145. A country setting brings guests to the Mineral Point area's **Old Granary Inn**, 608/967-2140. It has five rooms, a fireplace, and a porch; rooms cost $50 to $85; and it's all packaged in a pretty valley near Hollandale.

CAMPING

There is ample camping in the region, but this is a very popular summer vacation area. Campground reservations should be made early. Public campgrounds include **Blue Mound State Park**, off U.S. Highway 151/18, one mile northwest of Blue Mounds, 608/437-5711. (See the Planning Your Trip chapter for state park fees and reservation information.) The park has 78 sites, four sites with electricity, and showers. **Governor Dodge State Park**, north of Dodgeville on WI 23, 608/935-2315, has 268 campsites, 78 with electricity, and showers. **Tower Hill State Park**, off WI 23 on County Hwy. C, 608/588-2116, has 15 sites with no electricity or showers. The main attraction in the 77-acre park is an old lead-shot tower above the Minnesota River.

Private campgrounds include **Tom's Campground** near Dodgeville, on WI 191, 608/935-5446. From Dodgeville, go six miles east on U.S 151/18, two miles south on County BB, and left 700 feet on WI 191. There are 96 sites, 50 with electricity, 10 pull-throughs, pay showers, a playground, and basketball. It's open April through October, and rates are $14 to $16 for RVs and $8 to $10 for tents. At **Valley RV Park** in Spring Green on U.S. 14, 608/588-2717, there are 18 sites. Fifteen come with full hookups and cost $18; the other three include electricity. There are also showers, a grocery store, and a Laundromat. **Bob's Riverside Camp**, one mile west of Spring Green on Shifflet Rd., 608/588-2826, has RV and tent sites for $18 to $20, plus canoe and tube trips.

NIGHTLIFE AND SPECIAL EVENTS

The premier area entertainment is **American Players Theatre**, 608/588-2361 or 608/588-7401, a theatrical company performing Shakespeare and other classics in an outdoor amphitheater. Highly rated and professionally polished, the theater draws big crowds. Near Spring Green, it can be reached via WI 23, County Highway C, and Golf Course Road. The season, which begins in mid-June and doesn't wrap up until early October, features five plays with rotating repertoire. Tickets range from $19 to $35, and recent performances include Shakespeare's *Macbeth* and *Comedy of Errors* and Oscar Wilde's *The Importance of Being Earnest*. There are picnic grounds with a shelter, tables, and grills, or you can buy gourmet box lunches as well as desserts and beverages on the grounds.

Special events in and around Spring Green include the **Spring Green Arts and Crafts Fair**, 800/588-2042, downtown on Jefferson Street in June; and the nondenominational **Hymn Sings** at the Wyoming Valley Methodist Church, a historic church seven miles south of town on WI 23. In Dodgeville you can attend the **International Hog and Cow Calling Contest**, 608/935-5993, in July. There's also the **Annual Mount Horeb Art Fair** in July and **National Mustard Day** in August (888/765-5929). Fall brings Mount Horeb's **Fall Festival** in October and the November **Christmas Craft Fair**.

For an intimate encounter with Wisconsin's Hidden Valleys countryside, take WI 23 north from Spring Green to Reedsburg. If you're a Norman Rockwell fan, stop at the **Museum of Norman Rockwell Art** at 227 South Park (open year-round, 608/524-2123). Then follow picturesque WI 33 west as it twists and turns, passing through the quaint towns of Wonewoc and Hillsboro. The highway descends into a deep valley, then climbs the steep hills into wooded **Wildcat Mountain State Park**, 608/337-4775, where you can hike the bluff trails to "ooh" and "ah" over sweeping vistas of forested hills and green valleys. Head for the picnic area in the northern section of the park for glimpses of the Kickapoo River far below and to hike the **Old Settler's Trail** (about three miles long). Should you decide to linger, the park offers 38 campsites with showers but no electricity. There's also a horse-trail campground. Northwest of the park, between Ontario and Cashton, highway traffic includes horses pulling black buggies—evidence that a community of Amish live here. Wander down a few country roads, and you'll see bonneted women and barefoot children hoeing the gardens, and

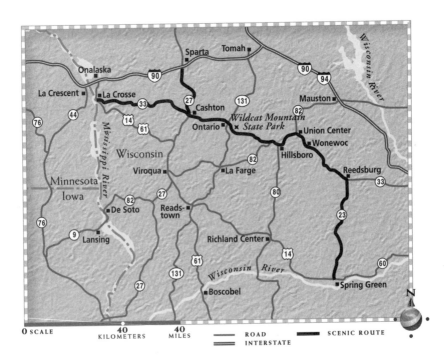

draft horses at work in the fields. In schoolyards during recess, long-skirted girls and black-clad boys play tag. Be sure to stop where signs offer goods for sale: The Amish sell maple syrup, quilts, handcrafted hickory furniture, and other wares, but not on Sundays. Leave your camera in the car—the Amish prefer not to be photographed. From Cashton, you can continue on WI 33 west into La Crosse and connect with the Great River Road. Or follow WI 27 north to I-90, which you can follow east to connect with I-94. From there you are poised to head northwest to the Twin Cities or southeast to Madison and Milwaukee. Whichever way you go, you can feel a little smug about having driven WI 33, one of the northern Heartland's prettiest roads.

APPENDIX

Consider this appendix your travel tool box. Use it along with the material in the Planning Your Trip chapter to craft the trip you want. Here are the tools you'll find inside:

1. Planning Map. Make copies of this map and plot out various trip possibilities. Once you've decided on your route, you can write it on the original map and refer to it as you're traveling.

2. Mileage Chart. This chart shows the driving distances (in miles) between various destinations throughout the region. Use it in conjunction with the Planning Map.

3. Special Interest Tours. If you'd like to plan a trip around a certain theme—such as nature, sports, or art—one of these tours may work for you.

4. Calendar of Events. Here you'll find a month-by-month listing of major area events.

5. Resources. This guide lists various regional chambers of commerce and visitors bureaus, state offices, bed-and-breakfast registries, and other useful sources of information.

PLANNING MAP: Minnesota/Wisconsin

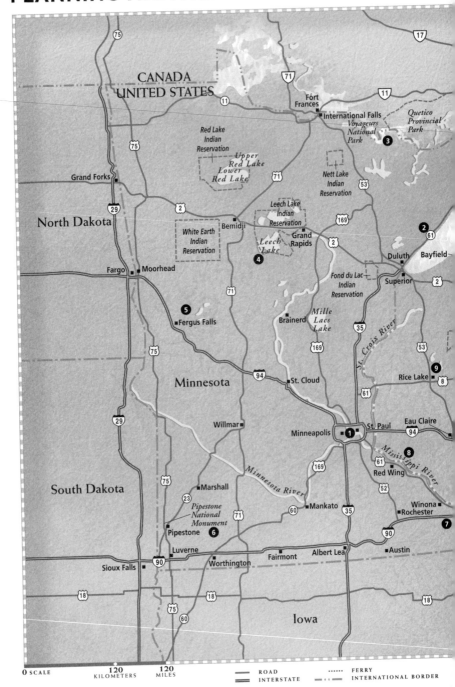

CANADA
UNITED STATES

Fort Frances

International Falls

Voyageurs National Park

Quetico Provincial Park

Red Lake Indian Reservation

Upper Red Lake
Lower Red Lake

Nett Lake Indian Reservation

Grand Forks

North Dakota

White Earth Indian Reservation

Bemidji

Leech Lake Indian Reservation

Leech Lake

Grand Rapids

Duluth   Bayfield

Fargo   Moorhead

Fond du Lac Indian Reservation

Superior

Fergus Falls

Brainerd

Mille Lacs Lake

St. Croix River

Rice Lake

Minnesota

St. Cloud

Willmar

Eau Claire

Minneapolis   St. Paul

South Dakota

Marshall

Minnesota River

Red Wing

Pipestone National Monument

Pipestone

Mankato

Winona
Rochester

Luverne

Mississippi River

Austin

Sioux Falls

Worthington

Fairmont   Albert Lea

Iowa

O SCALE   120 KILOMETERS   120 MILES

ROAD
INTERSTATE

FERRY
INTERNATIONAL BORDER

MINNESOTA
1. Twin Cities
2. Duluth and the North Shore
3. The Northern Wilderness
4. Minnesota's North Woods
5. Otter Tail Country
6. Prairie Lands
7. Bluff Country
8. Great River Road

WISCONSIN
9. Indianhead Country
10. Bayfield and Madeline Island
11. Wisconsin's North Woods
12. Door Peninsula
13. Lake Winnebago
14. Milwaukee
15. Madison
16. Hidden Valleys

Thunder Bay

Isle Royale National Park

Grand Portage

61

Lake Superior

Apostle Islands National Lakeshore

Madeline Island

Ashland
Hurley
Bad River Indian Reservation

28

28

41

41

Michigan

2

Lac du Flambeau Indian Reservation

11

Minocqua   Woodruff

Escanaba

Lac Courts Oreilles Indian Reservation

8

8

41

51

Menominee Indian Reservation

Wisconsin

29

Wausau

Chippewa Falls

29

Green Bay

12

Sturgeon Bay

Wisconsin Rapids

94

Petenwell Lake

41

Appleton

Manitowoc

Oshkosh

Lake Winnebago

La Crosse

33

13

Fond du Lac

Sheboygan

Reedsburg

14

16

151

41

43

Lake Michigan

Madison

15

Sun Prairie

18

14

Milwaukee

Waukesha

90

Janesville

43

94

Racine
Kenosha

151

Dubuque   Illinois

N

Most lakes and rivers not shown

MINNESOTA/WISCONSIN MILEAGE CHART

	Minneapolis	St. Paul	Luverne	Fergus Falls	Bemidji	Ely	Duluth	Red Wing	Lanesboro	Bayfield	Rice Lake	Minocqua	Spring Green	Madison	Milwaukee	Fond du Lac	Oshkosh
St. Paul	10																
Luverne	211	212															
Fergus Falls	186	186	216														
Bemidji	220	230	353	137													
Ely	242	238	453	292	173												
Duluth	151	147	310	212	145	108											
Red Wing	56	46	255	242	276	285	194										
Lanesboro	124	116	219	310	344	354	263	93									
Bayfield	217	207	397	299	232	195	87	222	309								
Rice Lake	111	101	322	297	239	202	94	101	188	121							
Minocqua	237	227	448	437	308	271	163	233	320	119	140						
Spring Green	258	248	363	428	460	423	315	180	144	360	221	241					
Madison	257	247	408	473	461	424	316	225	189	324	222	205	45				
Milwaukee	324	314	475	540	528	491	383	292	256	391	289	272	112	67			
Fond du Lac	300	290	439	496	500	463	368	270	220	324	261	205	114	69	73		
Oshkosh	284	274	423	480	484	447	352	254	204	308	245	189	130	85	89	16	
Sturgeon Bay	317	307	513	503	515	478	370	307	294	326	275	207	220	175	141	106	90

SPECIAL INTEREST TOURS

With *Minnesota/Wisconsin Travel•Smart* you can plan a trip of any length—a one-day excursion, a getaway weekend, or a three-week vacation—around any special interest. To get you started, the following pages contain six tours geared toward a variety of interests. For more information, refer to the chapters listed—chapter names are bolded and chapter numbers appear inside black bullets. You can follow a suggested itinerary in its entirety, or shorten, lengthen, or combine parts of each, depending on your starting and ending points.

Discuss alternative routes and schedules with your travel companions—it's a great way to have fun, even before you leave home. And remember: don't hesitate to change your itinerary once you're on the road. Careful study and planning ahead of time will help you make informed decisions as you go, but spontaneity is the extra ingredient that will make your trip memorable.

BEST OF THE REGION TOUR

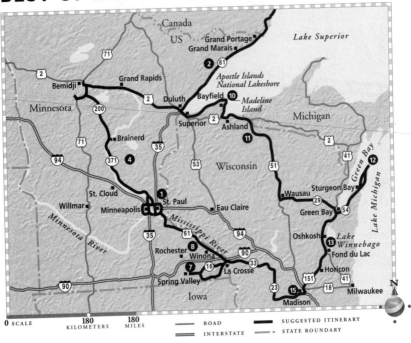

O SCALE 180 KILOMETERS 180 MILES ——— ROAD ━━━ SUGGESTED ITINERARY
═══ INTERSTATE ━ ━ STATE BOUNDARY

❶ **Twin Cities** (historic sites, museums, parks)
❷ **Duluth and the North Shore** (Boundary Waters Canoe Area, Gunflint Trail, museums, scenic drives)
❹ **Minnesota's North Woods** (Mississippi River headwaters, resorts)
❼ **Bluff County** (scenic drives, hiking and biking)
❽ **Great River Road** (historic buildings, river towns, scenic views, eagles)
❿ **Bayfield and Madeline Island** (hiking, boating, Madeline Island Historical Museum, Apostle Islands cruises)
⓫ **Wisconsin's North Woods** (hiking trails, fishing)
⓬ **Door Peninsula** (maritime museums, hiking, state parks, ferries, cruises, inns)
⓭ **Lake Winnebago** (glacial-moraine country, waterfowl habitat)
⓯ **Madison** (state capitol, arboretum, museums)

Time needed: three weeks

NATURE LOVER'S TOUR

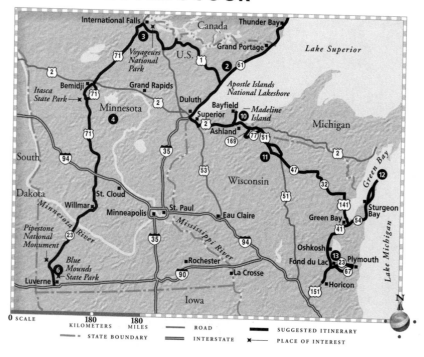

This tour includes wilderness areas and lots of state parks.

❷ Duluth and the North Shore (state parks, Gunflint Trail, Superior National Hiking Trail)

❸ Northern Wilderness (Voyageurs National Park)

❹ Minnesota's North Woods (hiking, Itasca State Park, Wilderness Drive)

❻ Prairie Lands (Blue Mounds State Park, Pipestone National Monument)

❿ Bayfield and Madeline Island (Big Bay State Park, Long Island)

⓫ Wisconsin's North Woods (Northern Highland-American Legion State Forest)

⓬ Door Peninsula (Newport and Whitefish Dunes State Parks)

⓭ Lake Winnebago (hiking trails, Ice Age Visitor Center, Horicon Marsh Wildlife Area, Horicon National Wildlife Refuge)

Time needed: two weeks

ARTS AND CULTURE TOUR

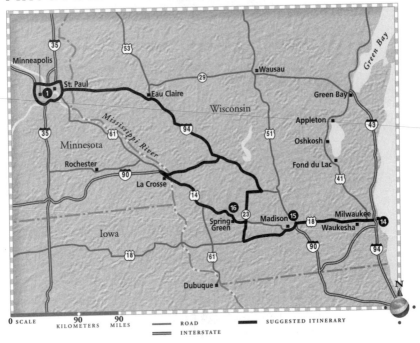

Both urban and rural areas are rich in art offerings.

❶ Twin Cities (Guthrie Theater, Institute of Art, Mixed Blood Theater, Walker Art Center, Weisman Museum; Minnesota Orchestra, Saint Paul Chamber Orchestra; Broadway productions, gallery shows, dance, literary readings, opera; Saint Paul's Summit Avenue Victorian architecture)

❹ Milwaukee (Charles Allis Art Museum, churches, ethnic festivals, mansions, Milwaukee Art Museum/War Memorial Building, walking tours)

❺ Madison (Canterbury Bookstore, Coffee House, and Inn; Elvehjem Museum of Art; Monona Terrace and First Unitarian Society Meeting House; Madison Art Center; Madison Repertory Theatre; Wisconsin State Historical Museum)

❻ Hidden Valleys (American Players Theatre, Frank Lloyd Wright's Taliesin and Hillside School, Little Norway)

Time needed: two weeks

FAMILY FUN TOUR

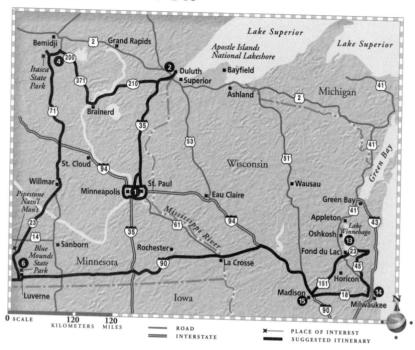

❶ Twin Cities (Children's Theatre Company, Como Park Zoo and Conservatory, Historic Fort Snelling, Minnesota Children's Museum, Minnesota Zoo, Science Museum of Minnesota, Valleyfair Amusement Park)

❷ Duluth and the North Shore (Canal Park, Lake Superior Railroad Museum, *William A. Irvin* scenic train rides)

❹ Minnesota's North Woods (Itasca State Park, water sports)

❻ Prairie Lands (Laura Ingalls Wilder Dugout Site and Museum, sod houses)

❸ Lake Winnebago (Fond du Lac's Galloway House and Village, marsh tours, Larsen's Clydesdales, Kettle Moraine Ice Age Visitor Center, walking trails)

❹ Milwaukee (Milwaukee County Zoo, Milwaukee Public Museum, Old World Wisconsin)

❺ Madison (Henry Vilas Park Zoo, Madison Children's Museum, Baraboo Circus Museum, North Freedom's train rides, Wisconsin Dells)

Time needed: two weeks

WATER LOVER'S TOUR

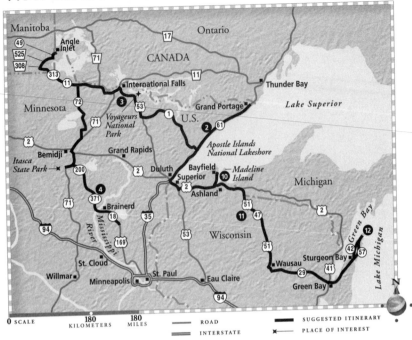

The states offer nearly 37,000 lakes, two Great Lakes, the Mississippi River, and clear trout streams.

- **②** **Duluth and the North Shore** (Canal Park and Lake Superior Maritime Visitor Center, Lake Superior)
- **③** **Northern Wilderness** (BWCA, Lake of the Woods, Voyageurs National Park)
- **④** **Minnesota's North Woods** (Mississippi Headwaters, sand beaches)
- **⑩** **Bayfield and Madeline Island** (Apostle Islands–hopping, canoeing, kayaking, sailing, sea caves)
- **⑪** **Wisconsin's North Woods** (lakes of the Northern Highland-American Legion State Forest)
- **⑫** **Door Peninsula** (fishing, maritime museums)

Time needed: two weeks

COUNTRY BACK ROADS TOUR

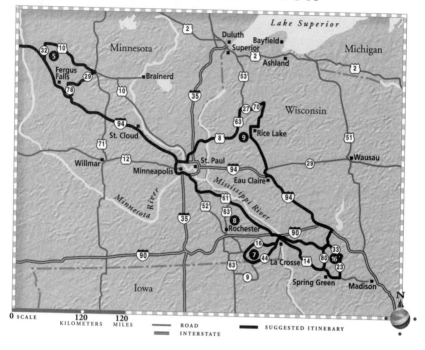

Wander the back roads and make your own discoveries as you go.

❺ **Otter Tail Country** (lakes, lush hardwood forests, small towns)
❼ **Bluff Country** (County Road 4)
❽ **Great River Road** (Apple Blossom Drive)
❾ **Indianhead Country** (Rice Lake, Birchwood, Stone Lake, Spooner, Shell Lake, Barronett, Cumberland shops)
⓰ **Hidden Valleys** (Highway 33: Reedsburg to La Crosse)

Time needed: two weeks

CALENDAR OF EVENTS

January

Annual Fond du Lac Farm Show (Fond du Lac)
The Fond du Lac Fairground hosts displays of farm machinery and dairy equipment during the Farm Show; 800/937-9123.

Bemidji Winter Events (Bemidji)
Polar Daze features a night-ski event, taste of Northern Minnesota, golf on ice, and more; 800/458-2223. At Old-Time Winter Carnival there are horse-drawn sleigh rides, downhill races, snowboarding exhibitions, and pioneer and historic displays; 218/243-2231.

Brainerd Jaycees $100,000 Ice-Fishing Extravaganza (Brainerd)
Snag a prize for catching fish on Gull Lake; 800/458-2223

Icebox Days (International Falls)
This annual event proves that winter can be fun with 10 days of outdoor insanity including a Freeze Yer Gizzard Blizzard Run and softball on frozen Rainy Lake; 800/FALLS MN.

Sled Dog Race and Weight Pull (Orr)
Folks bundle up to watch sled dogs do their work; 800/325-5766.

Winterfest (Grand Marais)
Events include cross-country ski competitions and snowmobile races with a bonfire and a fireworks finale; 800/622-4014.

February

Candlelight Ski (Door Peninsula)
Skiers follow a one-mile lighted loop through woods and meadow in Peninsula State Park; 920/868-3258. In Newport State Park, skiers gather around a bonfire for refreshments; 920/824-2500.

Fish Creek Winter Games (Door Penninsula)
Ice bowling, golf, volleyball tourneys, a carnival, sleigh rides, and cherry-pit spitting chase away winter doldrums in Fish Creek; 920/868-2316.

Saint Paul Winter Carnival (Saint Paul)
Parades, fireworks, car races on ice, ice carving and snow sculpting competitions, sleigh and cutter parades, and more; 800/488-4023.

Ski for Chocolate (Spring Green at the Springs Golf Club Resort)
A chocolate lovers fantasy: Cross-country ski then get rewarded with heavenly chocolate treats; 800-588-7000.

Snowfest (Minocqua, Arbor Vitae, Woodruff)
A hot-air balloon rally and other Snowfest events; 800/446-6784.

March

Buena Vista Spring Roundup (Bemidji)
Horses pull skiers at this spring roundup with barbecue cookouts, sleigh rides, downhill ski races, and more; 218/243-2231.

Country Fair Think Spring Art and Craft Show (Fond du Lac)
Shop for homemade arts and crafts at this juried show at the County Fairgrounds Expo; 800/937-9123.

Eagle Watch (Winona/Mississippi River)
An evening educational program on bald eagles and a bus trip to view migrating eagles on the Mississippi River; 800/657-4972.

Ski Jumping Championships (Minocqua Winter Park)
Watch ski jumpers compete; 800/446-6784.

Sugarbush Pancake Brunch and Maple Syrup Tour (Minnesota Landscape Arboretum in Chanhassen)
Enjoy a maple syrup–making tour and all the pancakes you can eat; 612/443-2460, ext. 105.

April

Annual Area Invitational Art Show (Fergus Falls)
Local/regional artists display their work at the Fergus Falls Community College show; 800-726-8959 or 218/739-7500.

Fond du Lac Jazz Festival (Fond du Lac)
Crowds gather for immersion in jazz at Marion College. Past performers include Dizzy Gillespie and George Shearing; 920/937-9123.

Mid-Wisconsin Chippers Woodcarving Exhibit (Oshkosh)
You can attend this woodcarvers' extravaganza at the Sunnyview Expo Center; 800/876-5250.

Octagon House Easter Egg Extravaganza and Tour (Fond du Lac)
Displays of Ukranian, jeweled, sugar, and ceramic eggs are the highlights on tours of a historic house in Fond du Lac; 920/922-1608.

Washington Island's Island Party (Door Peninsula)
Food, dance, and entertainment are highlights; 920/847-2179.

May

Annual Sheep Days (Greenbush)
Everything's wooly during sheep days; 800/382-FISH or 218/634-1174.

Blossom Festivals (Door Peninsula)
Egg Harbor hosts a Blossom Walk on Sunday mornings with a 45-minute

guided tour of the loveliest gardens; 920/868-3717. Numerous Door County blossom festivals celebrate blooming wildflowers, daffodils, and orchards in flower; 920/743-4456, ext. 806.

Door County Lighthouse Walk (Door Peninsula)
This is your chance to visit lighthouses (on the mainland and via boat tours) and select lighthouse-keepers' quarters; 920/743-5958

Polish Heritage Days (Winona)
A two-day celebration of the anniversary of the 1791 Polish Constitution and Commemoration Feast of Mary, Queen of Poland, features a banquet with Polish fare, a Hall of Fame induction, and a dance; 507/454-3261.

Sykkle Tur (Root River Trail, Bluff Country)
Bicyclists pedal the Root River Valley and Harmony-Preston Valley trails the third weekend in May; 800/247-6466.

June

Art in the Park (Lanesboro)
Enjoy a lively art happening held each year on Father's Day; 800/944-2670

Buffalo Days (Luverne)
On the first weekend in June, come for a gala Saturday parade, horseshoe toss, and buffalo-chip throw in Luverne, and a Sunday open house at nearby Blue Mounds State Park; 507/283-4061.

Cows on the Concourse (Madison)
Milk cows on Capitol Square, courtesy of University of Wisconsin farms; 608/266-6033

Grandma's Marathon (Duluth)
A testing ground for Olympic hopefuls, this popular event features three races on the North Shore of Lake Superior, plus guest speakers, live entertainment, and a fitness expo; 218/727-0947.

Great American Think-Off (New York Mills)
Essay finalists engage in a public philosophical debate; 218/385-3339.

Lady Slipper Festival (Lake Kabetogama)
This celebration of northland wildflowers includes nature hikes, naturalist-guided activities wildlife boat tours and cruises, craft/artisan shows, food, and workshops; 800/524-9085.

Walleye Weekend (Fond du Lac)
This festival, billed as the world's largest outdoor fish fry, also has family entertainment; 920/937-9123.

Wildflower Route Celebration (Williams)
This celebration honors the 75-mile wildflower corridor with a sea of blooming orchids along the Borderland Trail; 800/382-3734.

July

Bastille Days (Milwaukee)

A four-day celebration of French culture with wonderful food, entertainment, a marketplace, wine tasting, bicycle races, and more in Milwaukee's East Town; 414/271-7400.

EAA Fly-In (Oshkosh)

Air shows with acrobatic performers and 700 exhibitors displaying innovations are among the highlights at this popular annual event; 920/426-4800.

Great Circus Parade (Milwaukee)

All ages come for the downtown horse-drawn circus parade during a week of circus-related activities and fireworks; 414/273-7877.

Hiawatha Pageant (Pipestone)

A cast of 200 puts on a colorful show in an amphitheater north of Pipestone; 507/825-4126.

Laura Ingalls Wilder Pageant, "Fragments of a Dream," (Walnut Grove)

Not far from the site of *On the Banks of Plum Creek*, folks flock to see this production based on Laura Ingalls Wilder's life; 507/859-2174.

Phelps Mill Festival (Fergus Falls)

A two-day arts festival with arts and crafts displays, entertainment, and American and ethnic foods; 218/739-2884.

Red Cliff Cultural Days (Isle Vista Casino/Red Cliff)

Birch-bark wigwams and tepees spring up near the casino during Red Cliff Cultural Days. Events include a fish boil, powwow, beading and canoe-making demonstrations, Ojibwe storytelling, drumming, and dancing. The public is welcome; 800/226-8478.

Riverboat Days Festival (Wabasha)

Riverboat rides, food, and festivities add up to fun on the banks of the Mississippi River; 800/565-4158.

Spooner Rodeo (Spooner)

The rodeo's main events are a rodeo parade and competition, a chicken barbecue, and a cowboy church service; 800/367-3306.

Territorial Days Celebration (Mineral Point)

This small-town Independence Day celebration includes a parade, chicken barbecue, ball games, city band concert, and fireworks; 888/POINT-WI.

Viennese Sommerfest (Minneapolis)

A Viennese *markplatz* with colorful food tents and free live entertainment fills Peavy Plaza, next to Orchestra Hall, which holds classical music performances and concerts; 800/292-4141.

August

Annual Door County Museum Classic Wooden Boat Show (Door Peninsula)

Highlights include more than 50 wooden boats, maritime entertainment, a "quick and dirty" boat building contest, and U.S. Coast Guard demonstrations; 920/743-5958.

Annual Native American Artist Shows (Lac du Flambeau)

Beadwork, painting, weaving, birch-bark and other cultural and contemporary Native American art are featured; 715/588-3333.

Annual Smallmouth Bass Tournament (Ash River Trail/Voyageurs National Park)

Cash prizes are awarded for the largest fish, and there's a fish fry; 218/374-3181.

Bayfront Blues Festival (Duluth)

This three-day outdoor music festival hosts more than 20 national performers on two concert stages, North Shore Scenic Railroad "Blues Train" excursions, and live blues at local nightclubs; 715/394-6831.

Finn Creek Fall Folk Festival (New York Mills)

Yesteryear comes to life for two days with crafters, food, music, buggy rides, a threshing bee, and logging demonstrations at Finn Creek Open Air Museum; 218/385-2233.

Minnesota State Fair (Saint Paul)

This large fair includes animal barns and demonstrations, horticultural exhibits, machinery, midway, booths, grandstand shows, food, and more food (pronto pups are a dining tradition here); 800/657-3700.

National Mustard Day (Mount Horeb)

Come and see how this town celebrates mustard; 888/765-5929.

Rendezvous Days (Grand Portage Indian Reservation)

Held the second weekend in August, rendezvous events include a reenactment of the Old Northwest Company's annual fur trade rendezvous with an Ojibwe village, voyageur encampment, Native American arts, crafts, food, and a powwow; 218/387-2788.

Triangle Ethnic Fest (Madison)

This colorful celebration at Braxton Place features customs and cultures from all over the world; 608/256-7808.

Wisconsin State Fair (Milwaukee)

Ten days of agricultural traditions, booths, displays, rides, fireworks, and fun await fairgoers; 800/884-FAIR or 414/266-7000.

September

Annual North Shore In-Line Marathon (Duluth)
Thousands of skaters race in the country's largest in-line skating marathon, 218/722-0436 or 218/628-3464.

Apostle Islands Lighthouse Celebration (Bayfield/Madeline Island)
The annual lighthouse celebration brings eight days of boat tours to lighthouses, lectures, displays, and a Big Top Chautauqua lighthouse production; 715/779-3397 or 715/779-3335.

Apple Festival (La Crescent)
Apples are everywhere—in orchards, stands, and pies. The festival has a beer tent, carnival rides, food, and more; 800/926-9480.

Baileys Harbor Autumn Fest (Door Peninsula)
Lumberjack shows, hot-air balloon rides, a fish boil, arts and crafts, Western barbecue, a flapjack-fling contest, and other events are part of the fall fun; 920/839-2366.

Buckskinner's Rendezvous (Tower Hill State Park)
Demonstrations and music are highlights; 608/588-2166.

Fall Foliage Fest (Harmony)
You'll see southeastern Minnesota's hardwood forest in glorious hues; 800/247-MINN or 507/886-2469.

Tri-State Band Festival (Luverne)
Bands, bands, and more bands march in precision and play at this colorful, annual high school competition; 888/283-4061.

World Dairy Expo (Madison)
Cattle shows, farm tours, and more than 1,100 dairy exhibits bring people from near and far; 608/224-6455.

October

Annual Apple Festivals (Door Peninsula, Bayfield and Madeline Island)
Fall celebrations include the Cider Pressing Party and Fall Festival on Washington Island, 920-847-2179; the Annual Apple Fest in Bayfield, 800/447-4094; and the Annual Fall Festival in Sister Bay with parades, crafts, food and entertainment, 920/854-2812.

Annual Fall Festival (Mount Horeb)
You can buy produce off a farm truck, take a horse and buggy ride, listen to live music, see folk art demonstrations, and more; 888/765-5929.

Cranberry Festival (Stone Lake)
See cranberries being harvested, watch cranberry-crate races, eat cranberry ice cream or crandogs, and buy cranberries; 715/865-3302.

Fall Art Tour (Spring Green)
Get a map at the Jura Silverman Gallery and spend three days visiting regional artists' studios—some in town, some tucked away in the hills; 800/588-2042 or 608/588-7049.

Oktoberfest (LaCrosse)
Many people come for the music, carnival rides, and beer gardens of Oktoberfest; 608/784-FEST.

Oktoberfest (New Ulm)
German festivities abound: Hear the Concord Singers and eat sauerkraut, landjaeggers, and other German food; 888/4-NEW ULM.

Woodcarvers Show (Red Wing)
Woodcarvers gather for a show in Red Wing, the second weekend in October; 800/498-3444.

November

Annual Swan Watch (Winona)
Buses take you to see tundra swans at four viewing sites in Minnesota and Wisconsin along the Great River Road; 800/657-4972.

Christmas Craft Fair/Hospitality Day (Mount Horeb)
Downtown is decorated with white lights and greenery; merchants offer treats; and the community center hosts a craft fair; 888/765-5929.

Christmas Walk (Sturgeon Bay)
Three days of tours of decorated bed-and-breakfasts, caroling, tree lighting, a parade, Santa, and a Christmas tea put folks in a Christmas mood; 920/743-6246.

Egg Harbor Holly Days (Egg Harbor/Door Peninsula)
Enjoy a weekend of holiday shopping, a Christmas tree–lighting ceremony, caroling, and breakfast with Santa; 920/868-3205.

Sheldon Theatre Brass Band Holiday Concert (Red Wing)
Get tickets early for the two sell-out performances of this delightful holiday concert in the brass-band tradition; 800/899-5759.

Thanksgiving Arts and Crafts Show (Sister Bay)
Local artists and crafters exhibit and sell their wares in the village hall to benefit Gibraltar School; 920/854-5027.

December

Capitol New Year (Saint Paul)
This family-oriented, alcohol-free celebration throughout downtown features entertainment and a midnight countdown; 800/627-6101 or 651/265-4900.

Christmas by Candlelight (Sturgeon Bay)

Open houses in historic bed-and-breakfasts and inns, free hayrides between inns, Christmas tea, music, and refreshments; 920/743-6246.

Christmas Celebrations on the Mississippi River (Great River Road)

River towns celebrate the holidays at Hometown Holidays in Pepin, Wisconsin; Old Fashioned Christmas in Wabasha, Minnesota, and Maiden Rock, Wisconsin; Country Christmas in Stockholm, Wisconsin; and Christmas Housewalk in Alma, Wisconsin; 920/743-6246.

Christmas Crafts, Tea, and Tours (Bayfield)

This two-day happening has a Christmas craft show, a tea benefit for the Big Top Chatauqua, wassail dinners, a Christmas home tour, and sleigh rides; 800/447-4094.

Holiday Concert (Spring Green)

In the long-standing tradition of Frank Lloyd Wright's Taliesin Fellowship, the resident community of architects are encouraged to develop other artistic talents—hence this holiday concert in Spring Green's historic Gard Theater by the Rural Musicians Forum, made up of local, Taliesin, and professional musicians; 608/588-2042.

Holidays at the Allis (Milwaukee)

Lavish decorations adorn the Tudor-style Allis House-Museum including seven Victorian-style trees, boughs, and bows; 414/278-8295.

International Snowmobile Race of Champions Snocross Race (Brainerd)

See the fastest sleds race at the Crow Wing County Fairground; 800/450-2838.

New Year's Eve Fireworks Celebration (Minneapolis)

This family event features concerts, costumed characters, and fireworks on the Minneapolis riverfront; 612/673-5123 or 612/673/5126.

Oshkosh Holiday Events (Oshkosh)

Holiday happenings include the Annual Holiday Gala at the Oshkosh Public Museum and Holiday Open House at the Paine Art Center and Arboretum; 800/876-5250.

Victorian Christmas (Mineral Point)

The Gundry House Museum welcomes guests with holiday music and refreshments; 888/POINT WI.

RESOURCES

Minnesota Office of Tourism, 500 Metro Square, 121 Seventh Place East, St. Paul, MN 55101; 800/657-3700 or 651/296-5029, www.exploreminnesota.com.

Wisconsin Department of Tourism, Box 7976, 201 West Washington Avenue, Madison, WI 53707-7976; 800/372-2737 (Wisconsin and neighbor states), 800/432-TRIP (national), or 608/266-2161, www.tourism.state.wi.us.

Minnesota Department of Natural Resources Information Center, 500 Lafayette Road, St. Paul, MN 55155-4040; 888/646-6367 or 651/296-6157, License Bureau 651/296-2316, www.dnr.state.mn.us.

Wisconsin Department of Natural Resources, Box 7921, Madison, WI 53707-7921; 608/266-2181, www.dnr.state.wi.us. Call 608/266-2621 for fishing, boating, and hunting regulations and licensing.

Chambers of Commerce and Visitors Bureaus

Minnesota
Alexandria Lakes Area 800/235-9441, www.alexandriamn.org
Bemidji Area 800/458-2223, www.bemidji.org
Brainerd Lakes Area 800/450-2838, www.brainerd.com
Chatfield 507/867-3966
Detroit Lakes Region 800/542-3992, www.visitdetroitlakes.com
Duluth 800/4-DULUTH, www.visitduluth.com
Ely 800/777-7281, www.ely.org
Fergus Falls 800/726-8959, www.fergusfalls.com
Grand Marais 888/922-5000 or 218/387-2524, www.grandmaraismn.com
Grand Portage 800/232-1384 or 218/475-2592 (U.S.), 800/543-1384 (Canada)
Greater Minneapolis 800/445-7412, 612/661-4700, or 612/348-7000, www.minneapolis.org
Gunflint Trail Association 800/338-6932, www.gunflint-trail.com
Harmony 800/247-MINN, www.harmony.mn.us
Historic Bluff Country 800/428-2030, www.bluffcountry.com
International Falls 800/325-5766, www.intlfalls.org
Iron Trail Convention and Visitors Bureau 800/777-8497, www.irontrail.com
La Crescent 800/926-9480

Lake City 800/369-4123, www.lakecity.org
Lake of the Woods Area 800/382-3474, www.fishandgame.com/woods and www.lakeofthewoodsmn.com
Lanesboro 800/944-2670, www.lanesboro.com
Lutsen-Tofte 218/663-7804, www.mn-northshore.com
Luverne Area 888/283-4061 or 507/283-4061, www.luvernemn.com
Perham Area 800/634-6112, www.perhamcc.com or www.perham.com
Pipestone 800/336-6125 or 507/825-3316, www.pipestone.mn.us
Red Wing 800/498-3444, www.redwing.org
Redwood Falls Area Chamber and Tourism 800/657-7070, rwfchmbr@rconnect.com
St. Paul 800/627-6101 or 651/265-4900, www.stpaulcvb.org
Superior Hiking Trail (lodge-to-lodge hiking) 800/322-8327, www.boreal.org/adventures/hiking
Taylors Falls 800/447-4958 or 651/462-7550
Voyageurs National Park Headquarters 218/283- 9821
Wabasha 800/565-4158, www.wabasha.net
Winona 800/657-4972, www.visitwinona.com

Wisconsin

Bayfield 800/447-4094, www.bayfield.org
Bayfield County 800/472-6338, www.travelbayfieldcounty.com
Birchwood Area 800/236-2252
Cumberland 715/822-3378 phone and FAX
Dodgeville 608/935-5993, depot@mhtc.net
Door Peninsula/Wisconsin: Door County 800/52-RELAX or 920/743-4456, www.doorcountyvacations.com
Fond du Lac 800/937-9123, www.fdl.com
Governor Dodge State Park 608/935-2315
Greater Madison Convention and Visitors Bureau 800/373-6376, www.visitmadison.com
Greater Milwaukee Convention and Visitors Bureau 800/554-1448, www.milwaukee.org/visit.htm
Kettle Moraine State Forest Headquarters, North Unit 920/626-2116
Lac du Flambeau Chamber of Commerce 715/588-3346
Lac du Flambeau Tribal Center 715/588-3303, Heritage Tourism: 715/588-9052
La Crosse Area 800/658-9424, www.wi.centuryinter.net/lacvb
Madeline Island 888/475-3386 or 715/747-2801, www.madelineisland.com

Minocqua-Arbor Vitae-Woodruff Area 800/446-6784, www.minocqua.org

Mount Horeb Area 888/765-5929 or 608/437-5914, danenet.wicip.org/mthoreb

Northern Highland-American Legion State Forest 715/385-2704 or 715/385-2727

Oshkosh 800/876-5250 or 920/236-5250, www.oshkoshcvb.org

Rice Lake Area 800/523-6318, chamber.rice-lake.wi.us

Shell Lake 715/468-4477, www.shell-lake.com

Spooner 800/367-3306 or 715/635-2168, www.spooner-wi.com

Spring Green 800/588-2042 or 608/588-2042, www.execpc.com/~spring

Stockholm 715/442-2015

Stone Lake Area 715/865-3302, 715/865-2482, or 800/639-6822, www.stonelakewi.com

Trempealeau 608/534-6780

Washburn County 800/367-3306, www.washburncounty.com

Woodruff DNR 715/356-5211

INDEX

Map Index

ALICE M. VOLLMAR

ABOUT THE AUTHOR

Alice M. Vollmar routinely gets lost on purpose. That's how she discovers se-crets—in a city, tiny hamlet, or open countryside. "I try to go into an area with open eyes and mind, without expectations, willing to rub elbows with locals, eat where they eat, and tune into the daily rhythms of the community or re-gion," she explains.

Vollmar holds a B.A. in journalism from Metropolitan State University in Minneapolis. Her work has appeared in *Home & Away*, *Travel & Leisure*, *Ladies' Home Journal*, and other publications. She has won several awards for travel journalism.

Vollmar lives in Minneapolis with her husband, Craig. They have six children.